MW00909902

D. H. LAWRENCE AND THE PHALLIC IMAGINATION

D. H. Lawrence and the Phallic Imagination

Essays on Sexual Identity and Feminist Misreading

Peter Balbert
*Professor of English and
Chair of the English Department
Trinity University
San Antonio, Texas*

St. Martin's Press   New York

First published in the United States of America in 1989

Quotations from the published works of Ernest Hemingway are fully
protected by United States and international copyright. See page x
for full acknowledgement of dates and titles.

Printed in Hong Kong

ISBN 0-312-01357-4

Library of Congress Cataloging-in-Publication Data

Balbert, Peter, 1942–
D. H. Lawrence, and the phallic imagination.
  Bibliography: p.
  Includes index.
  1. Lawrence, D. H. (David Herbert), 1885–1930—
Criticism and interpretation.   2. Sex role in literature.
3. Feminism and literature.   4. Feminist literary
criticism.   I. Title.
PR6023.A93Z564   1989   823'.912   87-20561
ISBN 0-312-01357-4

TO A BEVY OF WONDERFUL WOMEN:

Lynne	my wife
Rebecca, Rachel, Reika, Risa	my daughters
Marjorie	my mother
Diana	my sister
Maria	my typist

Contents

Contents

Acknowledgements

The essays assembled here have appeared in earlier forms during the last ten years in various journals and books of collected essays, and portions of them have been presented at international Lawrence conferences in 1979 and 1985. I have altered and expanded each essay to achieve a more integrated publication in this volume. Yet I have resisted any temptation to adulterate an originally embattled tone that no doubt both contributed to the attention my remarks received and reflected the sense of literary urgency outlined in the Introduction.

Grateful acknowledgement is hereby given for permission to quote the substance of the following chapters of this volume where sections of my work were first published: for Chapter 1, to *The D. H. Lawrence Review*, in 11 (1978), 93–113; for Chapter 2, to *Papers on Language and Literature*, 19, 3, Summer 1983. Copyright © 1983 by the Board of Trustees, Southern Illinois University; and also for Chapter 2, to Cornell University Press, reprinted from Peter Balbert, ' "Logic of the Soul": Prothalamic Pattern in *The Rainbow*', in *D. H. Lawrence: A Centenary Consideration*, edited by Peter Balbert and Phillip L. Marcus, 45–66. Copyright © 1985 by Cornell University Press; for Chapter 3, to *Studies in the Novel*, in 17 (1985), 267–85. Copyright © 1985 by North Texas State University; for Chapter 4, to the *D. H. Lawrence Review*, 18 (1986), 255–73; for Chapter 5, to Southern Illinois University Press, reprinted from 'The Loving of Lady Chatterley: D. H. Lawrence and the Phallic Imagination', in *D. H. Lawrence: The Man who Lived*, edited by Robert B. Partlow, Jr. and Harry T. Moore. Copyright © 1980 by Southern Illinois University Press; and also for Chapter 5, to *The Hemingway Review*, in 3 (1983), 30–43.

For permission to quote from the works of D. H. Lawrence, as published in the list of titles, below, I gratefully acknowledge the estate of Mrs Frieda Lawrence Ravagli, and Laurence Pollinger Ltd:

Cambridge University Press: *The Letters of D. H. Lawrence*, vols 1, 2, and 3; *Mr Noon*
Penguin Books: *The Complete Short Stories*
Random House: *Lady Chatterley's Lover*
Gibbs M. Smith: *Mornings in Mexico*
The Viking Press, Inc: *The Collected Letters of D. H. Lawrence; Phoenix; Phoenix II; Psychoanalysis and the Unconscious* and *Fantasia of the Unconscious; The Rainbow; Sex, Literature, and Censorship; Sons and Lovers; Studies in Classic American Literature; Women in Love*
For permission to quote from the works of Ernest Hemingway, as published in the list of titles below, I acknowledge the Executors of the Ernest Hemingway Estate, and the following:
Ernest Hemingway, excerpted from *A Farewell To Arms*. Copyright 1929 Charles Scribner's Sons; copyright renewed © 1957 Ernest Hemingway. Reprinted with the permission of Charles Scribner's Sons and Jonathan Cape Ltd
Ernest Hemingway, excerpted from *The Sun Also Rises*. Copyright 1926 Charles Scribner's Sons; copyright renewed © 1954 Ernest Hemingway. Reprinted with the permission of Charles Scribner's Sons and Jonathan Cape Ltd
Ernest Hemingway, excerpted from 'The Short Happy Life of Francis Macomber' in *The Short Stories of Ernest Hemingway*. Copyright 1938 Ernest Hemingway; copyright renewed © 1966 Mary Hemingway. Reprinted with the permission of Charles Scribner's Sons and Jonathan Cape Ltd
For permission to quote from the works of Norman Mailer, as published in the list of titles below, I acknowledge the following:
Norman Mailer, excerpted from *The Prisoner of Sex*. Copyright © 1971 by Norman Mailer. Used by permission of the author and his agents, Scott Meredith Literary Agency, Inc., 845 Third Avenue, New York, New York 10022
Norman Mailer, excerpted from *The Armies of the Night*. Copyright © 1968 by Norman Mailer. Used by permission of the author and his agents, Scott Meredith Literary Agency, Inc., 845 Third Avenue, New York, New York 10022
Norman Mailer, excerpted from *Marilyn*. Copyright © 1973, 1975 by Alskog Inc., and Norman Mailer. Used by permission of the author and his agents, Scott Meredith Literary Agency, Inc., 845 Third Avenue, New York, New York 10022
Norman Mailer, excerpted from *Advertisements for Myself*. Copyright © 1959 by Norman Mailer. Used by permission of the author

and his agents, Scott Meredith Literary Agency, Inc., 845 Third Avenue, New York, New York 10022

Norman Mailer, excerpted from *The Deer Park*. Copyright © 1955 by Norman Mailer. Used by permission of the author and his agents, Scott Meredith Literary Agency, Inc., 845 Third Avenue, New York, New York 10022

Introduction

I

This study interprets five fictional works by D. H. Lawrence through his fundamental notions about sexual identity and self-definition. In each essay my argument is based on an integrated analysis of Lawrence's artistic technique and informing doctrine, with the underlying unity of his poetic intuition and philosophic thought always the prime concern. This organic methodology – an approach surely consistent with Lawrence's claims as a visionary artist – also expresses two correlative preoccupations that are persistent sub-themes in my criticism: I am interested both in related patterns of feminist misreading of the fiction, and (in more secondary fashion) in several suggestive speculations by Norman Mailer on a recognizable dialectic of love, sex, and ego in Lawrence's art. While my essays are arranged in the chronological order of Lawrence's fiction, they are not offered as the interlocking links in a progressively developed thesis; rather, each essay functions as a contributing piece of evidence, employing similar methods of critical investigation and pointing towards a verdict that highlights the profundity of Lawrence's achievement and the inadequacy of many recent commentaries by his most outspoken detractors. My response to feminist misinterpretations of Lawrence's achievement remains a consistent but subordinate mandate, as it is always the art of the fiction which is central to each chapter. It is in that spirit that my explicit rejoinders to critics are limited to their misreadings that impinge upon my own thematic discussion of each Lawrence work.

By now critical studies of Lawrence that present a unified approach to his fiction and ideology are not uncommon. My own perspective in this volume is different both in the narrow range

1

of its concern and in the precise issues that frame each of the essays. Indeed, I employ a 'selective intensity' of both scope and approach (that is, five fictional works, and one major theme) to relate moments in the fiction to the power of Lawrence's craft, to the meaning of his ideas, and to the errors of a distinct body of committed criticism. I have focused on several scenes in each work for extensive discussion; that selection process is based on my attention to those special qualities of a *dramatized* power in Lawrence's art and doctrine that receives insufficient recognition or understanding today. In short, it is my belief that this organic achievement by Lawrence in fiction, at its best, is as powerfully kinetic as it is expressly dialectic; despite that impressive fusion of the theoretical with the theatrical, it is still the latter appeal that needs more attention from the critics even as they clarify doctrine. Above all, Lawrence values the novel over the discursive essay because fiction captures the elusive 'man alive'.[1] Surely he acknowledges here that it is the montage of moving, passionate moments in the stories and novels that must captivate us before we respond to the sexual ethos that further illuminates a scene. In this regard my approach often highlights Lawrence's kinetic method by slowing the action of his fiction – that is, by freezing a particular vignette from which the novelist's vision gets its initial meaning. My intention is to suggest how a series of riveting episodes in Lawrence's four major novels and most controversial tale become resonant with significance when they are sufficiently 'suspended' to permit an additional clarification of the drama and doctrine that *jointly* inform the art.

Invariably the scenes I select for extensive analysis have an essential relation to Lawrence's vision; because of this integral connection to his 'metaphysic', such scenes tend to attract considerable feminist comment, and – as is often the case in my study – those critics invite responses to their misreadings. In the pages that follow I linger over such prototypical Lawrencian moments as Paul and Miriam's hypnotic fascination with the moon, Walter's poignant response to the news of William's death, Lydia Brangwen's childbirth at home, Anna Brangwen's dance of nullification, Ursula Brangwen's destructive consummations with Skrebensky, Birkin and Ursula's delicate communion at a pond, Connie Chatterley's evocative response to Mrs Flint's baby, and the revealing first reactions of the 'woman who rode away' to her captors. My study does not intend to function as any statement on the complex development and modification by Lawrence through his career of all his relevant notions on sexual identity and self-definition. I am not concerned with a delineation through his complete work of precise shifts in Lawrencian belief; it is the evocation and explanation of his bedrock ethic in selected fictions that I wish to convey. As the titles and preoccupations of several of my chapters suggest, and as the correlative arguments in the notes often indicate, it is through an engaged discussion of Lawrence's fundamental vision – what I call 'the phallic imagination' – that much of the feminist displeasure with him can be revealed as reductive and misleading.

My choice of the four novels is dictated by their recognized central significance in Lawrence's canon and by their documented susceptibility to an interrelated pattern of misreading. My selection of one 'long' short story quite simply reflects my desire to rescue its tarnished reputation from the persistent attacks of its detractors. In each of the essays my analysis of the fiction also suggests that a variety of feminist zeal and ideological sermonizing among critics has resulted in a litany of basic misinterpretation of character and technique, such as the following: an inadequate appreciation of Paul's intrinsic strengths and a sentimentalizing of Miriam's profound emotional flaws in *Sons and Lovers*; an inability to comprehend both Tom's important growth in *The Rainbow* or the archetypal dimensions of his struggle with 'the unknown'; a failure to fully note the purgative role of Ursula's self-defining sex with Skrebensky in *The Rainbow*, and her crucial corrective function in *Women in Love*; a general disinclination to understand both the central theme of marriage in *The Rainbow* and the emphasis on female instinct in *Women in Love*; a tendency to avoid a discussion of the connection between Connie Chatterley's appreciation of Mellors's mode of loving and her previous conditioning in Fabian pieties; a blindness to the incisive evaluative vision of the woman who rode away and an insensitivity to the extent of Lawrence's antagonism to her killers.

II

It may be helpful here to provide a short history of published feminist antagonism to aspects of Lawrence's visionary imagination. Its most standard case against him appears a year after his

death, and it is argued, ironically enough, not by a woman but by
an ex-friend and former collaborator of Lawrence's, J. Middleton
Murry. In *D. H. Lawrence: Son of Woman*, Murry essentially claims
that much of Lawrence's fiction (as well as the novelist's character)
is flawed by evidence of his 'hyper-sensitive masculinity'.[2] His
vindictive study attempts to reduce Lawrence's writings to the
service of a transparent, futile effort to compensate for unresolved
oedipal longings, which invariably emerge – in Murry's facile blue-
printing – as Lawrence's need to make all women 'subject again'
and to 'annihilate the female'.[3] Murry's criticism remains notable
as the first formulation of an attack against Lawrence that is echoed
constantly by many contemporary feminist critics: that Lawrence's
phallic preoccupation is the signature of his psychological weakness and inveterate sexism. Yet in the quarter century after
Murry's study, there is little sustained criticism of Lawrence along
such lines; not that feminists applaud his work in the ensuing
decades, but that his relatively low literary reputation seems to
exempt him from much attention at all during this period.
Prompted by that belated rediscovery of Lawrence around mid-
century (a renewal of interest and admiration spurred by – among
others – F. R. Leavis, Harry T. Moore, Mark Spilka, and Dorothy
Van Ghent), a second wave of feminist displeasure is initiated by
Simone de Beauvoir in 1953 in her short but engaged chapter on
him in *The Second Sex*. Although often respectful and even
admiring on aspects of his creative achievement, de Beauvoir
echoes Murry and anticipates the objections of the coming
women's liberation movement when she argues that Lawrence's
'phallic criticism' is demeaning to women; she concludes with the
simplistic assertion that the goal for a woman in relation to other
men in his fiction is 'for her to bow down before their divinity'.[4]

In the formalistic literary climate of the 1950s and amidst the
insulating directives of the reigning 'new criticism', de Beauvoir's
speculative look at Lawrence inspired minimal attention from
critics and little momentum for further feminist reconsideration of
him.[5] This period of relatively unpoliticized criticism of Lawrence
ended abruptly in 1970 with the publication of Kate Millett's *Sexual
Politics*, a seminal tract that contains a frontal assault on the
fictional vision of such alleged male chauvinists as D. H. Lawrence,
Norman Mailer, and Henry Miller. Millett displays little patience
for moderation in her argument and scant concern for crucial,
subtle nuances in Lawrence's fiction; she is avowedly and unab-

ashedly on an ideological hunt for male demons, as she concludes that Lawrence's work is reactionary and unwholesome for its 'absorption in "phallic consciousness" ' and a 'doctrinaire male-supremacist ethic'.[6]

Despite the occasional acknowledgment today of the qualities of overstatement and narrow partisanship in much of Millett's study, the lack of any sustained, documented response to *Sexual Politics* (except from Norman Mailer) at the time of its publication was not surprising.[7] Her work appeared precisely on the crest of that popular cause known as 'women's liberation', and the wave of movement support in 1970 was spreading into both the academic and commercial publishing markets. Thus her extreme analyses were ready to be received by many editors and feminists as an awaited theoretic manual as well as a retributive piece of revisionist criticism. Indeed, just two years before Millett's staid, heavily annotated text, Mary Ellmann's more breezy and often ironic study, *Thinking About Women*, received appreciative reviews from literary critics and cultural commentators. Her work is less about literature and society than it is about the urgencies of Ellmann's own revolutionary goals, as she continually makes exhortations in the familiar language of the late 1960s: she urges women to free themselves from the perils of misogyny by under-going a metaphysical transformation of self-image and ambition. For my purposes here the book is noteworthy not only for its antagonistic obsession with Norman Mailer, but also for its casual, passing mention – as if it were beyond question – that Lawrence claims 'the most a woman can do' is to be a baby-carrier and 'inspire the man'.[8]

Such an unscrutinized radicalism by Millett and Ellmann suggests the hospitable market by the early 1970s for their fervour. It became not only academically *de rigueur* for a woman to attack writers like Lawrence and Mailer, it was also rewarded in the market place. In 1971, for instance, Germaine Greer's fashionable best-seller, *The Female Eunuch*, sold thousands in hardcover on her version of the myriad institutions, habits, and societal forces that create the catchy oxymoron of her title. Greer's unprobing comments about Lawrence are instructive about the extent of the conformity in criticism induced by the mandates of feminist revalu-ation. Her remarks about him seem to proceed almost against her better aesthetic instincts, as if she feels the awkward obligation to her sister critics to establish her own credentials with the required

Lawrence slur. Greer first objects to what she calls Lawrence's 'inflated imagery'; then she revealingly states that she 'was not sure what was wrong with it' until she became sophisticated enough to understand how such language is part of a systematically manipulative ideal that invariably places women in 'imprisonment in the bourgeois temple'.[9] It is difficult to imagine any criticism of D. H. Lawrence more wide of the mark, as Greer preposterously employs a disingenuous cultural Marxism (a perspective that Lawrence despised) to paint him as the protector of the middle-class values that his fiction seeks to undermine.

Similarly, even the more determinedly academic studies by 1973 of purported sexism in literature reveal the ideological simplifications in the air about Lawrence's achievement. Carolyn Heilbrun's well-received *Towards a Recognition of Androgyny* contains a phrase so dated as to provide a reliable index to the easy trendiness of her critical procedure. Heilbrun (who a few years later would serve as President of the Modern Language Association) asserts – and does not even try to demonstrate – that Lawrence is 'a male chauvinist', and she then proceeds to refashion the ending of one of his major novels to suit the needs of that appeal embodied in her study's title.[10] Although such transparent misreadings and trite slogans of more than a decade ago by Greer and Heilbrun have lost much of their appeal today, there are now new critical tools that are often used both to support the programme of feminist critics and to continue the derogation of Lawrence. As has often been noted by observers of literary culture, beginning in the late 1970s the radical and often ahistorical biases of semiotics and deconstruction find an easy alliance with a variety of pet antagonisms held over from the women's movement of the previous decade. Robert Scholes, for instance, recently makes claims about Lawrence's 'fear of feminine sexuality', an assertion that he deduces from an insufficiently analyzed reference to Lawrence's hostility to clitoral orgasm in *Lady Chatterley's Lover*.[11] Scholes proceeds on the mistaken assumptions that such an alleged aversion can be considered apart from the sexual vision that organically informs the entire novel, and that Mellors's standard of sexual preference is some final word by D. H. Lawrence on the aesthetics of erotic appreciation.

The relative lack of response by critics and the academy to nearly two decades of unequivocal distortion of Lawrence's work carries with it a considerable risk in the province of education. Such silence can sound like community acquiescence to the charges of the revisionists, and that appearance of consensus can open the way to totalitarian 'reforms' that may permanently affect the structure of study in the liberal arts. For instance, the Associate Dean at a fine women's college recently mailed (with open administration endorsement) to each faculty member two attached and revealing items: a well-publicized *Newsweek* article that glowingly discussed the increasing momentum in 1983 towards curriculum revision at colleges to accommodate feminist priorities, and a copy of a more formal academic report, written under the auspices of the Association of American Colleges, titled 'Feminist Scholarship – the Extent of the Revolution', by Florence Howe.[12] Howe's report has a prominent concern with D. H. Lawrence; her perspective sounds like Germaine Greer's, except in the 1980s she writes with the tacit support and advisory power of an academic committee, a national organization of higher education, and a professional journal. In short, goals that once were regarded by idealistic revisionists as merely utopian and theoretical are now provided with mainstream attention and the sanctions of college leaders. In the report Howe explains that early in the 1960s she 'enjoyed reading Lawrence with students', even though 'he is shaped by a male vision that precludes women loving women or even managing deep and lifelasting friendships with women'.[13] In reference to her request for 'women loving women', it is never clear precisely what Howe wants or expects from Lawrence. On the associated issue of friends, one is hard pressed throughout his fiction to find much friendship even between men. Such a scarcity of enduring companionship is part of Lawrence's persistent emphasis on the difficulty of maintaining close relationships in the modern, mechanical world. Howe's remarks gradually develop into an advertisement for the kind of revised literature offerings discussed in the popular pages of *Newsweek*, and there is a real question whether any course slots have been saved for Lawrence in this sanitized curriculum of the future. She openly wonders whether he is fully relevant to the present decade, a period in which, she argues, women work, obtain friendships with women, and are generally liberated from the constrictions she believes Lawrence approves. She concludes her report by quoting out of context from *Sons and Lovers* to highlight her version of Lawrence's supreme ignorance about the basic sexual realities today.

In this contemporary world of burgeoning women's studies in

academia and fashionable androgyny in consumer culture, Lawrence's mystical emphasis on intense polarities between the sexes appears out of style. Thus Howe's confident revisionist zeal can both influence the direction of college curricula and – through her university report's semi-official status – attract positive notice to her subject by a gossipy news story in a popular middlebrow magazine. Even a talented writer like Edmund White uses a prominent review to express admiration for a female novelist through an opinion formulated in the mistaken pieties of 1980s revaluation; here he not only contorts the truth of Lawrence's achievement, but he also parades the misjudgment as recognized fact: 'Unlike Lawrence, she recognized that women are as complex and varied as men'.[14] Similarly, consider the concluding passage in a recent admiring review by a teacher of women's studies at a major university, as she contemplates a new study of 'sexual contradictions' in the life 'of a contemporary professional woman'. The reviewer's expressed idea of the good life cannot be dismissed as the eccentric hobbyhorse of an isolated academic, for her enraptured piece appears (as does White's essay) in that reliable index to acceptable liberal notions in America, the Sunday *New York Times Book Review*. Through the tortuous jargon of its praise, note that the vision extolled is precisely the horror that Lawrence satirizes in the perverse utopianism of the talkers at Wragby estate in *Lady Chatterley's Lover*:

> Ms. Dimen touches on the foundations of a new feminism when she points out that women must be free to assert their sexual desires directly and to infuse their capacity for emotional connections and empathy into an impersonal public sphere. Calling for a new round of feminist utopian thinking, Ms. Dimen offers a vague but intriguing proposition. She asks us to imagine a world without gender where sexual events occur between individuals of any persuasion and eroticism infuses everyday life with pleasure.[15]

III

I do not wish to argue either that the contemporary attack against Lawrence has gone totally unanswered, or that all feminists interpret him in a narrow and partisan manner. Indeed, as early as

1932, Anaïs Nin's modestly titled *D. H. Lawrence: An Unprofessional Study*, a work written in part as a response to Murry's bit of published revenge the previous year, provides a lively and sympathetic reading of Lawrence's vision and craft. Her perspective on him is from that of the alert and isolate 'female' contemplater – a stance, of course, that she will celebrate more famously in her diaries. Nin sees Lawrence's phallic obsessions as not only invigorating for men but also unthreatening, even liberating, to women. In this earliest of feminist appreciations of him, she praises Lawrence's fiction for its seminal understanding that 'it is inequality of sexual power which causes disintegration in sexual relationships. Each man and woman must find his own level';[16] she frequently finds in his work 'an extremely sympathetic feeling for the problems of the modern woman'.[17]

After Nin's appraisal and that extended period of dormancy in Lawrence studies, the 'rediscovery' of Lawrence by mid-century did not need to respond to feminist objections, for that adversarial view was not yet fully articulated. By the early 1960s the admiring Lawrence critics seemed to have won – or at least engaged – all the central aversions to Lawrence except those to be generated shortly by the issue of sexual politics. For instance, Mark Spilka's informative introduction in 1963 to the first major collection of essays by disparate hands on Lawrence provides a balanced summary of the history of critical response to him during the generation after his death. There is understandably a celebratory tone to Spilka's remarks and to the volume's essays, as both editor and contributors appear secure that the case for Lawrence has been made, and that he 'enjoys more widespread popularity and esteem than he knew in his lifetime'.[18] It is noteworthy that in Spilka's relevant litany of the antagonistic groups – 'possessive memorialists, sex cultists, hostile liberals, and religious purists'[19] – from whom Lawrence's reputation has been rescued, there is no term precise enough to anticipate the 'ideological feminists' who wait around the corner. Even Spilka's convenient bibliographical listing of relevant controversies over Lawrence as of 1963 does not suggest the imprisoning strictures of the new dogmatism from which Lawrence would need liberation in the next decade.

It was not until the first period of publicized feminist revisionism – from 1965 to its peak in 1973 with the absurd media event of the King-Riggs tennis match – began to subside that any extended, reasoned response to its attack on Lawrence appeared. Articles in

1975 by Lydia Blanchard and Charles Rossman provide the first more balanced overviews of Lawrence's depiction of women and of his unimpressed critics; both essays attempt some mild counter-attack against the ideologists. Blanchard's argument essentially separates herself from Millett's extreme revaluations, although she often undercuts her critical intuitiveness by a diplomatic willingness to see both Millett and Mailer as equally illegitimate, contrary poles of response to Lawrence. Yet Blanchard admirably seeks to praise Lawrence by demonstrating, in effect, what Florence Howe would not see a decade later: 'the power in his descriptions of intelligent women trapped by a society that provides them inadequate outlets for their talents and energies'.[20] Rossman's longer essay intelligently indicates where ideological hysteria has often demeaned the process of literary criticism with its use of 'reductive formulas and static phrases like "male supremacy" and "guidebooks for women" '.[21] But both Blanchard and Rossman's preliminary answers to a then unexamined body of feminist critiques are clearly self-conscious and tepid about their implicit mission to set the record straight. There is still an apologetic air about their own consideration of 'the woman issue' in Lawrence, as if in some sense Millett's contempt is often justified, and that Millett can be dismissed only if Mailer can be equally lambasted. There is also the inclination in both essays to applaud the most polemical arguments of feminist criticism as correct. For instance, Blanchard and Rossman are in a hurry to agree with the emphatic, unprobing attack against Lawrence's apparently vulnerable tale, 'The Woman Who Rode Away'. Rossman even sounds a bit like a righteous Millett when he argues that the tale 'suggests an animus against women verging on sadism',[22] and Blanchard affirms that it is surely the story with the most 'evidence for an indictment against Lawrence's attitudes toward women'.[23]

Apparently it continues to be difficult even in the 1980s for intelligent critics to drop the ideological baggage of a previous decade. For instance, Hilary Simpson's well-researched and often impressive book, *D. H. Lawrence and Feminism*, is a 1982 work that attempts a badly needed synthesis in Lawrence studies: Simpson supplies both an historical overview of Lawrence's relation to his own contemporary feminist culture, and a selective interpretation of his works in light of feminist ideas today. But her work is demonstrably strongest when it summarizes the relation of Lawrence to women's issues in England from 1914 to 1930, and predictably weakest when it seeks to denigrate Lawrence's fictional achievement by the current standards of emancipation ideology. Although more reasonable and sensitive than the doctrinaire feminists of the early 1970s, Simpson frequently misreads key moments in his novels by submitting them too willingly to the scrutiny of Millett's directives rather than to the more nurturant impulses of Lawrence's framing vision.[24] As my comments on the workings of 'the phallic imagination' in *Lady Chatterley's Lover* will indicate, I am quite willing to commend Simpson's study for its unusual willingness to argue that phallic preoccupations in Lawrence's fiction do not suggest that he is anti-woman. But once she establishes that essential understanding (lost to female critics since Anaïs Nin's study), Simpson often supplies consensus feminist doctrine rather than probing literary analysis of the works.

The first unequivocal response to that ideological disparagement of Lawrence was in a highly publicized set of essays by Norman Mailer, *The Prisoner of Sex*, first published in *Harper's Magazine*, and in book form several months later in 1971. The work is a significant rumination by a major writer (who is also the subject of feminist wrath) on sexuality, modern society, and the sense of self; his lyrical defence of D. H. Lawrence achieves a special power because of Mailer's wise strategy of advocacy: he willingly pits his own style of a passionate, speculative informality against the doctrinal resentments evident in Millett's reductive approach to life and literature. Above all, Mailer isolates with epigrammatic precision the essential direction of Lawrence's life and creative labour. That is, he identifies the dominant existential strain behind Lawrence's obsession with love and identity; he further relates that novelist's often enigmatic use of the 'unknown' to Lawrence's correlative mandate to lose one's ego in the act of sexual transcendence. Aspects of such a reading of Lawrence have occurred to other critics through the years. Yet it is only Mailer who – spurred no doubt by the urgencies of sexual politics and by the perception of Lawrencian influence in his own work – effortlessly demonstrates, in effect, Lawrence's fusion of the transcendental drift of mid-nineteenth-century romanticism with the existential *angst* of the modern world.

Thus Mailer rebuts Millett, not only by isolating several precise errors in her reading and methodology but also by suggesting that her one-track criticism leads to an obliviousness of the literary and philosophical traditions embodied in Lawrence's work. Perhaps what is more unusual about Mailer's provocative summary of Lawrence is the scant attention it has received from critics. Full-length studies of Lawrence or Mailer in the last fifteen years rarely do more than briefly acknowledge the *Prisoner of Sex* as a curious footnote in the history of Mailer's inevitable front-page skirmishes.[25] I do not pretend to offer in my essays more than various interrelated applications of Mailer's analysis to my own stated concern with Lawrence's fiction and patterns of feminist misreading. But there is often in my approach to Lawrence the implicit acknowledgement of the fundamental accuracy of Mailer's judgement of him, and I remain concerned that his criticism has still not received its necessary due.

IV

The record of the last decade in Lawrence criticism may show that it was left to me – by the virtual default of the academy – to supply a missing voice in response to feminist charges. Thus I add the following personal notes in this introduction to explain more fully the relevance of the essays in this volume, the motivations that produced them, and the several preoccupations they share. In 1975, the late Harry T. Moore, a pioneer Lawrence biographer and critic, prominently and generously reviewed my first book on Lawrence, which was a formalistic study of what I call 'the psychology of rhythm'. In the next few years my approach to Lawrence became less structural in its emphasis, as I felt an impatience with the ideological disparagement of Lawrence that was increasingly popular in the early 1970s. At that time I also wished to acknowledge my own debt to the inspiring defence offered by Mailer in *The Prisoner of Sex*. As my first major expression of these preoccupations, an essay of mine was published on *Sons and Lovers* that considered the issues of sexual identity and self-definition in relation both to the metaphoric structure of that novel and to feminist revaluations of it.

Harry T. Moore immediately sent me a warm letter of support for that article's argument, and he also conveyed his sad speculations about the relative silence in academia in the last decade to that extreme revisionism spear-headed by Millett. A few months later he invited me to give the featured lecture (as a late replacement for Leslie Fiedler) at the largest international conference on

Lawrence ever convened – a four-day, NEH sponsored event in 1979 at Southern Illinois University. I chose as my topic an unambiguous answer to the harsh recent attacks directed at the sexual ethics of *Lady Chatterley's Lover*. My intention was to provoke response not by denying the eminently phallic vision of the work but by stipulating the targets of Lawrence's emphatic attack in this fiction. I wished to demonstrate how the phallus as metaphor, participant, and metaphysical centre of the novel suggests Lawrence's renewing and existential view of love and sex. In that heyday of apparent acquiescence to feminist assaults, my remarks produced a storm of controversy and publicity along heated partisan lines, and the resulting skirmishes and tensions at that conference have been chronicled frequently in Lawrence journals and conferences through the years. The several other essays in this volume are a further testament to the concern that I uncomfortably carried from Illinois: if an academic consensus was so unsettled by my articulated response to feminist fervours, is it possible that any spirited defence today of Lawrence's sexual dialectic is perceived as a revisionist position?

There is another relevant circumstance that fuels my desire to elaborate on this theme of Lawrence's visionary imagination. The first versions of these essays appeared during my tenure as a Professor of English at Wells College, an excellent and venerable women's college in upstate New York. Like many women's colleges in the late 1970s, Wells had gradually accommodated aspects of its mission, curriculum, and campus life to the ideals and agenda of the women's movement; in my view such revisions were not always beneficial to the spirit both of liberal arts and the inquiring student mind. Motivated in part by my desire to teach against the grain of what I felt was a trendy accommodation, I had initiated an upper-level course at Wells in 1973, titled English 354, 'Studies in Fiction: Lawrence, Hemingway, and Mailer'; it has grown to be a popular if somewhat controversial elective through the years. In the spring of 1984 my scholarship, teaching and residence at Wells were all conjoined in an unusual and pleasant circumstance: Norman Mailer graciously responded to me after I had written a variety of articles on my perception of the influence of Lawrence and Hemingway on his work. I informed him of the intense interest in him and his work at Wells, and he cheerfully agreed to undertake his first visit to an all women's college in about fifteen years. During his stay he delivered a series of provocative remarks to a packed auditorium, provided a revealing reading of his own work, and met many of the current and former members of English 354, including many middle-aged alumni who had travelled many miles for the session. It is here that I wish to acknowledge a special debt to those students through the years who pushed me to battle them in class and forced me – on penalty of certain death – to defend many of the notions embodied in this study. A special thanks is here inscribed to Norman Mailer, both for his inspiring work and for tolerating the lovely chaos of that autumn visit.

Notes

1. Lawrence, 'Why the Novel Matters', in Edward D. McDonald (ed.), *Phoenix: The Posthumous Papers of D. H. Lawrence* (New York: Viking, 1972), 538.
2. J. Middleton Murry, *D. H. Lawrence: Son of Woman* (London: Jonathan Cape, 1954), 72. Hilary Simpson reaches the same point about Murry's early 'feminist' evaluation of Lawrence, but she is scrupulously non-judgemental about Murry's conclusions. Hilary Simpson, *D. H. Lawrence and Feminism* (Dekalb: Northern Illinois University Press; London: Croom Helm, 1982), 13.
3. Ibid., 118.
4. Simone de Beauvoir, *The Second Sex* (New York: Alfred A. Knopf, 1968; Harmondsworth: Penguin, 1972), 223.
5. Although by no means a feminist critic, Eliseo Vivas in 1960 objects to Lawrence's term 'phallic marriage', and wonders why it should not be replaced, or augmented, by a female term, *D. H. Lawrence: The Failure and the Triumph of Art* (Bloomington: Indiana University Press, 1960), 268.
6. Kate Millett, *Sexual Politics* (Garden City: Doubleday, 1970; London: Virago, 1977), 257.
7. An unusual exception is the characteristically blunt Midge Decter, who speaks of Millett's 'specific assertions and points of attack' as radiating 'a vulgarity almost not to be credited in this age of mass higher education'. In a related long footnote Decter documents the extent of Millett's faulty and manipulative appropriation of the Adam and Eve myth, in *The New Chastity and Other Arguments Against Women's Liberation* (New York: Capricorn Books, 1974), 100.
8. Mary Ellmann, *Thinking About Women* (New York: Harcourt Brace Jovanovich, 1968), 16.
9. Germaine Greer, *The Female Eunuch* (New York: McGraw-Hill; London: Paladin, 1971), 181, 182.
10. Carolyn G. Heilbrun, *Towards a Recognition of Androgyny* (New York: Harper & Row, 1974), 102.

11. Robert Scholes, *Semiotics and Interpretation* (New Haven: Yale University Press, 1982), 140.
12. Howe's essay is from 'Liberal Education and the New Scholarship on Women: Issues and Constraints in Institutional Change', from the *Report of the Wingspread Conference*, Association of American Colleges, 1981. The accompanying *Newsweek* article is entitled 'Out of the Academic Ghetto', from the issue of 31 October 1983.
13. Howe, 'Liberal Education and the New Scholarship on Women: Issues and Constraints in Institutional Change', 6.
14. Edmund White, 'The Woman who Loved Memory', *The New York Times Book Review*, 25 May 1986, 7.
15. Patricia McBroom, 'Envy in the Afternoon', *The New York Times Book Review*, 2 November 1986, 41.
16. Anaïs Nin, *D. H. Lawrence: An Unprofessional Study* (Chicago: Swallow Press, 1964; London: Black Spring Press, 1985), 27.
17. Ibid., 50.
18. Mark Spilka (ed.), *D. H. Lawrence: A Collection of Critical Essays* (Englewood Cliffs, Prentice-Hall, 1963), 1.
19. Ibid.
20. Lydia Blanchard, 'Love and Power: A Reconsideration of Sexual Politics in D. H. Lawrence', in *Modern Fiction Studies* 21 (1975), 443.
21. Charles Rossman, ' "You are the call and I am the answer": D. H. Lawrence and Women', in *The D. H. Lawrence Review* 8 (1975), 257.
22. Ibid., 257.
23. Blanchard, 'Love and Power: A Reconsideration of Sexual Politics in D. H. Lawrence', 441.
24. As a glaring evidence of this pattern, note Simpson's approval of Millett's silly statement that Paul 'nonchalantly disposes of' Clara. So nonchalant, one is tempted with pain and irony to remind Simpson and Millett, that Paul willingly undergoes a painful beating as the evidence both of a lack of concern and an absence of emotional stress. See Hilary Simpson, *D. H. Lawrence and Feminism*, 29.
25. Even Robert Merrill, in what stands as the most in-depth and sympathetic treatment of Mailer's work up to 1978, can say little more than 'the best that can be said about *The Prisoner of Sex* is that it is much better than its critics have insisted', in *Norman Mailer* (Boston: Twayne Publishers, 1978), 141. Similarly, Richard Poirier's earlier study of Mailer makes many scattered references to *The Prisoner of Sex*, a work that Poirier considers an uneven recapitulation of themes Mailer treats in greater depth elsewhere. There is little effort by Poirier to grapple with the full range of Mailer's argument and the structure of the work; an admiring passing reference to Mailer's reading of Lawrence is all Poirier offers on the issue of Mailer's unusual criticism of that novelist, in *Norman Mailer* (New York: Viking, 1972).

1

Forging and Feminism: *Sons and Lovers* and the Phallic Imagination

'Oh, I wish he would *stand up*.'
D. H. Lawrence, on seeing a statue of the Buddha.[1]

I

The seminal importance of the preoccupations and techniques of *Sons and Lovers* remains relatively unstated in recent years. Lawrence's emphasis on a 'priapic' ethos of masculine assertion and independence is widely regarded as inappropriate to the fashionable androgyny of contemporary culture. Clearly, this early work is a hymn to the phallus, as the shape of *Sons and Lovers* – from plot to moralism to metaphor – reflects Lawrence's purging effort, as artist and prophet, to dramatize his insistence on Paul's required sunderings; such 'separations' by Paul are depicted as part of the necessary struggle for mature and healthy sexuality both in the male protagonist and – by that felt extension of the doctrine and autobiography integrated in this novel – in the novelist and in his readers. What is purged before the novel can be completed is no less than a young man's accumulated experience of emotional and sexual confusion. The Lawrence–Paul character concludes his battle for identity not with any sentimental

16

security about the future, but with the knowledge, finally, o₁ ᵤ_
ordered and resolved past.

Feminist critics make allegations about Paul's confident 'faith in
male supremacy',[2] or his 'overtly manipulative'[3] strategies, or his
purported status as 'conqueror'[4] at novel's end, or his supposedly
'brilliant condition'[5] on the last page; these commentators mistake
the hero's implicit promise and brave resolution for a self-confi-
dence he cannot possess. Paul does gather together his resources
as he heads toward the glowing city. There is no indication of
some adamant strength in his character in the last chapter,
although such a trait is asserted by the feminists to be one measure
of the novelist's chauvinistic commitment to his fictional persona.
Lawrence's notorious delay in finishing *Sons and Lovers* is partly a
result of his instinctive sense that this novel would predict his
coming manhood as much as it dramatized his growth through
boyhood and adolescence.[6] He had to get it right. In writing his
version of the pubescent youth who struggles to become a sexually
emancipated adult – that is, in deriving a damaged but potent
Paul Morel, Lawrence, in effect, has derived himself as artist. He
is then free to speak poetry and doctrine to the world, for he has
made poetry in *Sons and Lovers* out of the tangled indoctrinations
of his own formative years.

But today there is reticence to discuss the fundamentality of the
phallic urgencies in *Sons and Lovers*; there is even less inclination
to justify Paul's difficult but necessary decisions to break off ties
with women who, in very different ways, have loved him and
have contributed to his growth as artist, lover, and man. Indeed,
as Alfred Kazin perceptively implies in an attack on the anti-
literary bias of so much current 'women's literature', such reticence
may be the symptom of cultural disease as well as of the vagaries
of critical disfavour.[7] Doctrines about phallic assertion are
dismissed as merely *macho*, or branded as the product of
subversive sexual politics – 'at a time when Freud's Victorian
illusion that women have penis envy has been replaced in up-to-
date America by penis hatred'.[8] Reconsideration of *Sons and Lovers*
is central in the current feminist momentum to camouflage, dislo-
cate, and misrepresent Lawrence's art and doctrine. Florence
Howe's casual dismissal of Lawrence's relevance for women in the
1980s, in her glowing college commission report on 'The Extent of
the Revolution' in feminist scholarship,[9] is representative of the
narrow ideological attacks this novel provokes today. Howe criti-

cizes Paul's pertinent questioning of the motivations in Miriam for her persistent preoccupation with her own career and with the issue of 'work' for women. Howe fails to note that Paul's scepticism about Miriam's answers results from his painful, developing understanding both of the nature of her emotional insufficiency, and of her attempt to mask her organic imbalance with lame excuses about institutional biases against women.

Other feminist critics are even more unprobing in their reactions to Lawrence's dramatized impatience in *Sons and Lovers* with merely political explanations for personal failure or inadequacy. In its most common form, such criticism of this novel reaches a variety of conclusions, most of which trivialize Lawrence and often allege nearly criminal behaviour on the part of Paul and his creator:

> Instead of examining the interactions of real men and women, what Lawrence actually wrote about was the relationship between men and a series of female stereotypes.[10]

> Lawrence is a ruthless user of women . . . the mother, Miriam, and Clara are all manipulated in Paul's painful effort at self-identity, the effort to become himself.[11]

> Paul kills or disregards the women who have been of use to him.[12]

> Readers . . . similarly allow themselves to be victimized by the narrator of *Sons and Lovers*.[13]

> As usual in Millett's criticism, there is much of a certain kind of truth in this savage account of the end of the novel.[14]

In short, Lawrence is often read today to see whether he fits into the straitjackets of feminist ideology, and consequently he is dismissed with condescending remarks about his deviation from our culture's latest celebration of party propaganda. To read or teach *Sons and Lovers* in this revisionist climate – 'in the teeth' of what Mailer acidly calls 'a growing piety in the treatment of women'[15] – is to sense the validity of a remark by a perceptive female critic, who warns that 'the trouble with feminist critics is that anything that passes for celebration of the male can be read as denigration of the female'.[16]

Even the more academic and undoctrinaire approaches to *Sons and Lovers* too frequently are unsatisfactory. Often the significance of the repetitive patterns of tension in Paul's sexual apprenticeship receives insufficient attention. Much of the criticism of *Sons and Lovers* is disturbingly fragmentary, refusing in a variety of ways to reckon with the cumulative burden of emphasis that unifies Paul's tripartite phallic struggle. It remains easier, apparently, to discuss his individual entanglements with Miriam, Clara, and Gertrude than to stress how the interrelating design of these involvements suggests the adamance of Lawrence's sexual ethic in the novel. The standard analysis of *Sons and Lovers* offers insight into Paul's relationship with one or more of the women, but the reiterated insistence of Lawrence's ethics – not to mention that supportive symmetry of his various metaphors of love and sex – all this unified superstructure of the novel largely is ignored.[17] Recent studies of this novel, despite various strengths in their critical perspective, tend to minimize an awareness of Lawrence's *fusion* of art and prophesy in favour of the more politicized issue of 'blame' for the negative nature of Paul's relationships.[18]

The direction of Paul's experience seems obvious enough: Paul Morel becomes sufficiently 'involved' with three women so that he finally recognizes, and for different reasons for each woman, the urgency of his need for sexual emancipation from them. Perhaps the reasons for D. H. Lawrence's emphasis on sexual survival is best stated by Norman Mailer, in his remarks on Lawrence in *The Prisoner of Sex*:

> And sexual transcendence, some ecstasy where he could lose his ego for a moment, and his sense of self and his will, was life to him – he could not live without sexual transcendence. . . . Each time he failed to reach a woman, each time he failed particularly to reach his own woman, he was dying a little. It is hopeless to read his books and try to understand the quirky changeable fury-ridden relationships of his men and women without comprehending that Lawrence saw every serious love affair as fundamental do-or-die: he knew he literally died a little more each time he missed transcendence in the act. It was why he saw lust as hopeless. Lust was meaningless fucking and that was the privilege of the healthy. He was ill, and his wife was literally killing him each time she failed to worship his most proud and delicate cock.[19]

Mailer's apocalyptic analysis is appropriate for the urgencies of

Sons and Lovers – Lawrence's early *Bildungsroman* of phallic worship and sexual baptism. The novel is insistent in its equation: Paul Morel will not have enduring love, or fulfilling work, or abiding faith, or meaningful friendships, or good relations with his family without the experience that Mailer calls 'sexual transcendence'. And Paul cannot transcend 'his ego . . . and his sense of self and his will' until he recognizes that the threats to him posed by Miriam, Clara, and Gertrude are different versions of the same problem. Each woman seeks to cripple that fundamental source of energy in him which I shall call his 'phallic imagination'. In this regard, Kate Millett's sneering description of Paul as 'the perfection of self-sustaining ego'[20] describes a state of power and confidence in him that never exists; in the essential paradox that fuels the poignant tensions of this novel, the three women who nourish his ego also provide emotional traps that nearly doom him to egocentric patterns of failure.

Thus each woman, by limiting or perverting the scope or quality of the love she offers Paul, also short-circuits Paul's ability to respond – as a confident male and with that proud existential assertion of self – to the daily challenges posed by work, family, and friends. The instinctive execution of such assertion by a male signifies organic health to Lawrence. Or put still another way, to catch the precise paradox of Lawrence's demand when it is subjected to Mailer's provocative terminology: Paul cannot surrender his ego to the realm of transcendent sex until he has confirmed, for himself, that bottom-line power of the self to discard the spurious appeal of bad love. Thus the demands of Lawrence's ethics, with all their categories of judgement, are vigorously puritanical: no transcendent sex without the death of bad sex, and no creative man until there is transcendent sex. It is in this prescriptive sense, once we grasp the full implications of Lawrence's sexual dialectic, that *Sons and Lovers* must speak to us of biographical secrets. It reveals how Lawrence–Paul promises to make love at least well enough to write his novel, as he learns to abandon those counterfeit passions which nullify the force of his phallic imagination.[21] Critic Faith Pullin has her own priorities here; she conveniently overstates Paul's erotic ability, as she refers contemptuously to Lawrence's alleged need to show how Paul's lover is 'swept away by [his] expertise'.[22] Such a view of him ultimately misses the tentative, baptismal nature of Paul's sexual awakening with Clara. Even through his most indulgent sex-play with her, Paul never appears even vaguely like a stud, for he cannot sustain himself with mere egoistic forays into manipulative passion. He remains a young man who senses – to use Mailer's distinction in the quotation above – that he can only *do* (and not die) when he fully exorcises those demon lovers who come to hinder his emergence into independent manhood. Feminists tend to misconstrue Paul's sexual experiences as achievement, while a cautious Lawrence depicts them as risky, necessary way-stations towards that ideal of transcendent, polarized sex he demands and describes in *Women In Love*.[23]

II

Just a few pages into *Sons and Lovers*, Gertrude Morel significantly reveals how ferociously at the age of only nineteen she holds account of a male's manhood. She has just ignored a suitor's praise of her hair and then directed their conversation to the issue of job choice. Now she cuts through his expression of vocational powerlessness with her unequivocal assertion of the sexual ethic that obsesses her throughout the novel:

> She held her head erect. He was rather timid before her.
> 'But my father's so stiff-necked. He means to put me into the business, and I know he'll do it.'
> 'But if you're a *man*?' she had cried.
> 'Being a man isn't everything,' he replied, frowning with puzzled helplessness.
> Now, as she moved about her work at the Bottoms, with some experience of what being a man meant, she knew that it was *not* everything.[24]

So even as a young woman Gertrude Coppard speaks with the energy and discontent that characterize her throughout the novel. Her insistence with timid John Field is only partly to her credit and only partially correct. Surely she is right to claim that manhood should mean a great deal, particularly in the often callous but unequivocally 'man's' world of competitive industry and coal mining in late nineteenth-century Nottingham. But even here, when her disgust appears legitimate, Gertrude comes off as a bit of a phallic taskmaster. She urges a similarly demanding ethic on

Walter with such wilful fervour early in their marriage that we suspect more may be at stake than the general outlines of Lawrence's emphasis on male assertion. For what is revealed is nothing less than her own nagging and neurotic sexual envy of the state of manhood itself. 'Not everything' is too strident in its emphasis, as it fails to disguise the germ of Gertrude's later bitterness over her station in marriage and her own gender's restrictions in this male-centred community. Her cynical phrasing also registers her unfair and insensitive reading of the imperatives under which the uneducated men of Nottingham must conduct their lives; that is, Gertrude is unable to empathize with the variety of pressures, competitions, and dangers that bedevil these intrinsically limited, male breadwinners in the harsh and unforgiving mining world.

Thus Gertrude's justifiable irritation with a cowardly suitor and an irresponsible husband should not obscure our perception of the organic confusions in this mother. Gertrude's source of irritation is not simply a socially conditioned envy of class, caste, or business opportunity. Lawrence suggests that a basic cause of Gertrude's baiting of Walter, and of her later smothering attachment to her sons, is in the insecure nature of her own female sexuality. Yes, the fertile Mrs Morel can raise and nurture children with a large degree of warmth and pleasure; but there remains in her a wasteful and manifest frustration – often perceived by Walter – that she was not born male, not born beyond the imposed social and intellectual limitations of her gender and her role as mother. In this sense Paul must be raised as Gertrude's compensating version of the effective, contributing mate. He must try to be man enough for both of them, but on the displaced terms established by an ambitious mother. He must be motivated sufficiently by the mother's influence to spurn the father's job at the mines and also to create, through his own artistic vocation, the new terms of family manhood dictated by Gertrude. Paul comes to see that it is not only Walter's work that Gertrude despises, but also the poison of a broken husband that gradually infects the atmosphere at home. Thus the son must do more than grow up as the embodiment of his mother's crusading standards about male demeanour and success. He must also grasp silently the lesson evident in Gertrude's attitude every day: that Paul must not fail – as Walter eventually does – to radiate strength and purpose in the family and at his chosen occupation. Paul knows the ferocity of disappointed love that flows from his mother, and he does not wish it to be directed at him.

Walter senses but cannot articulate the complex psychosexual scenarios and the underlying stakes that inform his own battles with Gertrude. For instance, after Walter vindictively cuts off the opulent hair of William because he senses that the boy will be feminized by his dominating mother, Lawrence describes the erotic compulsions of Gertrude's reaction:

> 'Oh – my boy!' she faltered. Her lip trembled, her face broke, and, snatching up the child, she buried her face in his shoulder and cried painfully. She was one of those women who cannot cry; whom it hurts as it hurts a man. It was like ripping something out of her, her sobbing.
>
> Morel sat with his elbows on his knees, his hands gripped together till the knuckles were white. He gazed in the fire, feeling almost stunned, as if he could not breathe. (15)

An impressively proud and isolated woman, no doubt. But in a revelatory scene of primal family tensions, she hurts suspiciously 'as it hurts a man' – with too much at stake for her to permit without great pain the luxurious cry of female anguish. Walter is often drunk and undependable, and he is fading from her sex life, yet she willingly inherits the male prerogatives of what he abrogates. The androgynous nature of her predicament is caught here in the contradictory imagery of that evocative sexual gesture with William. She becomes both the violator and the violated, as she both 'buries her face in his shoulder' to claim him for her own and also feels the 'ripping out' of a virginity that, being part of William, is now her own. Walter sits transfixed, a witness to a terror he can feel but not understand. It is the terror which he helps create by leaving the battle to his wife, and then accelerates by wounding her damaged sex with his profound admonition when he sees William's long hair: 'yer non want ter make a wench on 'im' (15).

Versions of this frenetic tableau of the father reduced to an emasculated but strangely moving reticence and of the mother racked with a passion which is resonant and displaced reappear throughout *Sons and Lovers*, particularly during those expressive moments of rites of passage. In one moving episode, years after Walter cuts the hair of their first-born son, the strength and purpose in the family is all Gertrude's, as she plays master to bring home the body of William. She is kept from emotional collapse – for her tie to William was, at the very least, abnormally close – by her determination to do what the official father has long since lost the ability to have done. Only a few pages earlier, when Paul comes to the pits to tell the father of the death of his son, Lawrence writes quietly and with a poignantly cadenced appropriateness:

> Morel walked on a few strides, then leaned up against a truck-side, his hand over his eyes. He was not crying. Paul stood looking round, waiting. On the weighing machine a truck trundled slowly. Paul saw everything, except his father leaning against the truck as if he were tired. (137)

Here is a son pained by the death of a brother, a son who is unable now to watch his father, not because of the torment the son will see, but because *even now*, in this moment of family tragedy, this son's connection is not with the father. Biological connections are askew at the Morels. Paul merely carries the news from his mother. Here is a father whose greatest measure of pain – and no small one at that – must be his persistent fatigue with it all: with the indomitable process of life and death for a collier, and with the inevitable exhaustion from a deadening job that provides his only manner of self-definition in the family. Walter must live at the mines for more hours than he spends at home, and in this incongruously delicate vignette, the machines shamelessly and appropriately still move in the hours of his son's death. So Walter must stop, for a brief moment, his self-protective dependency on the mindless whirring of machines, in order to assess a new turn of events. Yes, there is real pain in Walter's response, but Lawrence's muted portrait describes only what it must. The domain of Walter's male emotional assertion can scarcely reach beyond his job to the thought of death at home. Lawrence elaborates most fully in *Lady Chatterley's Lover* on this destructive relation between looming technological power and the province of the phallic imagination; in my final chapter I shall discuss the implicit sexual dialectic that he uses to highlight such a connection.

Yet Walter has given up more than William and Paul to Gertrude. While he is at the mines, Gertrude talks to Paul in such a way as to suggest to him both the inadequacies of his defaulting father and her own support for Paul's adherence to certain strict and traditional measurements of male potency: ' "I like Mr. Barker – I *do* like him. There's something so manly about him." Paul resumed his task silently' (87). Paul's silence speaks the pain of his understanding. Gertrude then pretends to appear apologetic about Walter's unmanly need for attention in the hospital. To young Paul Morel the message must be very clear: listen to me, his mother claims, and you will be a real man. It is a message affirmed by the climate of opinion Gertrude absorbs at the feminist conclaves of the Women's Guild that she periodically attends. There is the suggestion by Lawrence that perhaps such meetings contribute to the increasingly vitriolic attitude that Gertrude displays towards Walter; it is as if she now has a political right to undercut his fading authority at home, especially when he gradually fails in the man's traditional world of authority, money, and physical power. If he has so ruined his prospects away from home, and undercut his own presence in the family, then Gertrude henceforth shall vigorously set all standards for conduct and responsibility in the Morel household.

In her interesting discussion of the role of feminism in *Sons and Lovers*, Hilary Simpson praises the novel for its ability 'to portray with unusual clarity the economic basis of women's oppression'.[25] Her praise is justified as a record of Lawrence's awareness of the relative lack of institutional power in women during the period in which he writes. Yet Simpson significantly fails to note one of Lawrence's correlative observations in the novel that he dramatizes with equal force: that an awareness by a middle-aged mother like Mrs Morel of aspects of sexism against women, particularly as she becomes aware of such restrictions in the unbending mining community in which the Morels reside, may be the granting of a knowledge to her that will further undermine the family's emotional security. A little unefficacious learning can be a dangerous thing for one so striving, discontented, and frustrated as Mrs Morel; it fuels an unreserved spitefulness in her relation to Walter, and thus provides him with an anger from his wife that he can neither tolerate nor answer. Perhaps it even sparks that *organic* consciousness of lost power in Gertrude which will terminate in the cancerous stomach that too appropriately becomes her illness and her metaphor.

Gertrude is also a master with words, and Walter is no match for her verbal vengeance and honed rhetorical skill. To Gertrude, quite simply, a real man follows the letter of the law. On one occasion Walter returns home as an enraged drunk, although he is partly lost in liquor to escape that wife who would seek to change water to wine, who 'strove to make him moral, religious' (14). Gertrude then has the horrid judgement to use this occasion to demand a literal confession from her husband of his drunken state. She insists that he speak the words of proof for all to hear, as she invites him to further betray his manhood through her brutal epistemological game:

> 'Say you're *not* drunk!' she flashed. . . .
> ' "Say you're not drunk," ',' he repeated. 'Why, nobody but a nasty little bitch like you 'ud 'ave such a thought.' (22)

Walter is shocked that the issue here should be construed by his wife as verbal; it makes no sense to him that he should be requested to prove he is drunk by lying he is not. Only Gertrude, he claims with his incisive dialect, would use a chaotic time like this to assert the sophistic proofs of a rigged catechism.

Lawrence's belief years after the publication of *Sons and Lovers* that the portrait of Walter may have overemphasized the lack of his father's authority, and Lawrence's apparent need to adjust key episodes involving Gertrude, Paul, and Miriam to absorb his recent understanding of Freud's Oedipus theory – all this evidence of a delicate process of evaluation is consistent with his anguished attempt to balance the characterization of Gertrude.[26] He must always measure her possessive love for Paul against that fierce vitality Paul receives from her. Or in terms of the poignant and ironic burden of cause and effect in the drama itself of *Sons and Lovers*: Lawrence must balance Gertrude's destructive love for her son against that strength of character in Paul Morel, inherited from his mother, which permits Paul heroically to accept her death, to hasten it, and to promise to recover from it. We are meant to feel, with consequent sobering effects on an excessively negative opinion of Gertrude, that those large reserves of strength in Paul which take him through his mother's illness come from Gertrude herself, that his dogged ability to survive is her final gift to him, the bequest anticipated by Lawrence early in the novel: 'From his mother he drew the life warmth: the strength to produce' (58). As if one day he will have the strength to fashion, from the kindled warmth that becomes the fire of his phallic imagination, the story of his own emergent history.

III

For Lawrence will fashion a life and a novel in just those terms.
Fire, that energy which cleanses and kills, is a fundamental
resource of his metaphors of sexual revivification. *Sons and Lovers*
contains symbolic manipulations of the phoenix motif. His
patterned and insistent use in critical scenes of such words as
'flame', 'heat', 'melt', and 'fire' recalls the appropriateness of
Mailer's explanation of the do-or-die need for sexual transcendence
by Lawrence. Fire remains central to the notion that mature sexual
love burns off, in the actual forging heat of its passion, those
delimiting and personalized impurities of will, ego, and self in each
lover. Lawrence mandates a love which starts as the existential
assertion of the sexual 'separateness' of each lover and which
concludes with each lover's apprehension of the transcendent
force that animates the 'mystical, real otherness' of pure male and
female energies.[27] The lovers are balanced ('polarized') amid the
creative tensions of their separated sexual selves, which were
singled out in the intense forging of their union.[28] They move from
the *angst* of those clarifying flames to the awe at the recognition of
the energy beyond the fire. Thus the ideal impulse of love for
Lawrence embodies a species of existential transcendentalism; the
intrinsic power of lovers to get beyond their ego, will, and self
rests on the strength and willingness with which they assert the
raw power of their 'maximum selves' in the act of heterosexual
love.[29]

Late in the novel this metaphoric relation between flames and
sexuality is spelled out in a discursive explanation by Paul to
Miriam. Here Lawrence's theory of the phallic imagination is
broadened to include consideration of lovers who were 'baptized'
by the fire, but in middle age find the ashes of their marriage. The
passage is notable not only for the sustaining ethic that it formulates, but also for the timing of such remarks in relation to Paul's
developing experience. Tiring of Clara and frustrated with Miriam,
he still begins to sense the value of the engaged passion that
Lawrence will celebrate, in different ways, for years to come:

'That's what one *must have*, I think,' he continued – 'the real,
real flame of feeling through another person – once, only once,
if it only lasts three months. See, my mother looks as if she'd

had everything that was necessary for her living and developing. There's not a tiny bit of feeling of sterility about her.'

'No,' said Miriam.

'And with my father, at first, I'm sure she had the real thing. She knows; she has been there. You can feel it about her, and about him, and about hundreds of people you meet every day; and, once it has happened to you, you can go on with anything and ripen'. . . .

Miriam pondered this. She saw what he was seeking – a sort of baptism of fire in passion, it seemed to her. (317–18)

The fire metaphor reappears, of course, in key moments of many Lawrence works; it can suggest either the rebirth from ashes via Lawrence's familiar phoenix motif, or the signal, initial contact of erotic desire that transcends, in its potent heat, the cold enclosure of ego. In both instances (rebirth or desire), fire conveys the fourth-dimensional notion of *literal* flame that is basic to the texture of Lawrencian prose; Lawrence's trope of forging thus becomes less a matter of mere figurative speech in *Sons and Lovers* than a mode of perceived experience by a character. Although Miriam 'saw what he was seeking' in this passage, the vitalistic phrase 'baptism of fire in passion' has little more than merely descriptive significance for her. She can never look beyond metaphors, for she manages to distance experience from herself by interpreting symbols only as the easy signposts of correspondence. But Paul insists that the 'real flame' burns as well as describes, because it initiates the actual forging that results in the singling out he outlines to Miriam.

In one luminous scene earlier in *Sons and Lovers*, Lawrence had dramatized the accuracy of Paul's analysis of his parents' connection to each other. Here it is clear that the flames of Lawrence's phallic marriage do permanently unite the lives of those who long before would have parted, were it not for their sense of the organic eternality of their union – a sense that emerges in those subtle spaces between evocative memories, glib remarks, and the most mundane domestic habits:

Morel looked down ruefully at his sides.

'Me!' he exclaimed. 'I'm nowt b'r a skinned rabbit. My bones fair juts out on me.'

'I should like to know where,' retorted his wife.

'Iv'ry-wheer! I'm nobbut a sack o' faggots.'

Mrs Morel laughed. He had still a wonderfully young body, muscular, without any fat. . . .

'You've had a constitution like iron,' she said; 'and never a man had a better start, if it was body that counted. You should have seen him as a young man,' she cried suddenly to Paul, drawing herself up to imitate her husband's once handsome bearing.

Morel watched her shyly. He saw again the passion she had had for him. It blazed upon her for a moment. He was shy, rather scared, and humble. Yet again he felt his old glow. (197)

Although the atmosphere is teasing and affectionate in this family discussion, the banter is not a matter of superficial sexual flirtation or merely the product of a good mood. The innuendo is all about manhood. The tone of Gertrude's remarks is quietly passionate, and they amount to an insistence by her that what survives in this marriage is not trivial at all. Gertrude is charmingly transparent – 'had had' does not convey the timelessness of that truth. For there is a level captured by Lawrence in this scene, in which the wife cannot dramatize with unashamed pride before her family the memories of her man's manhood without also offering, in that significant and public disclosure, her judgement that he still retains adequate manhood for the present. The family vignette effectively dramatizes that which Paul proclaims later in his comments to Miriam: Lawrence's absolute faith in the immortality of a marriage baptized with the forging flames of polarized sexual love. When Gertrude compliments Walter, and he fluffs, glows, and finally – almost as a young lover! – 'watches her shyly', this couple is drawing on final reserves. Yet the phallic imagination insists that such primitive passion may be inexhaustible.[30] Lawrence returns to this seminal notion in *Lady Chatterley's Lover*, as Mrs Bolton explains to Connie that years after her husband's death, she can magically sense if any version of this forging process occurs: 'But there, when I look at women who's never really been warmed through by a man, well, they seem to me poor dool-owls after all, no matter how they may dress up and gad. No, I'll abide by my own. I've not much respect for people.'[31]

There has been ample and deserved critical attention to the subli-
mated sexuality in the swing scene. But there has not been
sufficient concern for the precise manner in which the scene's
supporting fire metaphors chart the dimensions of Paul and
Miriam's adamant incompatibility: 'She gripped the rope, almost
swooning. . . . It were almost as if he were a flame that had lit a
warmth in her whilst he swung in the middle air' (151). The sound
of 'almost' must ring loud in such an overtly copulatory scene.
Lawrence insists on that transition from the power of Paul's
'thrust' to the resultant 'hot wave of fear' which moves 'down to
her bowels', while Miriam 'gripped the rope' and he imploringly
asks, 'Won't you go any farther?' It is as far as Miriam can go,
and Paul lacks the experience to press his claim. Miriam does not
permit the forging process to be complete. She feels the heat from
his adolescent rhythms but only 'her heart melted in hot pain' –
the rest of her body remains taut and congealed, held in her typical
posture of restraint. Although she is aroused, she is unable to
lapse out in that necessary rendering into sexual essentiality:
'almost swooning' measures her compulsive need to keep some
hold on her consciousness. Thus Lawrence summarizes the unfortunate accuracy of Miriam's measured judgement of Paul's influence on her. 'It were almost as if he were a flame' is a statement
of the organic failure of Miriam to respond to the fire of real desire.

In addition to Millett's prominent attack on *Sons and Lovers*
(which has yet to be disavowed by her ideological cohorts), other
feminist critics continue to insist that Miriam's inability to forge
herself into Lawrencian pure 'otherness' is a positive trait in her
character; they often regard her restraint and coldness as an understandable and effective response to Paul's allegedly treacherous
use of her. For instance, Simpson's critique of Lawrence's depiction of organized feminism in *Sons and Lovers* leads her to
mistakenly praise Miriam for her 'resistance to the yielding of
identity that passion seems to demand'.[32] Diane Bonds even
suggests that Paul could easily rouse her more fully, except his
'view of Miriam is twisted by its oedipal determination'.[33] Indeed,
in relation to the resonant swing scene, such a scapegoating
approach to Miriam speaks admiringly of the supposed 'sexual
yearning that lies beneath Miriam's fear'.[34] Yet Bonds significantly
never substantiates where her evidence exists of such erotic poten-

tial in Miriam during the young woman's characteristically tormented experience with the swing. Lawrence's consistent depiction, throughout many scenes, of a resolute nullity in Miriam's sensual responses to life suggest that it is fear and loathing that lie beneath her occasional and sacrificial pretence of passionate desire. Paul's attempt at forging with her is doomed, for the kindling emotions of spontaneity and unreserved openness are noticeably absent in his intense girlfriend with dark hair.

Thus the 'warmth' roused in Miriam as Paul swings her, only emanates from the bodiless vibration of her melted 'heart'. Miriam cannot be 'forged' because she cannot be fully heated to the arousal of her naked passions – in short, she cannot be warmed because she refuses to be revealed. Lawrence's forging metaphor suggests a complementary symbol later when Miriam refuses the helping hand of nature, as the winds momentarily reveal, by *blowing up*, what Paul seeks to reach by melting down:

> They continued to mount the winding staircase. A high wind, blowing through the loopholes, went rushing up the shaft, and filled the girl's skirts like a balloon, so that she was ashamed, until he took the hem of her dress and held it down for her. He did it perfectly simply, as he would have picked up her glove. She remembered this always. (168)

Nothing wrong with Miriam's shame here, and nothing surprising about Paul's calculated pretence of business-as-usual. What lingers is all that Miriam missed. Miriam 'remembered this always' because the incident captures for her the skill of Paul's performance rather than the unspoken language of the moment. She admires his quick, direct movement, while she shows no sense of the adolescent passion which underlies the compulsions of his gallantry. The resonant sexuality is lost for her. The possibility of any awareness in her has been confounded, ultimately, by her coarse ability to translate the existential complexities of mood into the dull coordinates of an artistic observation. 'He did it perfectly simply' – but surely a minor point at this sexy moment. Paul did not adjust her dress as simply 'as he would have picked up her glove'. His movement appears unselfconscious in its simplicity, but she misses the emotional turbulence on the edge of his fluid gesture. On the winding staircase Miriam reduces a delicate mood to the fine point of perspective. Such a reduction, such a false and gratuitous levelling out, is her obsessive way of smoothing out the unexpected and jarring bumps of sexual proximity.

There is another more subtle, representative moment that depicts a relevant aspect of Paul's sexual frustration with Miriam during their courtship; the scene can also serve to illustrate the penchant of feminist critics occasionally to ignore the organic texture of a scene in favour of a rigged dismantling of its dramatic integrity. Millett has just quoted Lawrence's line about Miriam's relation to Paul, 'she mistrusted him as a teacher' (155). Millett then confidently adds, 'Well she might, in view of what follows'; here is the heinously *incomplete* passage from *Sons and Lovers* the critic supplies, followed by her interpretation of the emasculated scene:

> 'Do you see?' she looked up at him, her eyes wide with the half-laugh that comes of fear.
>
> 'Don't you?' he cried. . . . It made his blood boil to see her there, as it were, at his mercy, her mouth open, her eyes dilated with laughter that was afraid, apologetic, ashamed. Then Edgar came along, with two buckets of milk.
>
> 'Hello!' he said. 'What are you doing?'
>
> 'Algebra,' replied Paul.
>
> 'Algebra!' repeated Edgar curiously. Then he passed on with a laugh. (156)

Paul is roused by the mixture of tears and beauty; Miriam is beautiful to him when she suffers and cringes: 'She was ruddy and beautiful. Yet her soul seemed to be intensely supplicating. The algebra-book she closed, shrinking, knowing he was angered.'

As she is self-conscious and without confidence (Miriam's sense of inferiority is the key to her character) she cannot learn well: 'Things came slowly to her. And she held herself in a grip, seemed so utterly humble before the lesson, it made his blood rouse.' Blood roused is, of course, the Lawrentian formula for sexual excitement and an erection; the algebra lesson is something of a symbol for the couple's entire relationship. The sight of Miriam suffering or humiliated (she later gives Paul her virginity in a delirium of emotions) is the very essence of her attractiveness to him, but his response is never without an element of hostility and sadism.[35]

I include the scene (as quoted by Millett) and her response both to highlight the distance between the subtlety of Lawrence's 'art-speech' and the simplifications of preordained ideological readings, and to demonstrate the meretricious tendencies in Millett's pattern of quotation. In terms of her critical analysis, Millett is oblivious to Edgar's knowledgeable, ironic function in this scene, as the brother's passing choral comment is poignant and funny. He is a Leivers young man who is clearly familiar with his sister's agonized inhibitions and spiritual intensity; his concluding laugh reflects his immediate recognition that her suitor, Paul Morel, is in the process of a typical frustration by Miriam of a man's passionate intentions toward her. In essence, Edgar catches the awkward gist of the tableau spread before him, and he comprehends with a speed and conviction that is the product of a practised reading of a sister and a friendly regard for Paul: Edgar knows that Paul wants Miriam more than Paul wants to learn algebra; he also senses that the intensity of the couple's studious deliberations is a sham perpetrated by Paul's vulnerability to Miriam's sublimating games of the mind. So Paul and Miriam are caught memorably in a frustrating pose, and the brother laughs both at the secret they cannot conceal from him and at the pathos of their insufferable condition. In addition, Millett's dogmatic insistence that 'Miriam's sense of inferiority is the key to her character' makes that critic miss the real key to this meeting as it happens to be passingly noted by Edgar, dramatized by Lawrence, and suffered by Paul. That is, the scene turns on the fact of nullity at the core of Miriam's 'conscious being', and such emotional inadequacy has more to do with her intrinsic character than does the rationalization or extenuation offered by Millett. So the algebra lesson *is* 'something of a symbol for the couple's entire relationship', but not nearly in the way Millett suspects.

It is more than a decade since Mailer first exposed Millett's unreliable pattern of quotation in *Sexual Politics*. In his essay from *The Prisoner of Sex*, Mailer does not attempt any full-scale revelations of the liberties she takes; he only wishes to suggest, in biting summary fashion, that Millett's criticism often searches for too easy props to support its inherently unsteady thesis. But there has been little follow-up on Mailer's hints about Millett's suspicious strategies; indeed, it is fair to add that Millett's remarks on *Sons and Lovers* are often acknowledged and apparently admired by feminist critics of Lawrence.[36] While several critics do fault her for ideological stridency and a tendency to 'excess' in her doctrinal mission, the precise methodology she employs appears exempt from serious scrutiny by her fans or her detractors.[37] I wish to offer a few additional examples of Millett's typical approach to Lawrence's work, especially when it impinges on the issues of forging and feminism that are crucial to my reading of Lawrencian dialectic.

In the algebra scene quoted above, for instance, Millett buttresses her misreading by twice omitting lines in the quotation that patently undercut the evidence she presents. After she quotes 'Don't you,' Millett excises lines (noted by ellipses) and moves to her next quoted line from the novel: 'It made his blood *boil* to see her there' (156, my emphasis); thus Millett uses the connected lines to force an indictment of Paul for his anger and impatience. Here is how the scene reads with the missing lines included (indicated by my emphasis), with one additional adjustment of a word to correct what must be a typographical error by the critic:

> 'Do you see?' she looked up at him, her eyes wide with the half-laugh that comes of fear. 'Don't you?' he cried.
> *He had been too fast. But she said nothing. He questioned her more, then got hot.* It made his blood *rouse* to see her there. . . . (156, my emphasis)

Note that the actual phrase is 'blood rouse' and not Millett's 'blood boil'; not so minor an error here, as 'rouse' is as different from 'boil' as understandable sexual frustration is from an angry teapot. So Millett includes only what suits her legal brief – and then blithely transforms words themselves in the heat of her own indignation. Include the lines she omits and you sense a more pained, patient, and perplexed young man who struggles with a woman he cannot possess, reject, or understand. Similarly, Millett continues to batter Paul by linking the line of Miriam closing the algebra book with Millett's next quoted passage, 'Things came slowly to her'; the critic makes it appear as if the extenuating reasons for Miriam's conduct are there for our pity and indulgence – an illusion Millett perpetuates by eliminating the softening conjunction 'But' that Lawrence wisely includes before 'things came slowly to her'. Such a crucial qualification measures his (and Paul's) not insensitive awareness of Miriam's emotional disability, as does the important word 'when' which Millett also excises before 'she held herself in a grip'. What has Millett omitted in all these suspicious deletions? Only that Lawrencian sense of contradictory motives that influence the enacting by Paul of his conflicted love. Such a feeling makes all the difference in our reading of Paul's response to Miriam in this scene, for here is the line Millett discards for fear it suggests an emotion not helpful to the critic's case: 'and at the same instant he grew gentle, seeing her hurt because she did not understand' (156).

Kate Millett's treatment of *Sons and Lovers* is nothing if not relentless. She remains so insistent on finding evidence of some overriding and exculpatory sense of insecurity in Miriam (caused, of course, by Paul's insensitivity) that she continues to quote lines remarkably out of context. She rarely feels the metaphoric drama of forging that infiltrates a scene in delicate ways, as now she mistakenly interprets another evocative moment between the constrained lovers:

> Lawrence describes with aplomb how Miriam idolizes Paul; even stealing a thrush's nest, he is so superior that she catches her breath: 'He was concentrated on the act. Seeing him so, she loved him; he seemed so simple and sufficient to himself. And she could not get to him.' Here we are treated not only to idealized self-portraiture but to a preview of the later godlike and indifferent Lawrentian male.[38]

Such is all Millett provides about the scene, and all that she quotes from it. How she emasculates the poised art of Lawrence's fiction and evades his doctrines of fire and transcendence! 'She could not get to him' not as a result of any gratuitous aloofness in him, but because the forging warmth of living passion, which is natural to Paul's being, is closed off to Miriam, as her counterpointed isolation is typically cold and objectifying. The lines that directly introduce the scene declare the reasons for Millett's omission of them. They establish through a vitalistic and pastoral imagery that the issue dramatized is the organic fire in Paul played off against a wilful spirit in Miriam that would extinguish his fundamental energy:

> At the bottom of the Mow Close they found a thrush's nest. 'Shall I show you the eggs?' he said.

'Do!' replied Mrs Leivers. 'They seem *such* a sign of spring, and so hopeful.'

He put aside the thorns, and took out the eggs, holding them in the palm of his hand.

'They are quite hot – I think we frightened her off them,' he said.

'Ay, poor thing!' said Mrs Leivers.

Miriam could not help touching the eggs, and his hand which, it seemed to her, cradled them so well.

'Isn't it a strange warmth!' she murmured, to get near him.

'Blood heat,' he answered.

She watched him putting them back, his body pressed against the hedge, his arm reaching slowly through the thorns, his hand folded carefully over the eggs. (223)

Thus the complete scene commemorates Miriam's most characteristic relation to Paul. She tries to appropriate moments, to 'personalize' situations, in order to get near to him; but she desires the proximity without sharing any presence in the warm world he inhabits. Paul's knowledge here of 'blood heat' is both stated and enacted. The dramatized evidence in this scene of his radiated passion refutes Millett's reductive notion of Paul's 'indifference'. A compulsive Miriam typically 'could not help touching the eggs', but Paul remains, for once, beyond her grasp.

Miriam's clutching, spiritualized intensity constricts him frequently in their early courtship, and it is not surprising that Paul often smashes a stick into the ground to express his sexual frustration: 'He picked up a stick and began to stab the earth with it. . . . He thrust, thrust, thrust at the ground with the pointed stick. . . . He flung the stick into the currant-bushes . . .' (220). 'They were sitting on the bank of a stream, where the lip of turf hung over a hollow bank of yellow earth, and he was hacking away with a stick. . . . He still dug the earth viciously' (295–6). What redeems Lawrence's obvious and belaboured use of a phallic stick and vaginal mound is the implication of the stick's appearance always in the context of an agonizing conversation between Paul and Miriam. His sexual frustration becomes a reflection of his inability to pierce Miriam's self-protective shield of language. He plays with the stick and then throws it away not only because of his unsatisfied lust, but because he has been unmanned by Miriam's words. Paul's awful need to clarify his relation to Miriam becomes stalled, through her indoctrination, on the level of verbal metaphysics. For instance, in a crucial disagreement about a painting of Paul's, their relation to fire documents the difference between the energy of forging and the stasis associated with Miriam's restraint:

> Another day she sat at sunset whilst he was painting some pine-trees which caught the red glare from the west. He had been quiet.
>
> 'There you are!' he said suddenly. 'I wanted that. Now, look at them and tell me, are they pine trunks or are they red coals, standing-up pieces of fire in that darkness? There's God's burning bush for you, that burned not away.'
>
> Miriam looked, and was frightened. But the pine trunks were wonderful to her, and distinct. (152)

Paul's organic vision of painting, which encourages suggestion, resonance, and open-ended implication, clashes with Miriam's restrained, enclosed, and literalist interpretation. As she is frightened of Paul's phallic hunger for the 'beyond', and consequently attempts to bottle him up, here she is anxious about her inability either to know the co-ordinates of this painting or to understand the strange directions of Paul's excitement. To Paul the fact that the burning pines look like red coals (and vice-versa) is no accident and no fault of the painting. The setting sun, which spreads shadow and glare across the painting, suggests to Paul both the forging into the component energies of all that lives and – for that twilighted sun will shortly disappear – the mysterious, transcendent source of life itself. No matter to him that the force of such natural energy, when it is reflected in his painting, makes one object resemble another. For Paul 'wanted that': he wanted the grandeur of real life to enter his painting, and an obliging sun gives him the gift of cosmic autograph. The wording of Miriam's tepid appreciation catches her need to reduce the heat of the fire metaphor to the dullness of fluorescent illumination. She merely wants to confirm her known world, to keep her eye out for what is only 'distinct', and hence she avoids any awareness of the necessarily blurring flames of transcendence.

Paul still must play out the sexual failure with Miriam before he turns to Clara: 'He courted her now like a lover. Often, when he grew hot, she put his face from her, held it between her hands, and looked in his eyes. He could not meet her gaze' (284). Although Paul is 'hot', her eyes seek to mentalize and restrict the unknown, 'existential-edge' of his sex. He cannot burn off any sense of his will or ego under the harsh lights of her probing stare.[39] The pattern remains the same when Miriam greets Paul for the final time in the novel, and she appropriately fingers the dying freesias and scarlet anemones on Paul's table. Nothing much has changed for her. She still seeks to know the flowers with the absorbing wilfulness that must track down and enclose all evidence of Paul's vitality. She still tries to sniff out the unknown so she can kill it with knowledge. But this final time she is a parody of herself, reduced to finding evidence of her man as a detective hunts for fingerprints. 'Everything he had touched, everything that was in the least personal to him, she examined with lingering absorption' (414). Miriam senses the immediate vulnerability of Paul more than she does her own awkwardly compulsive posture. She suddenly suggests to Paul that they marry; but she phrases the proposition with words that give her away, and now the issue is clear to Paul:

> 'And if we married?' he asked.
> 'At any rate, I could prevent you wasting yourself and being a prey to other women – like – like Clara.'
> 'A prey?' he repeated, smiling. (417)

One looks in vain for other scenes of Paul smiling with Miriam, and he chooses the right time. For Paul at least knows for certain he was not Clara's 'prey'. He is suddenly aware of the spiteful and warped sexuality of Miriam, expressed in her bitter ignorance of the significant mutuality in Paul's affair with Clara. Now the language turns around, as Lawrence writes of her state with a phallic metaphor that measures the extent of Miriam's contorted sexual roots: 'Her impotence before him, before the strong demand of some unknown thing in him, was her extremity' (417). She is finally powerless to interfere with his struggle for transcendence. When Miriam leaves Paul, he stands alone on the platform. It is evident he will not take the deathly direction towards his mother's grave. He will walk towards the city's golden vitality because he understands the pathology of Miriam's offer of marriage: the offer was phrased in the neurotic terms of a mother substitute. He turns away from his mother in the last paragraph because his rejection of Miriam was described as the emancipation of a young man from mother-love, in *any* of its varied forms: 'He could not bear it – that breast which was warm and which cradled him without taking the burden of him. So much he wanted to rest on her that the feint of rest only tortured him. He drew away' (418).

In Diane Bond's revaluation of Paul's role in the novel, she is correct to note that Miriam 'reanimates' one of 'Paul's revered images of his mother'.[40] Yet Bonds also confesses to an odd uncertainty about 'whether such a reanimation would lead him to identify Miriam with his mother'.[41] Such perplexity on this issue is understandable in her criticism. Her frantic indictment of Paul and the narrator invokes both the name and perspective of Millett on several occasions; Bonds manipulatively undermines the narration of *Sons and Lovers* to construct a more favourable image of Miriam, and finally praises her through an almost Conradian reading of the novel that presents 'an alternate picture of Miriam that emerges from the action'.[42] There is no attempt in her revisionist essay to determine if Miriam's actions toward Paul often resemble maternal solicitude because of Miriam's sexual confusion rather than Paul's oedipal requirements. Bonds joins Millett, Faith Pullin, and Anne Smith,[43] among recent feminist critics of *Sons and Lovers*, in an ultimate dismissal of Paul as little more than an oedipal casualty; she also praises Miriam to the point of claiming that Miriam 'actually seems to embody the "shimmer" which Paul associates with vitality'.[44] Such 'shimmer', of course, is that mistaken interpretation of Miriam's luminous intensity that it is a critic's responsibility to see beyond; at its best the shimmer is a surface light, a self-reflecting and egocentric warmth that lacks the deeper, pulsating heat that Paul often produces and occasionally describes in the novel.

V

It is through Clara Dawes that Lawrence depicts the fundamental antagonism of the phallic imagination to the restrictive ideologies of feminism. Clara's pose as the 'liberated female' does not blind Lawrence to the fact of her anguish. He merely insists that her pain is personal and not – as she insists – the political result of institutionalized sexism. Lawrence locates the source of the feminist obsession with government in the refusal of women to come to grips with dislocating stages in their sexual history. This issue of sexual fundamentality versus institutional responsibility is spelled out in an interesting exchange that involves Paul, Clara, and Clara's mother:

'Do you like jennying?' he asked.

'What can a woman do!' she replied bitterly.

'Is it sweated?'

'More or less. Isn't *all* women's work? That's another trick the men have played, since we force ourselves into the labour market.'

'Now then, you shut up about the men,' said her mother. 'If the women wasn't fools, the men wouldn't be bad uns, that's what I say. No man was ever that bad wi' me but what he got it back again. Not but what they're a lousy lot, there's no denying it.'

'But they're all right really, aren't they?' he asked.

'Well, they're a bit different from women,' she answered. (261)

It takes Clara's mother, Mrs Radford, to state the crux of Lawrence's belief. The mother is appropriately more angry at the easy analysis of her daughter than she is about the issue of 'men'. Mrs Radford's anger at men has that authentic tone of respect and humour which is the product of this experienced woman's democratic battles with them in the proverbial sexual wars. She is unwilling to avoid admissions of the responsibilities of her female sex: she will not resort to the apologetics of her daughter. The mother cuts through the pretentiousness of her daughter's self-pitying question, 'Isn't *all* women's work?' For Clara talks rhetorically of 'markets' or 'labour' or the conspiracy of 'tricks', while her mother argues substantively that each man or woman remains his or her own fool. Mrs Radford realizes that the power struggle between men and women occurs, most properly, as a one-to-one conflict. Mrs Radford claims that a man and a woman fight as singled out, polarized sexual energies. 'They're a bit different from women,' she asserts about men, with no sense she would have it any other way. Her no-nonsense antagonism to the reductive interpretations of her daughter, combined with her own implicit acceptance of essential differences between the sexes, is persuasive because of the varied authority of her history.[45] She has been

lover, mother, worker, and abandoned wife, and she has presided
for a generation longer than her daughter over those principles of
sexual essentiality that Clara glibly reduces to a function of job
discrimination. Mrs Radford is not without the force of her own
moral vision. She is impressive as she tries to make Clara observe
the strict amenities of courtship in the Radford home, rules that
Mrs Radford supports even though the mother seems fond of her
daughter's suitor. She tells her daughter, who has been recently
recruited as a suffragette, to shut up and never lose track of what
really counts, as Mrs Radford exhorts Paul: 'Don't you listen to
her. She's for ever on that 'igh horse of hers . . .' (262). That, at
least, even young Paul did not need to be told.

Hilary Simpson develops an unusual argument that is cumulat-
ively in defence of Clara's position in *Sons and Lovers*, in opposition
to Lawrence's perception of Clara's needs, and in support of
feminist principles that appear to order Clara's life. She writes the
following as a summary statement of her indictment of Lawrence's
perspective: 'Because the novel betrays little appreciation of the
relationship between the personal and the political, the character
of Clara lacks coherence.'[46] But Simpson does not engage the more
compelling notion that it is Lawrence's purpose to demonstrate
that Clara *herself* lacks coherence; that is, Clara is unable to accept
personal responsibility for the sequence of emotional failures in
her life, as she looks with displaced anger at institutions and
collective 'men' as the primary cause of her malaise. Simpson's
misreading is most evident when she isolates precise scenes in
support of her argument about Lawrence's incomplete consideration of Clara. For instance, she discusses the conversation
between Paul and Clara on Margaret Bonford, the prominent
feminist leader of the time. Simpson asserts that 'the discussion
is a good example of the way in which Paul consistently ignores
the larger implications of feminism and reduces it to a series of
personal issues'.[47] She then quotes the following exchange to
support her assertion:

'I think she's a lovable little woman,' said Paul.
'Margaret Bonford!' exclaimed Clara. 'She's a great deal
cleverer than most men.'
'Well, I didn't say she wasn't,' he said, deprecating. 'She's
lovable for all that.'

'And of course, that is all that matters,' said Clara witheringly. (230)

Simpson concludes the passage as stated above; such selective quotation does wonders for her argument, for it avoids the qualifications of Lawrence's more complex verbal games between the lovers. The scene really completes itself as Paul makes a telling counter-point that insists on the rudiments of Lawrencian prophesy, while Clara responds with a materialist ideology that the novelist early in his career warningly associates with the demands of feminism:

> He rubbed his head, rather perplexed, rather annoyed.
> 'I suppose it matters more than her cleverness,' he said; 'which after all, would never get her to heaven.'
> 'It's not heaven she wants to get – it's her fair share on earth,' retorted Clara. She spoke as if he were responsible for some deprivation which Miss Bonford suffered.
> 'Well,' he said. 'I thought she was warm, and awfully nice – only too frail. I wished she was sitting comfortably in peace –'
> 'Darning her husband's stockings,' said Clara scathingly.
> 'I'm sure she wouldn't mind darning even my stockings,' he said. 'And I'm sure she'd do them well. Just as I wouldn't mind blacking her boots if she wanted me to.' (230–1)

Thus Clara Dawes and Hilary Simpson apparently share the belief that the direction of 'heaven' favoured by Paul is an indulgent, impossible goal amid the problems of poverty, chauvinism, and cultural deprivation on earth. But the scene's additional lines, as included above, demonstrate that Paul does not 'ignore the larger implications of feminism' – he simply considers them alarming and ultimately evasive. He is visionary enough to consider sexual transcendence – the escape from the petty inhibitions of ego – as more important than the demands, ambitions, or political complaints articulated by Clara. Paul begins to formulate Lawrence's developing doctrine that sensually reformulates Robert Browning's idea that 'a man's reach should exceed his grasp, or what's a heaven for?' In Lawrencian terms, heaven becomes embodied in the striving achievement of a polarized relationship between a man and a woman; such a state results – as Lawrence would say in *Mr Noon* – 'out of the sheer, pure, consummated fight' between lovers, as they finally 'burst out into a new heaven and a new earth, delicious'.[48] Paul argues that Clara uses an easy bill of institutional indictment against him, and thus she avoids the real risk of spontaneous electricity in the 'pure', unhampered connection between them. Paul's concept of emotional primacy, he is quick to add, is neither sexist nor demeaning, but the expression of homage when and where it is deserved; his little exchange over boots and socks suggests the democracy of gender that animates Paul's conviction.

Mrs Radford is right to suspect sour grapes behind Clara's embittered sexual politics. The mother senses that Clara must feel the confidence and pride of a renewing sexual assertion before Clara can speak of men without political rhetoric. As this pride develops in her affair with Paul, Clara becomes confident enough to submit herself to the 'unknown otherness' of her lover. Unlike Miriam, Clara is organically whole. She remains sufficiently female, with the requisite warmth, passion, and stability nearly to conquer her self-protective aversion to Lawrence's forging sex – to that existential baptism which burns off ego and personality in the fires of a sexual rendering:

And soon the struggle went down in his soul, and he forgot. But then Clara was not there for him, only a woman, warm, something he loved and almost worshipped, there in the dark. But it was not Clara, and she submitted to him. The naked hunger and inevitability of his loving her, something strong and blind and ruthless in its primitiveness, made the hour almost terrible to her. She knew how stark and alone he was, and she felt it was great that he came to her; and she took him simply because his need was bigger either than her or him, and her soul was still within her. (353)

Lawrence's qualification that 'her soul was within her' gently measures the incomplete singling out process for her. Clara is without any sense of permanence in her relation to Paul, so she still protectively holds on to some consciousness of herself. She can never 'melt' down to sexual essentiality while she remains aware of the transient demands of Paul's passion. But Clara feels the value of what she has received from him. While she anxiously ponders her insecure relation to Paul, she also feels sufficiently sexually renewed to permit him to experience his intense 'baptism of fire in passion'.

Hilary Simpson recognizes the supreme value Lawrence ascribes to sex that moves beyond the shackles of ego, a sex that embodies what Lawrence calls in *Sons and Lovers* 'the great hunger and impersonality of passion' (284). Her succinct summary in *D. H. Lawrence and Feminism* of the salient features of such communion provides a fair judgement of its function in Lawrence's singling out 'delivery to the unknown'[49] that is central to his visionary ethics. Simpson also acknowledges that Lawrence's doctrines about impersonal passion make equally fierce demands for each sex; both male and female, in a comparable manner of self-definition, are expected to strive for transcendence in their sexual experience. Simpson's commentary can function as a pertinent answer to Millett's charge that Lawrence uses his brand of impersonality as a shield for his closet-belief in the necessity of a woman merely to 'submit' to – in Millett's words – a man's 'bullying' that comes as the product of his 'consummate emotional manipulation'.[50]

But if Simpson effectively attempts to calm some feminist rage at this novel, she also falls short of the understanding Lawrence requires. As she describes, for example, the radical nature of Lawrence's imperatives about passion and ego, Simpson commits the same conventional error that the Paul–Clara affair warns us to avoid:

> Paul complains, 'Love should give a sense of freedom, not of prison. Miriam made me feel tied up like a donkey to a stake. I must feed on her patch and nowhere else. It's sickening.' To Clara's retort, 'And would *you* let a *woman* do as she likes?', Paul says 'Yes' (360). He is genuinely unconcerned about the double standard of morality. He does not expect his women to be 'pure.' In fact, Paul's concept of sexual love . . . really *requires* that both partners should be equal, free to plunge together into the baptism of fire. Yet this theory ignores the facts – the fact, for example, that women have traditionally had a larger stake in love and marriage than men, and that society expects the sexual relationship to be a woman's principal mode of self-definition.[51]

Simpson again misses Lawrence's essential point in her familiar zeal to indict him for daring to disregard political or institutional solutions to the problems of women; Lawrence's theory does not 'ignore the facts' of established social patterns 'in love and marriage'; he merely regards their existence as irrelevant to the implementation of his revolutionary expectations about sexual roles. In effect, Simpson quotes the spectre of the status quo to suggest that its looming presence defeats Lawrence's agenda; Lawrence believes, however, that his existential vision of erotic potential *surmounts* the facts by transforming the constricted relations between men and women. He agrees with Simpson that society expects the conventional sexual role for women in marriage that she describes. But Lawrence is less willing than the feminist critic to delimit a woman's self-defining sexuality, less willing than Simpson to deny woman that 'equal' partnership and freedom 'to plunge . . . into the baptism of fire'.

It is true that Clara does not sacrifice herself in the passive, uninterested manner of a Miriam Leivers. But Clara does 'submit' in the associated sense that she too easily defines her role as primarily an erotic stimulus for Paul; she too does not participate in the process of forging, but settles for that contentment evident in her young lover's 'baptism of fire in passion' (354). Clara remains unwilling to fully engage for herself that risky impersonality of passion that is her due as much as it is Paul's. No doubt the extenuating facts of her unresolved status with Baxter, and her working girl's insecurity with an unusually intelligent lover contribute to her aloofness with him when they make love. Yet both reasons for her sexual uninvolvement – marital commitments and feelings of inferiority – are related by Lawrence to a modern, social conditioning of her that he despises. Virtually everyone who writes about *Sons and Lovers* seems willing to dismiss Clara Dawes as an unsuitable long-term mate for Paul, which is probably a correct judgement. Who can say with certainty, however, that Clara's unwillingness to join Paul unreservedly in his lust for impersonality does not contribute to the speed with which their sex deteriorates?

In the next few years in such works as *The Rainbow, Women In Love,* and *Mr Noon,* Lawrence will repeatedly dramatize the mutuality of participation required from both sexes to attain that forged singling out that is the gateway to the unknown. Simpson argues with reformist energy that Lawrence remains insensitive to the extant social realities of women, and thus that he cannot see the unrealistic aspects of the demand that women accept his visionary dialectic. Lawrence later suggests in essays like 'À Propos of Lady Chatterley's Lover' and 'Pornography and Obscenity' that such a feminist argument relies on political panaceas and programmatic indoctrination to make meek, mechanical changes rather than the revolutionary fire he requires. The Lawrence of *Sons and Lovers* wants social regeneration only if it begins and ends with the revivification of sexual energy in individual men and women. He will chronicle that seminal desire most explicitly in *Lady Chatterley's Lover*, a work that he writes, ironically, after several years of infatuation with the institutional realm of reform that he undermines in his early novel, *Sons and Lovers*.

Mailer's summary of Lawrence's impulse to liberate the passionate potential of man is embodied in a provocative passage from *The Prisoner of Sex*. The lines are coincidentally resonant with the issues that order my concern with this novel, and Mailer manages, in effect, to integrate the facts of Clara's aversion to complete exposure through sex, of Millett's antagonism to Lawrence's view of Clara, and of Simpson's discomfort with Lawrence's preference for erotic transformation rather than reformist colloquy:

> So Millett will accuse him endlessly of patriarchal male-dominated sex. But the domination of men over women was only a way station on the line of Lawrence's ideas – what he started to say early and ended saying late was that sex could heal, all other medicines were part of the lung-scarring smoke of factories and healed nothing, were poison, but sex could heal only when one was without 'reserves or defenses.' And so men and women received what they deserved of one another. Since Women's Lib has presented itself with the clear difficulty of giving modern woman a full hard efficient ego, Lawrence's ideas could not be more directly in the way.[52]

VI

Paul Morel, who barely contributes to that conversation between Clara and her mother about work and the lot of women, had to remember an earlier conversation with Miriam on a similar subject. He must have felt that Mrs Radford was speaking for him as she

argued with her daughter, for here is the relevant exchange
between Paul and Miriam:

'What do you want then?'
'I want to do something. I want a chance like anybody else.
Why should I, because I'm a girl, be kept at home and not
allowed to be anything? What chance *have* I?'
'Chance of what?'
'Of knowing anything – of learning, of doing anything. It's
not fair, because I'm a woman.'
She seemed very bitter. Paul wondered. In his own home
Annie was almost glad to be a girl. She had not so much
responsibility; things were lighter for her. She never wanted to
be other than a girl. But Miriam almost fiercely wished she were
a man. And yet she hated men at the same time.
'But it's as well to be a woman as a man,' he said, frowning.
'Ha! Is it? Men have everything.'
'I should think women ought to be as glad to be women as
men are to be men,' he answered.
'No!' – she shook her head – 'no! Everything the men have.'
(154)

Paul tries to argue from what he regards as the elemental facts of
life, while Miriam relies on escaping the responsibility of her sexual
existence with statements like 'men have everything' or 'because
I'm a woman'. Paul is not insensitive to Miriam's strong desire to
succeed, and neither is he unaware of the boredom she suffers at
home. He also senses that her 'fierce wishes' are fuelled by her
displeasure with gender. 'But Miriam almost fiercely wished she
were a man' is no casual acknowledgement of Miriam's view of
the job market. It is Lawrence's criticism of her lack of healthy
organic roots: she has been cut off from her courses of female
sexual passion and sexual self-respect. Paul's assertion that men
and women should be glad of their own sexuality is the simple
and unadorned wording of the cornerstone belief of Lawrence's
phallic imagination: that the denial or degradation of sexual 'otherness' in oneself is a sin, denying as it does the organic connection
from the singled out self to the essential energy 'beyond'.[53] In
response to Paul's balanced defence of this principle of sexual
polarities – 'it's as well to be a woman as a man' – Miriam responds
with an ideologue's assertion about possessions: 'men have every-

thing'. Thus she provides nothing more than a theory that speaks
to what each sex *has* rather than what each sex *is*. Her primary
values depend on nothing organic, as she repeats a sophomoric
generalization about the province of property and power. Like
Clara in the matching conversation, Miriam argues that she does
not have enough of something for her to enjoy being female; but
Miriam's 'men have everything' comment bespeaks a biological
self-disgust that is more alarming than Clara's postured politics.

Unlike Clara, Miriam never changes. When Miriam returns to
Paul for the final meeting, that crucial issue of 'work' also returns
once more. Only now Paul will not fall silent to Miriam's evasions:

> 'Oh, I don't think it won't be a great deal. Only you'll find
> earning your own living isn't everything.'
> 'No,' she said, swallowing with difficulty: 'I don't suppose it
> is.'
> 'I suppose work *can* be nearly everything to a man,' he said,
> 'though it isn't to me. But a woman only works with a part of
> herself. The real and vital part is covered up.'
> 'But a man can give *all* himself to work?' she asked.
> 'Yes, practically.'
> 'And a woman only the unimportant part of herself?'
> 'That's it.'
> She looked up at him, and her eyes dilated with anger.
> 'Then,' she said, 'if it's true, it's a great shame.'
> 'It is. But I don't know everything,' he answered. (416)

It is a dead end. Paul cannot provoke Miriam into any awareness
of how her compulsion for work, in so far as it masks her organic
confusions, contributes to the denial of her fulfilment as a female.
It is even with difficulty that he provokes her to look him in the
eye. Miriam has denied the primacy of her womb for the specious
satisfaction of getting a nine-to-five job. Both in manner and
speech she is corrosive and awkward. Paul's tired, ambiguous
conclusion to their conversation reveals that he knows how
doomed his plea is: that 'real and vital part' of Miriam, Paul realizes
in this final scene, is not so much denied or covered up as non-
existent. She is dead and empty inside. His phallic imagination
cannot reach what does not exist. As Miriam now leaves with him
she sees the 'scarlet anemones flaunting the table', and she thinks,
'it was like him to have those flowers' (419). Perhaps she is right,

for these are the mythological flowers of poison and death, and they can stand as natural reflections of the bitterness and despair in Paul in recent weeks. Paul, who momentarily will turn with quickened life to the lights of the city, is well enough even now to give Miriam the flowers. So she is finally left, in the last view of her, with that symbolic correspondence which recalls her only manner of perception, while the precise symbol she holds also insists on her lack of life:

'Have them!' he said; and he took them out of the jar dripping as they were, and went quickly into the kitchen. She waited for him, took the flowers, and they went out together, he talking, she feeling dead. (419)

Yet the feminists variously persist in their belief that Paul's final meetings with Miriam illustrate his cruelty and the inadequate treatment by Lawrence of her legitimate needs. The subject again of 'work' is the key issue that persistently surfaces about the novel's conclusion. It is the theme that not only preoccupies Miriam in her conversation with Paul; it also both informs the representative criticism of *Sons and Lovers* evident in Florence Howe's college report on the feminist revolution, and is central – as I suggested earlier – to the critical perspective of Simpson, Millett, and Bonds. An additional example may be useful here, for it conveniently focuses on several relevant concerns about the ending of the novel. In a vitriolic attack on Paul Morel's character, Faith Pullin writes without irony that 'we know from *A Personal Record*, that Jessie Chambers was much more dominant in the relationship than Lawrence is willing to allow, and that she never really expected him to leave her, since she fully understood how necessary she was to his work'.[54] Thus Pullin appears to express the same confusion about organic priorities that is evident in Miriam's unwise estimation of some ultimate, sustaining value in vocation. No-one can doubt Miriam's important, often energizing function in Paul's young manhood, as this committed woman takes his warmth and 'urged it into intensity like a white light' (158). As their courtship develops, however, Paul never loses sight of where an obsession with money or job opportunity infringes on the more enduring goals of imaginative freedom, sexual satisfaction, and resolute independence. In short, can Pullin really summon up those biased lines from *A Personal Record* and not sense their corroborative relation to the pathology in Miriam and the growing strength in Paul that is dramatized in the novel? For it is Paul's persuasive ability to leave Miriam at the end – at a time of great need and vulnerability in him – that boldly testifies to the inaccuracy of Chambers's self-serving assertion. Similarly, it is Miriam's inability to anticipate the unswerving adamance of his departure which suggests precisely her manipulative, over-confident use of him that he is about to escape. A major reason that Chambers, Miriam, and Pullin cannot empathize with the strength evident in Paul's rejection of Miriam is their misreading of his decision as the residue of oedipal difficulty. So Pullin quotes without scrutiny the transparent evidence of Lawrence's girlfriend to support her own contention that Paul chooses to leave her out of weakness: 'As Jessie Chambers pointed out, the climactic rejection of Miriam does not come about because Paul has made a conscious decision but because he cannot successfully resist his mother'.[55]

Finally, all that is correct in Pullin's reductive approach may be her awareness that Paul's choice of rejection, and his later departure, are not really conscious decisions. When Paul proceeds toward that town alone, he is both brimming with life and bruised by it. He is shorn of a variety of emotional, sexual, and maternal supports; he appears to have accepted, in his soul, that individual responsibility for future failures and achievements that is the crucial step in the emergence of the Lawrencian phallic imagination. For several hundred pages Paul has acted passively, asserting himself only in those decisions that initiate or terminate his love affairs with Miriam and Clara. For much of his early years he lets events happen to him, and he still manages a bumpy but functioning love-life and the start of a promising artistic career. His final decisions to leave his women suggest a willingness to undergo sunderings that leave him wounded, alone, and oddly secure; he is 'derelict' in that last chapter in the dictionary sense that he has 'to leave or forsake (with intention not to resume)',[56] but that amounts to a dereliction of conventional duty that Lawrence is proud to dramatize. As Norman Mailer discusses the necessary, intrinsic qualities of manhood that he uses to begin his defence of Lawrence's art, he writes lines that nearly encompass the precise experience of Paul Morel at the end of *Sons and Lovers* as he walks while 'on every side the immense dark silence seemed pressing him' (420):

The primary quality of man was an assertion, and on the conse-
quence an isolation, that one had to alienate oneself from nature
to become a man, step out of nature, be almost as if opposed
to nature . . . that being a man was by this extreme sense not
even altogether natural, not if the calm of the seas is seen as
the basic condition of nature, that man was a spirit of unrest
who proceeded to become less masculine whenever he ceased
to strive.[57]

Notes

1. Harry T. Moore, *The Priest of Love: A Life of D. H. Lawrence*, rev. edn
   (New York: Farrar, Straus & Giroux, 1974; London: Penguin, 1980),
   346.
2. Kate Millett, *Sexual Politics* (Garden City: Doubleday, 1970; London:
   Virago, 1977), 249.
3. Diane Bonds, 'Miriam, The Narrator, and the Reader of *Sons and
   Lovers*', *The D. H. Lawrence Review* 2 (1981), 146.
4. Millett, *Sexual Politics*, 252.
5. Ibid., 257.
6. The history of the composition of *Sons and Lovers* is told objectively
   and comprehensively in Part One of the Moore biography, which
   he calls 'The Nottingham Years'. Scholarly disagreement about the
   composition of *Sons and Lovers* concerns many issues of biography
   and secondary source material, and among the most recent preoccupations of controversy is the issue of Lawrence's emotional reliance
   on his wife, Frieda, as he completed the novel. Martin Green claims,
   in *The von Richthofen Sisters: The Triumphant and the Tragic Modes of Love*
   (New York: Basic Books, 1974), that Frieda was nothing less than the
   source of Lawrence's genius from the time of *Sons and Lovers*. Emile
   Delavenay gives that version a convincing rebuttal in 'Making
   Another Lawrence: Frieda and the Lawrence Legend', *The D. H.
   Lawrence Review*, 8 (1975), 80–98.
7. Alfred Kazin, 'Women are not all alike: 1,' *Esquire*, June 1977, 42–52.
8. Ibid., 44.
9. Florence Howe, 'Feminist Scholarship: The Extent of the Revolution',
   in 'Liberal Education and the New Scholarship on Women: Issues and
   Constraints in Institutional Change', from the *Report of the Wingspread
   Conference*, Association of American Colleges, 1981.
10. Faith Pullin, 'Lawrence's Treatment of Women in *Sons and Lovers*,' in
    Anne Smith (ed.), *Lawrence and Women* (New York: Barnes & Noble;
    London: Vision, 1978), 73.
11. Ibid., 49.
12. Millett, *Sexual Politics*, 248.
13. Bonds, 'Miriam, the Narrator, and the Reader of *Sons and Lovers*', 52.

14. Hilary Simpson, *D. H. Lawrence and Feminism* (Dekalb: Northern Illinois University Press; London: Croom Helm, 1982), 36.

15. Mailer, *The Prisoner of Sex* (New York: New American Library, 1971), 24.

16. Carol Dix, *D. H. Lawrence and Women* (Totowa: Rowman & Littlefield; London: Macmillan, 1980), 89.

17. I must mention a number of the many exceptions. Although she oddly misinterprets the ending of *Sons and Lovers*, to find Paul destroyed rather than liberated, Dorothy Van Ghent's essay in *The English Novel: Form and Function* (New York: Holt, Rinehart & Winston, 1953) provocatively probes the relation of Lawrence's formal technique to the priorities of his vision. It was followed by Mark Spilka's *The Love Ethic of D. H. Lawrence* (Bloomington: Indiana University Press, 1955), and despite its limited design, that study remains the pioneer attempt at what Spilka calls 'whole knowledge' of Lawrence. Among more recent studies of this novel, Frank Kermode, in *D. H. Lawrence* (New York: Viking, 1973; London: Fontana, 1985), shows a fine perception of the lack of sentimentality in *Sons and Lovers*, but I feel he lacks sufficient concern for that structural balance which sets off Lawrence's theories. In *The Deed of Life* (Princeton: Princeton University Press, 1963), Julian Moynahan advances many patterns which display Lawrence's fusion of a sexual ethos with an awareness of the form of fiction. And a final remark on an early and influential advocate of Lawrence: F. R. Leavis, whose ethical passions and scrupulous concern for drama and style in Lawrence's fiction are evident in his discussion of *The Rainbow* and *Women in Love* in *D. H. Lawrence: Novelist* (New York: Simon & Schuster, Clarion edn, 1969; Harmondsworth: Penguin, 1970), dismisses adequate consideration of *Sons and Lovers* with the assertion that 'remarkable as it is, its qualities and its achievement, on the one hand, are obvious enough, and, on the other, they are not, I think, such as to suggest that the author was going to be a great novelist' (Leavis, 19).

18. For two generally solid studies of Lawrence that still lose sight of the 'organic' nature of Lawrence's art in *Sons and Lovers*, see the relevant chapters in Keith Sagar's *D. H. Lawrence: Life Into Art* (Athens: University of Georgia Press; Harmondsworth: Penguin, 1985), 77–101, and Daniel Schneider's *The Consciousness of D. H. Lawrence* (Lawrence: University Press of Kansas, 1986), 69–87.

19. Mailer, *The Prisoner of Sex*, 112.

20. Millett, *Sexual Politics*, 247.

21. To what exact extent there is biographical correspondence between Paul's story and Lawrence's life is a matter impossible to know. I would not think it inappropriate, however, to regard Paul's experience – for the purposes of my argument – as very similar to Lawrence's, and many of his theoretical pronouncements are virtually identical to Lawrence's. See Sagar's *D. H. Lawrence: Life Into Art*, for several provocative speculations on the relation of the novel to Lawrence's own life.

22. Pullin, 'Lawrence's Treatment of Women in *Sons and Lovers*', 65.

23. See both the 'Mino' chapter in *Women in Love* for the most relevant explanation of this theory, and Chapter 19 in *Mr Noon* for a more precise look at the Lawrencian sense of battle, polarity, and accommodation between passionate lovers.

24. Lawrence, *Sons and Lovers* (New York: Viking; London: Heinemann, 1958), 8. Page numbers in my text refer to the Viking edition.

25. Simpson, *D. H. Lawrence and Feminism*, 27.

26. For relevant discussion of the Freud issue in relation to *Sons and Lovers* see Frederick J. Hoffman's *Freudianism and the Literary Mind* (Baton Rouge: Louisiana State University Press, 1957), 144–80, and Spilka's chapter, 'Counterfeit Loves', in *The Love Ethic of D. H. Lawrence*, 60–89. In a passage from *The Priest of Love*, Moore summarizes the recorded memories of Lawrence's sister on the related issue of Lawrence's portrait of his parents. The sister clearly documents Lawrence's distaste for the self-righteous abrasiveness of his mother (Moore, 11–12).

27. Lawrence writes explicitly of this combination of what he considers 'vital self-realization' (the separateness) and a 'recognition of abysmal otherness' (the move to transcendence) in *Psychoanalysis and the Unconscious* (New York: Viking, 1960; Harmondsworth: Penguin, 1971), 40–41. The Viking edition also contains *Fantasia of the Unconscious*.

28. This process is described throughout *Psychoanalysis and the Unconscious* and *Fantasia of the Unconscious*, but Rupert Birkin's explanation to Ursula – set off smartly by the supporting metaphors of the battling cats – in the 'Mino' chapter of *Women in Love* (New York: Viking, 1960; London: Heinemann, 1984), 136–46, provides the clearest description. Although *Women in Love*, with its specific terminology, did not appear until 1920, Lawrence's earlier works anticipate most aspects of his later and more formalized theories of love; as my next chapter suggests, *The Rainbow* offers a three-generation dramatization of the quest for this 'unknown' in marriage.

29. Lawrence does not dwell on the precise term 'maximum' in *Sons and Lovers*, but it becomes his shorthand for the signified completion of the forging process. As Lawrence explains in *Fantasia of the Unconscious*, the passion to be 'maximum' is, in effect, the drive for existential purification: 'And only at his maximum does an individual surpass all his derivative elements and become purely himself' (71). In short, by burning off the dross of will and ego (those 'derivative elements') in the act of love, a lover becomes 'maximum'. In my chapter on *The Rainbow*, I provide a more precise analysis of how this lust for self-identity functions in the engaged, spirited life of a young woman.

30. In the first collection of posthumously published Lawrence papers, *Phoenix* (New York: Viking, 1972), there are two excellent reminiscences, one about a pet rabbit called 'Adolph', and one about a pet dog called 'Rex', 7–21. Both pieces are important for their emphasis on the strong passions between his parents, the warmth of his family life, and the unexpectedly strong sense of his father's charm and authority.

31. Lawrence, *Lady Chatterley's Lover* (New York: Grove Press, 1959; London: Heinemann, 1963), 218–19.
32. Simpson, *D. H. Lawrence and Feminism*, 56.
33. Bonds, 'Miriam, the Narrator, and the Reader of *Sons and Lovers*', 148.
34. Ibid., 150.
35. Millett, *Sexual Politics*, 253.
36. See relevant comments on Millett in Simpson, *D. H. Lawrence and Feminism*, 29, 36; in Diane Bonds, 'Miriam, the Narrator, and the Reader of *Sons and Lovers*', 146, 153; in Carolyn Heilbrun, *Towards a Recognition of Androgyny* (New York: Harper & Row, 1974), 6–7, 102.
37. For welcome exceptions to this tendency, see Patricia Meyer Spacks, *The Female Imagination* (New York: Avon, 1976), 34–41, and Juliet Mitchell, *Psychoanalysis and Feminism* (New York: Random House, 1975), 351–55.
38. Millett, *Sexual Politics*, 250.
39. 'Sex is not living till it is unconscious: and it never becomes unconscious by attending to sex', from George J. Zytaruk and James T. Boulton (eds), *The Letters of D. H. Lawrence*, II (Cambridge: Cambridge University Press, 1981), 426.
40. Bonds, 'Miriam, the Narrator, and the Reader of *Sons and Lovers*', 145.
41. Ibid.
42. Ibid., 150.
43. See Anne Smith's reductive oedipal reading of Lawrence's life and art in 'A New Adam and a New Eve – Lawrence and Women: A Biographical Overview', in *Lawrence and Women*, 9–48.
44. Bonds, 'Miriam, the Narrator, and the Reader of *Sons and Lovers*', 151.
45. No doubt the basis for such acceptance would have been obvious to most readers of Lawrence in 1913. Perhaps Lawrence sensed how the whims of cultural, political, and sexual fashion might seek to refute those distinctions that to him seemed so organically incontrovertible. For here are the introductory comments of a letter distributed to all faculty in 1975 at a liberal arts college in the United States by the Office of Special Programs for Women: 'I am sending you a summary (from *Psychology Today*) of a book by the leading authority (E. E. Macoby) on sex differences. I think it is useful to question our assumptions about the differences between men and women. The article points out that most of what we believe about the behavioral and psychological characteristics of the two sexes is either false or has not yet been confirmed.'
46. Simpson, *D. H. Lawrence and Feminism*, 29.
47. Ibid., 30.
48. Lawrence, *Mr Noon* (Cambridge: Cambridge University Press, 1984), 290.
49. See Simpson's *D. H. Lawrence and Feminism*, 34.
50. Millett, *Sexual Politics*, 255.
51. Simpson, *D. H. Lawrence and Feminism*, 35.
52. Mailer, *The Prisoner of Sex*, 107.
53. The concepts of 'otherness' and 'male and female integrity' in relation

to sexual pride and health are discussed in 'The Birth of Sex' in *Fantasia of the Unconscious*, 137–49.
54. Pullin, 'Lawrence's Treatment of Women in *Sons and Lovers*', 60.
55. Ibid., 52.
56. *The Compact Edition of the Oxford English Dictionary* (Oxford and New York: Oxford University Press, 1971), 226.
57. Mailer, *The Prisoner of Sex*, 97.

2

'Logic of the Soul': Marriage and Maximum Self in *The Rainbow*

I

Lawrence's letters during a confident stage in his composition of *The Rainbow* and *The Lost Girl*, in which he claims that his work is 'not a bit visualized' and 'really a stratum deeper' than the fiction of other novelists, suggest the importance of focusing on the internal emotional life of his characters.[1] In his many comments on the fiction of this period, no evidence exists of an attempt to duplicate the pictorial documentations of England such as those in *Sons and Lovers*. Critics generally recognize the focus on emotional life in *The Rainbow* and properly relate it to that novel's concern with habits of love and courtship through three generations. Yet relatively little attention has been drawn to the significance of such repetitive domestic struggles. Similarly, there has been insufficient discussion of the seminal theme of marriage in *The Rainbow*, a theme that Lawrence uses as a form of visionary ligature to integrate the pattern of repetition and to provide the doctrinal insistence so important to him.[2]

The tired Paul Morel who emerges from the conclusion of *Sons and Lovers* is both memorably individualized and an archetypal victim of a post-Victorian age. His varied experiences of passion and disappointment suggest that his emotional malaise is not unrelated to his culture's atmosphere of fear and spiritual confusion

56

just before the first world war. In a letter written in 1913 shortly after he completes this autobiographical fiction, Lawrence seems to echo the likely awareness of Paul as the novelist's *persona* resolutely heads for that new life he has earned; Lawrence writes with fresh conviction about his own reading of the root causes for a national frustration with which he was intimate only a few years earlier: 'And I am so sure that only through a readjustment between men and women, and a making free and healthy of their sex, will she [England] get out of her present atrophy.'[3] His confident assertion is inspired, no doubt, from a comfort over his current lovelife with Frieda. He has graduated from the fatiguing rites of passage outlined in *Sons and Lovers*; he has rejected the possibility of marriage with Jessie Chambers and Louie Burrows, whom he senses cannot offer him his holy grail of a 'free and healthy' sexual connection with a mate. His affair with Frieda von Richtofen will soon be formalized in marriage, and it becomes primary source material for that obsessive focus on sexual 'readjustment between men and women' that permeates *The Rainbow* as he starts to write it in 1913 just a few weeks before the above letter. In a seminal essay that Lawrence writes more than a decade after his elopement with Frieda, Lawrence implies a provocative conjunction between the movement of transcendent forces and the eternality – on earth – of formalized sexual union: 'Mankind has got to get back to the rhythm of the cosmos and the permanence of marriage.'[4] The significance of this basic formulation is central to the thematic and doctrinal patterns I wish to isolate in *The Rainbow* about marriage, the maximum self, and the quest for the unknown.

As he relentlessly travels in exile, works through disagreements with Frieda over her commitment to her Weekley family, and struggles with what would become a companion novel to *The Rainbow*, Lawrence conveys a preoccupation of both his impassioned life and his recent fiction when he tells his friend McLeod: 'I think *the* one thing to do, is for men to have the courage to draw nearer to women, expose themselves to them. . . . Because the source of all life and knowledge is in man and woman, and the source of all living is in the interchange and the meeting and mingling of these two.'[5] Lawrence thus insists (implicitly in his acceptance of the ostracism caused by his then 'illicit' connection to Frieda) that marriage amounts to an organic necessity; it remains the only institution that can sanction, legally and socially, the rigours of the mandate contained in his remarks to McLeod.

We must marvel at Lawrence's characteristic ability here to put his courage where his doctrine is: he permits his own instinctive sense of what is right to triumph over the natural temptation, which had to be strong in his beleaguered period early in the war, to renounce marriage altogether. Who could begrudge him resentment towards an institution so central to the bourgeois society that was attacking Lawrence for his alleged draft evasion, pornography, and libertinism? But he provocatively creates, in the midst of destroying one marriage in favour of the promise of his own, a virtual hymn in *The Rainbow* to the spirit of marriage; the creation becomes, in effect, a prothalamic embodiment of the kind of union he wishes to achieve with Frieda, which Frieda lacks in the marriage she abandons. He writes a novel that describes the continual 'exposure' and 'interchange' he regards as 'the source of life'. Lawrence never seriously considers, throughout these years of turmoil, any compromise in his stress on *legal* status; his letters show a resolute discomfort with the idea of a private romance with Frieda that would lack the contractual obligations of official marriage.[6]

Feminist criticism on *The Rainbow*, not surprisingly, is often condescending about Lydia, Anna, and their consuming involvement in marriage and motherhood. Critics such as Carolyn Heilbrun, Hilary Simpson, and Kate Millett concentrate approvingly on the radical, 'liberated' nature of Ursula, the third-generation Brangwen; their remarks on the novel tend to minimize or confute the value of that singling out into essential female being that Lawrence imputes to Ursula's mother and grandmother.[7] Their predictable perspective on this work fails to convey the poignant drama and the doctrinal principles that the novelist uses to highlight the sexual magnetism of the earlier Brangwen women. The existential strength of Lydia and Anna is certainly confined to a domestic and maternal setting; yet for both mothers – and for Lawrence – their sexual power remains admirable and authentic precisely because it *is* derived from the unharnessed, unmechanized expression of the pure and isolate self. Thus the sense of identity prominent in Ursula's blood ancestors exists apart from any notion of occupational achievement, political favour, or institutional support. Feminists are quick to note, and perhaps to overestimate, the crusading possibilities inherent in an allegedly emancipated woman like Ursula; they are openly unsympathetic to that self-definition by Lydia and Anna that remains content with an archetypal involvement in marriage, children, and the transcendent 'beyond'.

Heilbrun, for instance, speaks of her version of the subtle transpositions of the 'patriarchal myth'[8] in the novel, and maintains, not very convincingly, that androgynous mythologies are a prime component of Lawrence's depiction of the Brangwens. In essence, she is struggling to make the work palatable for her own ideological reading of culture, power, and the 'prison of gender'.[9] There is little awareness in Heilbrun's comments that a more primitive and subsuming dialectic of *polarized* sexuality informs the action of the novel. Millett writes reductively about the early generations of *The Rainbow*; she describes them as a reflection of Lawrence's view of women as 'marry and smother them', and then she adds with a sneering contempt (I presume) for marriage, such views embody 'curiously related gestures here'.[10] But there are no smothered Brangwen women. Lydia and Anna are proud to use their innate connection to the Lawrencian 'unknown' to assert an impressive and fertile 'maximum self', and that profound expression of their femaleness nearly smothers their typically insecure mates. One of the major reasons for Millett's confusion over what Ursula does to Skrebensky under the moon – Millett calls it, with frank perplexity, 'extremely tenuous and hazy bouts of magic'[11] – is that this critic does not wish to define Ursula's power through Lawrencian doctrine; she wishes to argue that Ursula and Lawrence are products of the feminist influence during the first world war, and such claims of influences bear little relation to the visionary aspects of Lawrence's sexual doctrine. Simpson even quotes Millett to confirm her own belief that 'the driving force behind Ursula's efforts is, of course, the feminist movement at its height during the years of *The Rainbow*'.[12] Although Simpson corrects Millett's sweeping misjudgement about Lawrence's preoccupations in *The Rainbow* with an important qualification – 'but the type of feminism represented by the suffrage movement is specifically rejected'[13] – both critics fail to acknowledge that it is Lawrence's emerging faith in marriage, and not feminism, that is the driving force in his composition of *The Rainbow*.

The Rainbow is a testament to the conservative impulse in Lawrence that is at the heart of his most apocalyptic doctrines; it reflects a sensibility inclined towards traditional forms of worship, stability, and passion, even though he wishes to transmute and invigorate the forms. Indeed, his radical notions of the vital relations between men and women in *The Rainbow* are framed by an affirmation in each Brangwen generation of the legal state that sanctions a marriage. The words of another writer, whose self-proclaimed designation is 'left-conservative', help illuminate significant aspects of Lawrence's beliefs. In a summary of the ethical imperatives that he believes underlie Lawrence's fictional representations of love and sex, Norman Mailer writes: 'Lawrence's point . . . is that . . . people can win at love only when they are ready to lose everything they bring to it of ego, position, or identity – love is more stern than war – and men and women can survive only if they reach the depths of their own sex down within themselves. They have to deliver themselves "over to the unknown." No more existential statement of love exists, for it is a way of saying we do not know how the love will turn out.'[14] Mailer's lines suggest the demands of the dual process of self-definition and transcendence that is central to the many communion scenes in Lawrence's fiction. Lawrence insists on passion that begins as the unharnessed assertion of the sexual apartness of each lover – a drive towards a sexual singling out – identified by a character's unintimidated acceptance of the 'otherness' of his partner. Through this balanced (or 'polarized') forging of male and female energies, each lover – in separate and often uneasy ways – is then able to recognize the spirit of the overarching 'unknown' that is the animating force in Lawrence's universe. In Lawrence's necessarily circular dialectic, just as self-definition relies on a person's initial faith in the beyond, so a person must desire this unknown to legitimize the process of singling out. The circularity becomes a fail-safe testament to the organic nature of Lawrence's vision, which never envisages a felt connection to the transcendent without a perception of the pristine, sexual self.

In *The Rainbow*, men have the greater difficulty in accepting this pure unknown in their mates; thus they exhibit, in moments of extreme stress, a fear and uncertainty about the cosmos (that is, fear of the sky, wind, stars, moon, and so forth) – the looming 'beyond' that is both animator and confirming principle of the sexual otherness they struggle to accept in each other. The quest for the unknown is no less intense in the men than in the women, but often inhibitions and egocentric worry hamper the male. Tom,

Will, and Skrebensky wish to feel the impulse to the transcendent even as they draw back from that naked exposure to their wives or lovers; Lawrence believes that such restraint compromises the courage he mentioned to McLeod for 'the one thing to do'. When Lawrence returns late in his life to these basic beliefs about marriage and the unknown, he describes in 'Pornography and Obscenity' the necessary interrelation between self-realization and transcendence; his words provide a fair summary of the doctrinal tenets that operate on the men in *The Rainbow*: 'In his adventure of self-consciousness a man must come to the limits of himself and become aware of something beyond him. A man must be self-conscious enough to know his own limits and to be aware of that which surpasses him.'[15] Similarly, and with the same retrospective tone so relevant for *The Rainbow*, Oliver Mellors in *Lady Chatterley's Lover* virtually describes Tom Brangwen, as the gamekeeper explains that men have difficulty in sustaining such acts of existential faith and ego suspension: 'A man has to find and battle for the best, and then trust in something beyond himself.'[16]

The consistent depiction in *The Rainbow* of the willingness in women to embrace the unknown, and the strength imputed to them because of such courage, is Lawrence's fictional version of a doctrine of female speciality that has ample precedent in religious, mythic, and psychological structures of belief. In his essay 'The Crown', which Lawrence wrote while revising *The Rainbow*, he expresses a faith in the innate power of women that sounds like a shorthand fusion of the clinical concepts of anatomic destiny promulgated by Freud and Erikson, the mystical awe of Mary urged by the Catholic Church, and the poetic adoration directed at Dante's Beatrice and Eliot's *Lady of Silences*. Put simply, Lawrence envisages women as a step closer to the unknown than men, since 'the womb is full of darkness and also flooded with the strange white light of eternity'.[17] Although the lack of a uterus puts the male at an unbridgeable distance behind the female in proximity to the transcendent, his need to perceive that unknown is as urgent as the female's. Yet in the discriminatory nature of Lawrence's vision, the stabilizing biology of a womb, that ingrown potential for linking with eternity, makes a woman's search for the beyond less fraught with self-consciousness and fear of failure. Her body's structure thus gives confident direction to her quest.

Lawrence portrays the men in *The Rainbow* as always looking to the institution of marriage as the social instrument for delivery to the unknown. That portrayal is consistent with his views in another work simultaneous with *The Rainbow*, the 'Study of Thomas Hardy', in which he claims that man 'dare not leap into the unknown save from the sure stability of the unyielding female'.[18] The women in *The Rainbow* try to show the men that as males they instinctually desire a link to eternity through their wives. But their civilized male egos, which have been conditioned to settle for the wages of a protective day's work on the farm, urge them to avoid risking their souls in enterprises that depend on acts of faith. The novel becomes a three-generation battle between female persuasion, which can become vindictive, and male inhibition, which can become self-destructive. In a letter to Sir Thomas Dunlop in July 1914, Lawrence writes prescriptive lines that could serve as an introduction to the preoccupations he dramatizes in *The Rainbow*:

> One must learn to love, and go through a good deal of suffering to get to it, like any knight of the Grail, and the journey is always *towards* the other soul, not away from it. . . . It is damnably difficult and painful, but it is the only thing which endures. You mustn't think that your desire or your fundamental need is to make a good career, or to fill your life with activity, or even to provide for your family materially. It isn't. Your most vital necessity in this life is that you shall love your wife completely and implicitly and in entire nakedness of body and spirit.[19]

II

The opening page of *The Rainbow* introduces a theme that reverberates through more than fifty years of Brangwens: 'There was a look in the eyes of the Brangwens as if they were expecting something unknown, about which they were eager.'[20] A 'look' is all Lawrence provides about this eagerness, as if only a glance can catch the inarticulate quality of the Brangwen desire. The men are in the grip of a need as powerful as the lust for sex or the drive for success in their farming occupation. It is the instinctive urge to find a reason for existence, to feel a sense of affirmation beyond the duties of work, to connect with something 'foreign' and beyond familial responsibility. But they are farming men, aware that the requirements behind their look must somehow be accommodated to their working presence at Marsh Farm. For the men this look stays in living suspension in their blood and circulates only when the men feel ready both to embrace a woman 'in entire nakedness of body and spirit' and to affirm the presumed permanence of that embrace in matrimony.

The inexorable drift towards that 'vital necessity in life' is first chronicled in Tom Brangwen. Although a robust and capable young man, he matures slowly; his experiences with a prostitute and a flirtatious young woman do little to confirm his sense of manhood. Yet his immaturity does not delay his need to deliver himself to that unknown embodied in Lydia Lensky. He feels ready for her, motivated by what Lawrence soon calls 'a logic of the soul' (36). All Tom requires is the slightest glance at this inscrutable woman: ' "That's her," he said involuntarily' (24) – an involuntary mutter from his instinct, his soul, and not from his knowledge or experience. That Lydia is also literally 'foreign' accelerates Tom's sense of polarized attraction to her when they first meet. Later this foreign element will demand the full measure of Tom's adjustment when he undertakes marriage with a wife whose history and manner are so unusual in his community. The early scenes between Tom and Lydia convey a sense of anticipatory tension beneath the apparent nonchalance of the encounters; they show the heightened readiness in Tom that results from months of eager waiting for 'something to get hold of. . . . Steadfastly he looked at the young women, to find a one he could marry' (20). The slightest gesture becomes filled with meaning, as it moves like a luminous movie, run strangely slow motion through an imagination in Tom that is vibrantly alive with his desire:

> And he also stooped for the button. But she had got it, and she stood back with it pressed against her little coat, her black eyes flaring at him, as if to forbid him to notice her. Then, having silenced him, she turned with a swift 'Mother –,' and was gone down the path.
> The mother had stood watching impassive, looking not at the child, but at Brangwen. He became aware of the woman looking at him, standing there isolated yet for him dominant in her foreign existence. (28)

The perspective here is multiple and resonant, for as Tom makes his discovery, the widow carefully measures him as her potential man, and even the daughter is vaguely aware – 'Mother' sounds the frightened declaration of *her* allegiance – that stakes of family destiny are silently enacted at this encounter. Several pages later Tom's decision to propose is captured in a poignant scene with his wise servant:

> All these things were only words to him, the fact of her superior birth, the fact that her husband had been a brilliant doctor, the fact that he himself was her inferior in almost every way of distinction. There was an inner reality, a logic of the soul, which connected her with him. . . . Tilly brought down one of the linen shirts he had inherited from his father, putting it before him to air at the fire. She loved him with a dumb, aching love, as he sat leaning with his arms on his knees, still and absorbed, unaware of her. . . . 'It's got to be done,' he said as he stooped to take the shirt out of the fender, 'it's got to be done, so why baulk it?' (36)

For years Tilly has lovingly ministered to the Brangwen family's needs, and as she recognizes why there is ritual in Tom's preparations, so must she prepare him for a man's most crucial calling even as she loses the part of him that was her own. Although Tom senses the momentousness inherent in his marital decision, he seems uncertain about where all this ceremonial fuss might lead.

Mailer's comment about the existential uncertainty in Lawrence's work of how the love will turn out seems particularly appropriate to that lingering image of Tom walking to Lydia as a man who has exposed himself to forces larger than he can manage: 'He went up the hill and on towards the vicarage, the wind roaring through the hedges, whilst he tried to shelter his bunch of daffodils by his side. He did not think of anything, only knew that the wind was blowing' (37). Tom walks as if under the spell of a private god; he is motivated by 'an inner reality' and 'he did not think of anything' – he moves toward his woman with that combination of mystical mandate and deductive conviction conveyed by the oxymoronic phrase 'logic of the soul'. When Tom reaches Lydia's house to make the actual proposal, Lawrence establishes the risk involved with Tom's faith in his soul's logic. Tom peers in at a world separated by barrier and prohibition:

There was a light streaming on to the bushes at the back from the kitchen window. He began to hesitate. How could he do this? Looking through the window, he saw her seated in the rocking-chair with the child, already in its nightdress, sitting on her knee. The fair head with its wild, fierce hair was drooping towards the fire-warmth, which reflected on the bright cheeks and clear skin of the child, who seemed to be musing, almost like a grown-up person. The mother's face was dark and still, and he saw, with a pang, that she was away back in the life that had been. The child's hair gleamed like spun glass, her face was illuminated till it seemed like wax lit up from the inside. The wind boomed strongly. Mother and child sat motionless, silent, the child staring with vacant dark eyes into the fire, the mother looking into space. The little girl was almost asleep. It was her will which kept her eyes so wide. . . .

Then he heard the low, monotonous murmur of a song in a foreign language. (37–8)

The warmth of maternal blood connection, the magic of shared history, the sensuous allure of flesh and soft hair, and the tacit link between the hidden past and the transcendence of nature – Lawrence is rarely better and never more composite. Tom is as cut off from the world beyond the glass as Heathcliff is when he looks through the window at the foreign domain of the Lintons. But Tom Brangwen wants to join the tableau spread before him. He understandably hesitates before the bond of history and blood between mother and daughter that he can never share. The sounds of foreign words and a 'life that had been' with a husband he can never know intimidate him. Their contented contact with each other and their indecipherable murmurs keep him imprisoned outside. He perceives the scene through a window that is as admonishing as it is transparent; are they priceless artifacts, wax museum pieces he dare not touch, much less propose to protect?

As the window passage concludes, Lawrence characteristically moves, in the second of several analogous movements in the novel, from the issue of a Brangwen's struggle to experience the unknown, to a complementary depiction of the overarching cosmos that is source and overseer of the primal force Tom struggles to comprehend: 'Then a great burst of wind, the mother seemed to have drifted away, the child's eyes were black and dilated. Brangwen looked up at the clouds which packed in a

great, alarming haste across the dark sky' (38). The impulsive
feel of the wind and the hasty, alarming clouds reflect both the
immediate proximity of Tom's quest – just *beyond* the glass, as it
were – and his fear of the confrontation itself. Although Tom
enters the house and Lydia accepts his proposal, the frozen
moment of his observation at the window, filled with his sense of
desire and fear, anticipates the rhythm of his relation to her during
their engagement and marriage. The foreign element in Lydia that
spurs his attraction is also a wedge that complicates his emergence
from the strait jacket of ego and consequently hampers delivery
to the unknown demanded by her: 'When he approached her, he
came to such a terrible painful unknown. . . . What was it then
that she was, to which he must also deliver himself up, and which
at the same time he must embrace, contain?' (53) At the end of
the proposal scene Tom still has not won the struggle to abide by
the logic of his soul.

Although he knows 'it's got to be done' he cannot give himself
up to her. As Tom leaves his betrothed, Lawrence again turns to
a view of the firmament that insists, as a choral reminder
throughout the novel, that his struggle take place: 'He went out
into the wind. Big holes were blown into the sky. . . . And all
the sky was teeming and tearing along, a vast disorder of flying
shapes . . . then the terror of the moon running liquid-brilliant
into the open for a moment, hurting the eyes before she plunged
under cover of cloud again' (44). The enveloping cosmos presents
no merely symbolic correspondence to Tom's unpredictable
relations with Lydia and not any pantheistic celebration of inscrutable natural energy. It becomes a felt and *participatory* reflection
of what Tom has achieved with his fiancée; in effect, his vitalistic
perception of the unknown in her will lead him to his fundamental
appreciation of the energy beyond her. What Tom perceives in
Lydia is as actual as the wind and moon that take part in the
prescient feeling with which he leaves. 'Hurting the eyes before
she plunged under cover of cloud again' – a celestial body becomes
Lawrence's counterpoint, in a universe that itself ebbs and flows,
to Tom's strained willingness, just a page earlier, to meet Lydia
in a kiss 'till he could bear no more' and must retreat, as 'he drew
away, white, unbreathing' (43).

It is not surprising that Tom's greatest difficulty in accommo-
dating himself to his wife's 'unknown' occurs when she is pregnant, when she is most adamantly 'other'. During this period

Lydia remains isolated and confident, her body brimming with the confirmation (which Lawrence describes in 'The Crown') of her direct connection to the forces of creation. Tom returns home with a mixture of trepidation and excitement to the bedside of a womb-aloof wife who is about to give birth:

> There was the sound of the owls – the moaning of the woman. What an uncanny sound! It was not human – at least to a man.
>
> He went down to her room, entering softly. She was lying still, with eyes shut, pale, tired. His heart leapt, fearing she was dead. Yet he knew perfectly well she was not. He saw the way her hair went loose over her temples, her mouth was shut with suffering in a sort of grin. She was beautiful to him – but it was not human. He had a dread of her as she lay there. What had she to do with him? She was other than himself.
>
> Something made him go and touch her fingers that were still grasped on the sheet. Her brown-grey eyes opened and looked at him. She did not know him as himself. But she knew him as the man. She looked at him as a woman in childbirth looks at the man who begot the child in her: an impersonal look, in the extreme hour, female to male. Her eyes closed again. A great, scalding peace went over him, burning his heart and his entrails, passing off into the infinite.
>
> When her pains began afresh, tearing her, he turned aside, and could not look. But his heart in torture was at peace, his bowels were glad. (76)

The scene is alive with the paradox of the 'logic of the soul' that motivates Tom. He is roused to anticipation of death by the portentous darkness, owls, and silence while he waits with tentative pleasure for the first life he created. Here is a man who cannot comprehend the 'suffering grin' of his woman, for hers is the painful joy that belongs to an anatomy unlike his own. Here is a husband in love with his pregnant wife; yet here also is man so bewitched by the transformations of parturition that he feels his woman's humanity as something 'not human'. Lawrence dramatizes the developing breach in her body as establishing a necessary breach with him – an archetypal singling out of the pure polarity of pregnant mother and expectant father. Tom fears this separation from Lydia, and he remains more perplexed than respectful that she is 'other than himself'. Although Tom cannot fully appreciate its primeval simplicity, her look at him is the regard of ultimate recognition. The scene works not only as a faithful and poetic rendering of the most essential aspects of Lawrencian doctrine but also as an appropriate depiction of the truths about childbirth a century ago.

Once again Mailer supplies direction, this time with a clue to the reason for the relative absence of such a haunting vignette in the technologized world often reflected in contemporary fiction:

> Sometimes the Prisoner thought women had begun to withdraw respect from men about the time pregnancy lost its danger. For once Semmelweiss uncovered the cause of puerperal fever, and the doctor could take over from the midwife, once anesthesia, antiseptics, obstetrics, and delivery by flourescent [sic] light were able to replace boiling water, the lamp by the bed, and the long drum roll of labor, then women began to be insulated from the dramatic possibility of a fatal end. If that had once been a possibility real enough for them to look at their mate with eyes of love or eyes of hate but know their man might yet be the agent of their death, conceive then of the lost gravity of the act, and the diminishment of man from a creature equally mysterious to woman (since he could introduce a creation to her which could yet be her doom) down to the fellow who took lessons on how to satisfy his wife from Masters and Johnson.[21]

Such is the gravity of this scene in *The Rainbow* as Tom and Lydia are reduced to 'creatures'; they are shorn of the habits of civilized discourse by the silence and metamorphosis that accompany the fate that Lydia risks. Finally Tom leaves the room while 'his heart in torture was at peace', which suggests that he begins to comprehend the measuring look by Lydia, who sees him as 'her man'. Tom's functioning instinct, which is summarized in the beats of his pacified heart and the message of his 'entrails', is the pulse of the transcendent as he begins to accept the otherness of Lydia.

Mailer's dialectical rumination in *The Prisoner of Sex* on the difference between the sexes often sounds like an incisive commentary on the drama evident in the depiction of marital tensions in *The Rainbow*. Lawrence is not Mailer's preoccupation in the following passage. But it is difficult not to recall Tom's doubt of Lydia's humanity while she awaits the birth of her child. She is blessed with more intrinsic strength, even in her weakened condition, than is present in her overawed husband; Mailer crystallizes the distinction dramatized by Lawrence in that stirring scene in Lydia's room: 'Women, like men, were human beings but they were a step, or a stage, or a move, or a leap nearer the creation of existence – they were – given man's powerful sense of the present – his indispensable and only connection to the future.'[22] It is a summary of the young husband's inscrutable mixture of desire and fear that underlies his relation to Lydia; it recalls Tom's unarticulated sense that Lydia has a self-defining power denied him. Lawrence continues to measure Tom's maturity by the extent to which he can learn to admire and embrace that human channel to the transcendent whom he can neither understand nor control.

In the early pages of *The Rainbow* there is also an implicit notion of 'separateness' between the sexes that is related to the stress on polarized sexuality in the novel. That is, Tom must learn to accept the otherness of Lydia, but he must not linger as a voyeur before those ultimate, 'female' manifestations of that unfathomable quality in her. He must not observe her birthpains for long, but only quickly acknowledge her separate domain and then leave the room. During that valedictory period of Lawrence's life and art more than a decade after *The Rainbow*, Lawrence lets Mrs Bolton in *Lady Chatterley's Lover* spell out the reasons for such necessary distance; in effect, she also describes why Tom can be at peace with Lydia's otherness without staying to watch the magic:

> The way he sat when my first baby was born, motionless, and the sort of fatal eyes he looked at me with, when it was over! I had a bad time, but I had to comfort *him*. 'It's all right, lad, it's all right!' I said to him. And he gave me a look, and that funny sort of smile. He never said anything. But I don't believe he had any right pleasure with me at nights after; he'd never really let himself go. . . . I always blamed his mother, for letting him in th' room. He'd no right t'ave been there. Men makes so much more of things than they should, once they start brooding.[23]

Thus Mrs Bolton describes a dramatic example of the cautionary elements in the mysteries of singling out; in *Mr Noon*, which chronicles many of Lawrence's experiences with Frieda shortly before he begins work on *The Rainbow*, the narrator formulates the doctrines of polarized otherness in unequivocal terms that strike at the heart of feminist ambitions for social revolution:

But man must remain man, and woman woman. There is something manly in the soul of a man which is beyond woman, and in which she has no part. And there is something in woman, particularly in motherhood, in which man has no part, and can have no part. For a woman to trespass into man's extremity is poison, and for a man to trespass into woman's final remoteness is misery.[24]

So Lawrence, for the fourth time in thirty pages, moves from Tom's organic struggles to the climate of the infinite, but this time – caught in his first acceptance of the proper sense of awe – Tom has moved from fear to the larger truth that overwhelms: 'He went downstairs, and to the door, outside, lifted his face to the rain, and felt the darkness striking unseen and steadily upon him. The swift, unseen threshing of the night upon him silenced him and he was overcome. He turned away indoors, humbly. There was the infinite world, eternal, unchanging, as well as the world of life' (76). Tom seems properly initiated to the visionary sensations he has begun to accept. Years later when he is present at the wedding of Anna, his stepdaughter, he tries to defend marriage to his unconvinced elder brother, Alfred: 'There's very little else, on earth, but marriage. You can talk about making money, or saving souls. You can save your own soul seven times over, and you may have a mint of money, but your soul goes gnawin', gnawin', gnawin', and it says there's something it must have. In heaven there is no marriage. But on earth there *is* marriage, else heaven drops out, and there's no bottom to it' (134). Tom's remarks conveniently allude to both the matrimonial urge felt as the logic of the soul and the connection to transcendent truth provided on earth through marriage. The young man who once timidly peered through a window at his future family now speaks for a vision he has grown to understand.

III

The intention of this analysis is not to detail Lawrence's painstaking portrait, 'really a stratum deeper', of the emotional history of Will and Anna's marriage, but it needs to be stressed that the primary struggle between Tom and Lydia is recapitulated in the second generation in more elaborate terms. Although the assignment of 'blame' for specific periods of their discord varies according to the prominence of Anna's self-involvement or Will's inhibitions, Lawrence presents their problem with a language that holds the husband primarily at fault: 'Always, her husband was to her the unknown to which she was delivered up . . . he seemed to expect her to be part of himself, the extension of his will' (166).[25] Like his father-in-law, Will experiences an immobilizing insecurity when he confronts his wife in her pregnancy. When she reveals to him that she is pregnant, the turbulent wind again charts a comment on his fear: 'And he trembled as if a wind blew on to him in strong gusts, out of the unseen. He was afraid. He was afraid to know he was alone. For she seemed fulfilled and separate and sufficient in her half of the world' (175). When Anna understandably becomes alienated by Will's obvious resentment of this 'fulfilment' in her, she punishes him by means of her naked dance. This primitive pantomime of his emasculation and execution summarizes the concern with marriage and the unknown that constitutes the ethical core of this novel. It is an extraordinary scene, not only for its sexual intensity and unrestrained cruelty, but also for its reflection of the special dispensations of Lawrence's art: it stands as both symbolic and literal rendering of that final recourse that Will's abrogations have forced Anna to take. Although the logic of Will's soul urges his marriage to Anna, he still resists delivery to the unknown, the essence of marital communion. Anna's pregnancy provides her with the natural temptation – doubly attractive because of her bitterness over Will's failure – to reach for the transcendent without her husband. So a pregnant Anna mobilizes within herself. She enacts a blasphemous version of Lawrence's prothalamic vision. She takes a cruel, logical, and heretical shortcut to the 'beyond' that is the ultimate direction of the logic of the soul. In essence, she capitalizes on her self-contained link with the infinite, bypasses her defaulting husband, and communes with the unknown by herself: 'She would dance his nullification, she would dance to her unseen Lord. . . . And she lifted her hands and danced again, to annul him' (180). The legalistic ring of 'nullification' and 'annul' registers a contractual failure by her husband. Will has not adhered to the marriage sacrament, so Anna sidesteps her man to engage her 'Lord' directly. Will senses that her pre-emptive dance signifies his ritual murder, and the pain he feels is more organic than analogical, as was the wind 'out of the unseen' that earlier had made him tremble. These fires burn through the real flesh of people who default on sacramental responsibility: 'Her face was rapt and beautiful, she danced exulting before her Lord, and knew no man. It hurt him as he watched as if he were at the stake' (181).

The revivifying potential of sex in a Lawrencian marriage is evident when Will and Anna re-establish their vital connection to each other. In his 'Study of Thomas Hardy' Lawrence proposes a doctrinal explanation for the logic in a husband that urges him to conceive children despite his fear of the profound 'separateness' in his wife occasioned by her pregnancy and maternal commitments. Lawrence writes of a man who, 'taking the superb and supreme risk, deposits a security of life in the womb', but he immediately clarifies the reasons for undertaking such a risk with a terminology that infiltrates *The Rainbow*: 'It is so arranged that the very act which carries us out into the unknown shall probably deposit seed for security to be left behind.'[26] Thus Will undergoes the penalty implicit in the risk when he observes his wife's annihilating dance, as an angry Anna presides over his emasculation in that confident period of her life that Lawrence describes as the 'fecund of storm life', when 'she felt like the earth, the maker of everything' (205). Only when Will rouses her to a sensual duel of discovery – as if to call her back after her frenzied years of pregnancy – do they demonstrate how they remain each other's crucial link to the beyond. The inviolable primacy of sexual intercourse, apart from procreation, Lawrence stresses in his 'Study of Thomas Hardy': 'But the act, called the sexual act, is not for the depositing of the seed. It is for leaping off into the unknown.'[27]

Lawrence concludes the Will and Anna section with an interlude that links the fate of young Ursula with the prothalamic theme that frames the novel. Ursula listens intently to Lydia's nostalgic and contemplative description of her two marriages. Lydia shows that she loved both men, and she emphasizes the importance of her granddaughter's understanding that her grandmother's loving and varied life was given baptismal form and meaning through the institution of marriage. Lydia's advice to Ursula was prompted by the child's curiosity about the wedding rings on her fingers. The next mention in *The Rainbow* of a wedding ring (aside from its use as the early title of *The Rainbow*) occurs several years later and is so strategically casual that it recalls the contrasting context of Lydia's warm and serious remarks about the significance of her

rings. It happens in the midst of Ursula's courtship with Skrebensky immediately after Ursula remarks, 'I don't think I want to
marry you' (453). There is nothing unexpected about this renunci-
ation of Skrebensky's proposal of marriage, an offer that he makes
with a characteristic pretence of aplomb: 'I suppose we ought to
get married' (452). Ursula's refusal reflects her developing sense
of his inadequacy for her, even as the phrasing also suggests her
inability to break off sexual dependency on him, for she does not
offer to end the affair. Yet a few lines later, as if she had not just
declined his offer, she happily joins him in a conventional playact of young lovers by purchasing 'a wedding-ring for a shilling,
from a shop in a poor quarter' (453). Her participation in this
charade of betrothal contrasts with her earnest attention to her
grandmother's benedictive consideration of marriage. Ursula's
adolescent behaviour with a wedding ring functions as a denial of
her awareness of Skrebensky's inadequacy, and it anticipates her
perverse proposal of marriage that she writes to him late in the
novel.

The history of Ursula's long affair with Skrebensky, which
concludes with the antiprothalamic trappings of a miscarriage, an
emasculated male, and a sick female, stands as Lawrence's
warning of the pathology in a love that does not produce a joint
singling out. Through her early sexual experiences with Skrebensky, Ursula realizes that she can never reach the unknown
with him because 'as a distinct male he had no core' (321);
however, Ursula later realizes she at least can attain self-definition
at his expense.[28] Mailer's earlier comments about the modern tendency to adulterate the apocalyptic possibility in sex provide a
pertinent index to the pattern of Skrebensky's decline; his gradual
physical and emotional deterioration, urged on by that 'terrible
knowledge' Ursula gains of him under the moon, recalls Mailer's
fears about 'the lost gravity' of the sexual act and 'the diminish-
ment of man from a creature equally mysterious to woman'. Yet
it would be wrong to castigate Ursula's exploitation of their sexual
relationship. Her compulsion to follow the logic of her soul into
an affair with him is not merely the manifestation of either physical
desire or ego. Her sexual triumphs over Skrebensky are apprentice
efforts at her own singling out. So she indulges in a form of
competitive sex with him that is both necessarily at his expense
and necessary for her own growth into the woman who marries

Rupert Birkin, a man who will demand that otherness be achieved through polarity or 'star-equilibrium'.

In *Psychoanalysis and the Unconscious*, which explores certain 'pollyanalytical' principles dramatized in his fiction, Lawrence provides a doctrinal explanation for the relentless impulse behind Ursula's treatment of Skrebensky: 'It is perhaps difficult for us to realize the strong, blind power of the unconscious on its first plane of activity. It is something quite different from what we call *egoism* – which is really mentally derived – for the ego is merely the sum total of what we conceive ourselves to be. The powerful pristine subjectivity of the unconscious on its first plane is, on the other hand, the root of all our consciousness and being, darkly tenacious.'[29] In a complementary letter to his friend Edward Garnett, Lawrence in effect discourages criticism of Ursula's manipulative but instinctive brand of sex. He also provides an explanation for the abrupt sequence of changes in Ursula's mood and health in the novel's last pages: 'You mustn't look in my novel for the old stable ego of the character. There is another ego, according to whose action the individual is unrecognizable, and passes through, as it were, allotropic states which it needs a deeper sense than any we've been used to exercise.'[30] This passage through allotropic states, which seems to demand obedience of a person's instinctive passion, is dramatized when Ursula and Skrebensky make love: 'It was begun now, this passion, and must go on, the passion of Ursula to know her own maximum self, limited and so defined against him. She could limit and define herself against him, the male, she could be her maximum self, female, oh female, triumphant for one moment in exquisite assertion against the male, in supreme contradistinction to the male' (301). Such language, with its repetitive emphasis on isolated male and female movements towards self-definition, is revealing for what it suggests about both the prerogatives of Ursula's singling out and the instrumentality of Skrebensky's role in that process. Once the allotropic process begins, once Ursula begins to exert her primal female self, 'her own maximum self', the forging to elementals develops a momentum of its own; the porous Skrebensky, who cannot single out, is easy prey for the slaughter. Why should Ursula enjoy such predatory behaviour, and why should Lawrence devote so many scenes to the chronicling of this victory over Skrebensky? Lawrence's response in *Fantasia of the Unconscious*, with its distinct echo of phrasing from *The Rainbow*,

goes to the crux of Ursula's instinctive achievement; he summarizes why the stakes implicit in her intercourse with Skrebensky
under the moon seem heightened beyond the needs of orgasm or
ego: 'And only at his maximum does an individual surpass all his
derivative elements and become purely himself.'[31] Ursula's quest
for her maximum self is most graphically described in the act of
love, where the potential for singling out is greatest, and where
Lawrence can employ the moon and stars as participatory
representatives, respectively, of Ursula's quest for self-definition
and for transcendence.[32]

The act of intercourse is not the only context used by Lawrence
in the Ursula section to dramatize aspects of his prothalamic
theme. In the barge scene, for instance, he re-establishes the
novel's emphasis on the values of stability and vitality in marriage
that Lydia had enunciated years earlier in her talk with Ursula.
The husband and wife whom Ursula meets on their boat exist in
that state of lively and delicate balance that Lawrence would
describe in *Women in Love*. The man exhibits a competent independence without resorting to the chauvinistic slogans that Skrebensky had just praised in a previous conversation with Ursula.
Although the husband loves his wife, speaking of her 'with just
pride' (311), he also demonstrates an appreciation of Ursula's
charm; he has a respectful flirtation with Ursula that moves beyond
Skrebensky's games of ego and conquest. Similarly, Ursula's abandonment of Uncle Tom's necklace during her visit on the barge
anticipates her coming awareness, for she soon identifies Uncle
Tom with a cynical view of love and marriage. It is not surprising
that, after she breaks off with Winifred, because she senses the
mechanization and organic dislocation that underlie Winifred's
flaunted independence, she realizes the appropriateness of Winifred's union with Tom.

In her book on Lawrence and feminism, Hilary Simpson fails to
understand that Lawrence's criticism of Winifred stems from the
sexual contempt that pompous 'Miss Inger' masquerades as trendy
radicalism and graceful independence. Simpson is seduced by the
political interests of Winifred to the extent of believing that
Ursula's teacher legitimately offers what current jargon might
ponderously call 'a viable and alternative lifestyle'. For here are
Simpson's oddly misleading remarks about Winifred's motives
and relation with Ursula, followed by the lines she directly quotes
and misinterprets from *The Rainbow*:

Winifred also initiates Ursula into a different aspect of her female heritage from that of the uninterrupted domesticity and child-bearing of her mother. 'Miss Inger was telling Ursula of a friend, how she had died in childbirth, and what she has suffered; then she told of a prostitute, and some of her experiences with men.' (338)[33]

Thus Simpson appears not to realize that Winifred's preoccu-pations with suffering, dirty sex, and death in childbirth tell more about Winifred's relation to love and sexuality than about norma-tive realities of passion and nurturing affections.

When Ursula begins to sense the truth about Winifred, she is content to lose her to the equally manipulative Uncle Tom. Lawr-ence's deadpan description of the motivations and hopes for such a marriage reads as a litany of the values he despises:

Brangwen and Winifred Inger continued engaged for another term. Then they married. Brangwen had reached the age when he wanted children. He wanted children. Neither marriage nor the domestic establishment meant anything to him. . . . He had the instinct of a growing inertia. . . . He would let the machinery carry him. . . . As for Winifred, she was an educated woman, and of the same sort as himself. She would make a good companion. She was his mate. (351)

It is instructive to contrast Uncle Tom's needs with the instinctive 'look in the eyes' of the Brangwens on the first page of the novel. He has no real interest in either marriage or the unknown, for he only 'wanted children' to propagage his mechanical view of existence. He is spurred in this desire by no vital logic of his soul but only by 'the instinct of growing inertia', which recognizes a kinship with the deadness at the core of Winifred. The flat repetition of 'he wanted children', with its suggestion of apathy and pragmatism, makes Uncle Tom appear as an early version of Clifford Chatterley. Like the paralyzed magnate, who literally 'let the machinery carry him', Uncle Tom speaks without respect for institutions and metaphors such as marriage, fatherhood, and the infinite – all of which exist beyond the easy control of a machine or marketable idea. As for Winifred, Lawrence mocks her fashionable pretence with his use of 'an educated woman', 'a good companion', and a 'mate'; those vapid and trendy terms indicate her lack of connection to the flesh and blood realities of passionate marriage.

IV

But, it may be argued, does not the apocalyptic conclusion of the novel contradict the bedrock celebration of marriage that Lawrence develops throughout *The Rainbow*? Are not the final pages – as much feminist criticism insists – a declaration of the birth of an eminently single and 'modern' woman, an ending that shows conclusively the influence on Lawrence of his recent exposure to the radical ideas of Cambridge? In the independence and stoic optimism that Ursula's vision of the rainbow seems to suggest, does she not reject the prothalamic doctrines of this work?

Feminist critics of this novel continue to admire Ursula for her supposed opposition to middle-class values of marriage and fecund motherhood that apparently are contrary to some 'modern' spirit of female freedom. Their criticism not only fails to see how Ursula is deftly integrated by Lawrence into those preoccupations about marriage and the maximum self I have discussed; it also misunderstands the paradoxical role of Skrebensky in sufficiently stimulating Ursula's primitive desire for the unknown so that she fully exposes the nothingness at the core of his being. Heilbrun, for instance, speaks of Ursula as a 'new woman' at the end who 'is entirely alone'. She remarks, 'Hindsight suggests that there was no one less likely than Lawrence to have created her', but she never subjects the purported isolation to an analysis that would reveal the unlikeliness of her own interpretation. Heilbrun sees Ursula's only future option as 'ordinary marriage for the sake of social recognition',[34] when, in fact, the final page posits something quite apart from the 'ordinary'. Millet distorts the compulsions that operate in Ursula's treatment of Skrebensky, as she argues that 'Anton must be sacrificed as an object lesson in how monstrous the new woman can be'.[35] This peculiar reading results from such an overriding desire in Millett to charge Lawrence with sexism that she ironically misses the justifications of Ursula's attack on the man. More recently, Lydia Blanchard mars an otherwise balanced appraisal of familial structures in *The Rainbow* with her stress on Adrienne Rich's delimiting theories of motherhood and power relationships. Blanchard is one of the few critics to realize that 'the ending of the novel is not a resolution', but she steers clear of any crucial admission that Ursula's quest for self-definition requires the opposite sex.[36]

The ending of *The Rainbow* reflects neither a rejection of Ursula's need and desire for marriage nor Lawrence's de-emphasis of the critical importance of marriage in shaping the instinctive life of men and women. Indeed, it is not really an ending at all but an announcement of Ursula's realization of the kind of marriage she needs – a declaration, in effect, of her intention to prepare for that 'discovery' of the proper husband in *Women in Love*. Lawrence's companion novel begins with a discussion between Ursula and Gudrun Brangwen on the subject of marriage; although Ursula confesses that she has rejected several offers, it is the inadequacy of the men in her life rather than an abiding antagonism to the institution that has kept her single. One of the offers of marriage was from Anthony Schofield, a generous and competent young man from *The Rainbow*, whom Ursula turns down because the life he offers her is unstimulating and unsuitable. Before she rejects him Lawrence scarcely hides the continued importance Ursula places on a husband when he writes with odd coyness: 'But having more freedom she only became more profoundly aware of the big want . . . she wanted to know big, free people; and there remained always the want she could put no name to' (406).

Several reasons exist for the unfortunate consensus in much Lawrencian criticism that finds Ursula more determinedly isolated and self-contained at the conclusion of *The Rainbow* than she really is. A willingness to see the Ursula on the last page as complete and emblematic tends to serve the fashionable interests of sexual politics. Ignorance of some relevant facts about the composition of *The Rainbow* deflects needed attention from the suspiciously pre-emptory nature of the novel's concluding incidents; a tendency not to be wary of an interpretation of the ending that contradicts Lawrencian belief permits a reading that strangely asserts Lawrence's celebration of Ursula's glorious chances for spinsterhood. These interpretations distort the significance of an aspect of Ursula's rainbow vision by not considering the concluding lines in a context broad enough to integrate notions in Ursula's dramatized past, her 'realized' present, and her likely future.

No doubt the subservient letter that she writes to Skrebensky persuades many readers that Ursula's fortuitous escape from marriage to him suggests her intention to pursue life without a man.[37] But Ursula's ultimate realization about her pathetic letter and the threat posed by Skrebensky have taught her to be wary of flawed men and inadequate marriages. It is important not to give Ursula's fawning letter to Skrebensky any weight on the subject of normative marriage. Its tone of maudlin imploring – ' "It was given to me to love you" ' (484) – describes a nearly hysterical Ursula not seen before; the self-abnegating sentiments she expresses about marriage and her wifely role stand in contradiction to the portrait throughout the novel of Ursula's reliable instinct and developing insight. In short, the letter must be construed as a reflection of her understandable panic and illness when she discovers she is alone and pregnant and not as a programme for recommended wedlock. Even her analysis of her parents' marriage is glib and reductive, failing to catch the complexity of the adjustments between Will and Anna: 'Was it not enough for her as it had been enough for her mother? She would marry and love her husband and fill her place simply' (484). There is nothing 'simple' about either Lydia's or Anna's definition of 'place'.

College-educated and emancipated Ursula is an adamantly different woman than her mother and grandmother, and she entertains ideas about her destiny that do not rest comfortably with Lydia's and Anna's emphasis on maternity. Lawrence accommodates his understanding of Ursula's special power and requirements in the implications of the novel's final lines. Lawrence forecasts without any self-consciousness a kind of 'royal' marriage for Ursula that he memorializes in *Women in Love*; he has created the only woman who might be an appropriate wife for Birkin: 'Who was she to have a man according to her own desire? It was not for her to create, but to recognize a man created by God. The man should come from the Infinite and she should hail him' (493). This inflated style, with its sense of grandiose expectation, is not mere metaphor; it suggests that Ursula readies herself for neither the submissive marriage to Skrebensky nor the traditional marriage of the previous two generations of Brangwens but for that advocate of star-equilibrium whom she will meet in the novel originally conceived as *The Sisters*, before Lawrence split it into *The Rainbow* and *Women in Love*.[38] Only a Lawrence would dare suggest the coming of Birkin–Lawrence in terms so hyperbolic, but he never was modest about his talent or mission. When Birkin does 'arrive' for Ursula in *Women in Love*, his significance for her recalls the tone and imagery suggested by Ursula's concluding mandate in *The Rainbow* 'to recognize a man created by God': 'It was here she discovered him one of the sons of God such as were in the beginning of the world, not a man, something other, something more.'[39]

There is a more crucial reason for anticipating the next novel. The history of the composition of *The Rainbow* and *Women in Love* supports the view that the end of *The Rainbow* is really the beginning of Ursula's search for the right husband. In a concise discussion of the final revisions of *The Rainbow*, Harry T. Moore writes: 'Apparently Ursula's experiences towards the end of *The Rainbow* had occurred near the beginning of *The Sisters*; the surviving manuscript of *The Rainbow* indicates, with its alterations of page numbers and in order of chapters, that these experiences had been moved back, a process which evidently pushed Birkin (the school inspector) into the second book.'[40] Such information helps explain the 'addendum' tone of *The Rainbow*'s final lines that makes many readers feel the end amounts to a beginning. Ursula's final experiences were originally part of a longer work that would more decisively chronicle her straight-line movement from Skrebensky to a suitable mate. Lawrence's final revisions and his decision to write two novels make the ending of *The Rainbow* more declarative than dramatized; the assertion of the conclusion tends to disguise the original function of the final episodes as a mediating stage in Lawrence's prothalamic vision.

Just a few months before Lawrence began work on what would become *The Rainbow* and *Women in Love*, he wrote a letter to Frieda that not only reveals something about himself but also summarizes a pattern of concern in his fiction: 'Can't you feel how certainly I love you and how certainly we shall be married. . . . Do you know, like the old knights, I seem to want a certain time to prepare myself – a sort of vigil with myself. Because it is a great thing for me to marry you, not a quick, passionate coming together. I know in my heart "here's my marriage." '[41]

Notes

1. James T. Boulton (ed.), *The Letters of D. H. Lawrence*, I (Cambridge: Cambridge University Press, 1979), 526.
2. There has been much discussion of the 'special' qualities of each generation in *The Rainbow*, and several essays deal with the recurrent

motifs and images that unify the Brangwen saga; but critics rarely
stress in an integrated fashion both Lawrence's vision of marriage
and the compulsions in his characters that inform the doctrine and
structural repetitions. F. R. Leavis was among the first to note that
'the effort of realization and discovery starts again in each
generation . . . and it is an essential part of the undertaking of *The
Rainbow* to deal with three generations', in *D. H. Lawrence: Novelist*
(New York: Simon & Schuster, 1969; Harmondsworth: Penguin, 1970),
101. But Leavis isolates this pattern primarily to make his argument
about class, English culture, and the tradition of the novel, while
the correlative themes of marriage and instinctive need receive little
attention from him. Leavis makes partial amends for such omission in
his later essay when he examines the rainbow symbol to demonstrate
Lawrence's concern with the interrelationship of marriage and individual growth; Leavis shows 'how the distinctive offer of *The Rainbow*
is to render development concretely – the complex change from generation to generation and the interweaving of the generations', in
Thoughts, Words and Creativity (New York: Oxford University Press,
1976), 125. Julian Moynahan emphasizes that 'the crucial relation in
The Rainbow is between a man and a woman in marital and sexual
experience'; Moynahan sees marriage 'as the major recurring event
in *The Rainbow*', and he stresses a doctrine of 'individuation' within
the context of Lawrence's depiction of marital struggle, in *The Deed
of Life* (Princeton: Princeton University Press, 1963), 43–4. Yet Moynahan's analysis of the passionate scenes between the Brangwens under-
estimates the extent to which Lawrence documents an intrinsic,
instinctive momentum in marriage toward reconciliation and compromise; Moynahan seems more concerned with Lawrence's mystical
ideas on salvation and transfiguration than with the tensions in the
marital discord. H. M. Daleski integrates the marriage theme with
both Lawrence's doctrine and the structure of the novel. He maintains
that *The Rainbow* is more than 'a psychological study of marriage',
and he shows how it functions as the 'first stage in an attempt to
discover the necessary conditions for a meaningful life'. Although
Daleski illustrates how 'Lawrence deals with three generations in
order to discover what is consistent in the lives of men and women',
he does not sufficiently explain the seminal relation of Lawrence's
use of the 'unknown' to the sense of primitive urgency that operates
in many of the scenes Daleski discusses. See Daleski, *The Forked Flame:
A Study of D. H. Lawrence* (Evanston: Northwestern University Press,
1965), 75.

3. Lawrence, *Letters*, I, 544.
4. Lawrence, 'A Propos of *Lady Chatterley's Lover*', in Harry T. Moore
   (ed.), *Sex, Literature, and Censorship* (New York: Viking, 1959), 105.
5. Reported by Harry T. Moore, in *The Priest of Love: A Life of D. H.
   Lawrence*, rev. edn (New York: Farrar, Straus & Giroux, 1974;
   Harmondsworth: Penguin, 1980), 197.
6. Here are a few of the many relevant comments contained in *The
   Letters*, I: 'Remember, you are to be my wife' (393). '*Is* the divorce

coming off? . . . Have you settled anything definite with Ernst? . . .
My next coming to you is solemn, intrinsically – I am solemn over it
– not sad, oh no – but it is my marriage, after all, and a great thing
– not a thing to be snatched and clumsily handled' (401). 'Dear God,
I am marrying you, now, don't you see. It's a far greater thing than
ever I knew' (403).

7. See Carolyn Heilbrun, *Towards a Recognition of Androgyny* (New York:
   Harper & Row, 1974), 102–10; Hilary Simpson, *D. H. Lawrence and
   Feminism* (Dekalb: Northern Illinois University Press; London: Croom
   Helm, 1982), 37–42; Kate Millett, *Sexual Politics* (Garden City:
   Doubleday, 1970; London: Virago, 1977), 257–62.
8. Heilbrun, *Towards a Recognition of Androgyny*, 102.
9. Ibid., ix.
10. Millett, *Sexual Politics*, 257.
11. Ibid., 262.
12. Simpson, *D. H. Lawrence and Feminism*, 37.
13. Ibid.
14. Norman Mailer, *The Prisoner of Sex* (New York: New American Library,
    1971), 107. Mailer first refers to himself as 'left-conservative' in *The
    Armies of the Night* (New York: New American Library, 1968), 185.
15. Lawrence, 'Pornography and Obscenity', in *Sex, Literature, and Censor-
    ship*, 79.
16. Lawrence, *Lady Chatterley's Lover* (New York: Grove, 1959; London:
    Heinemann, 1963), 373.
17. Lawrence, 'The Crown', in *Phoenix II: Uncollected, Unpublished, and
    Other Prose Work by D. H. Lawrence* (New York: Viking, 1970), 367.
18. Lawrence, 'Study of Thomas Hardy' (Cambridge: Cambridge Univer-
    sity Press, 1985) is also found in Edward D. McDonald (ed.), *Phoenix:
    The Posthumous Papers of D. H. Lawrence* (New York: Viking, 1972),
    446–7. Mark Kinkead-Weekes provides significant criticism on the
    relation of Lawrence's doctrine in 'Study of Thomas Hardy' to both
    the theme of marriage in *The Rainbow* and the function of the novel's
    tripartite structure. Kinkead-Weekes's essay is based on the develop-
    ment of Lawrence's thoughts about marriage and selfhood from the
    manuscript of *The Wedding Ring* to the completion of *The Rainbow*. His
    essay focuses on how Lawrence's basic ideas on 'male' and 'female'
    principles in the 'Study of Thomas Hardy' provide insights into the
    complexities of characterization in *The Rainbow*. My major objection
    to that essay is the degree to which it relies on the dialectic in the
    Hardy study to corroborate (or initiate) the conclusions Kinkead-
    Weekes reaches about the revisions in Lawrence's composition of the
    novel. Although Kinkead-Weekes maintains that the 'Study of
    Thomas Hardy' is not a 'skeleton key' for *The Rainbow* 'and must not
    be misused as one', he does not clearly observe his own warning, in
    'The Marble and the Statue: the Exploratory Imagination of D. H.
    Lawrence', from Ian Gregor and Maynard Mack (eds), *Imagined
    Worlds: Essays in Honor of John Butt* (London: Methuen, 1968), partly
    reprinted in Mark Kinkead-Weekes (ed.), *Twentieth-Century Interpret-
    ations of 'The Rainbow'* (Englewood Cliffs: Prentice-Hall, 1971), 110.

Except for his interpretation of the Lincoln Cathedral scene, he does not subject his conclusions about marriage to a close scrutiny of relevant scenes in the novel.

19. George J. Zytaruk and James T. Boulton (eds), *The Letters of D. H. Lawrence*, II (Cambridge: Cambridge University Press, 1981), 191.
20. Lawrence, *The Rainbow* (New York: Viking, 1961; London: Heinemann, 1954), 1. Page numbers in my text refer to the Viking edition.
21. Mailer, *The Prisoner of Sex*, 93.
22. Ibid., 47.
23. Lawrence, *Lady Chatterley's Lover*, 217.
24. Lawrence, *Mr Noon* (Cambridge and New York: Cambridge University Press, 1984), 212.
25. See Charles L. Ross, 'The Revisions of the Second Generation in *The Rainbow*', in *Review of English Studies* 27 (1976), 277–95, and *The Composition of 'The Rainbow' and 'Women in Love': A History* (Charlottesville: University Press of Virginia, 1979), who builds on several of Kinkead-Weekes's conclusions.
26. Lawrence, 'Study of Thomas Hardy', 441.
27. Ibid.
28. My explanation in this paragraph of Ursula's sense of self is a reformulation of my original discussion in *D. H. Lawrence and the Psychology of Rhythm* (The Hague: Mouton, 1974), a book that discusses in greater detail the relation of *The Rainbow* to the principles Lawrence enunciates in his major psychological essays.
29. Lawrence, *Psychoanalysis and the Unconscious* (New York: Viking, 1960), 28.
30. Lawrence, *Letters*, II, 183.
31. Lawrence, *Fantasia of the Unconscious* (New York: Viking Press, 1960; Harmondsworth: Penguin, 1971), 71.
32. Mark Spilka first stressed the significance of the moon scenes in his pioneering work on Lawrence more than a quarter of a century ago. He explains that Ursula resembles both Diana, the moon goddess who protects women, and the daughter of Aphrodite, whom 'Lawrence calls the goddess of dissolution and death'. *The Love Ethic of D. H. Lawrence* (Bloomington: Indiana University Press, 1953), 112. Thus as Ursula seeks rhythmic communion with the moon, she asserts her triumphant female self as a woman whose psychology calls upon her to destroy the oppressive weight on her (for example 'Skrebensky, like a load-stone weighed on her', 317) and as a mythical goddess (beyond psychology, as it were) whose very triumph is ensured by her name and the moon environment. When Ursula makes love to him late in the novel, she brings to a climax her need to bypass his enclosed self – 'not on any side did he lead into the unknown' (473) – and she has her intercourse with the stars. It is a version of the legitimate sexual bypass of a lover that Lawrence depicted in Anna's dance in front of Will.
33. Simpson, *D. H. Lawrence and Feminism*, 338.
34. Heilbrun, *Towards a Recognition of Androgyny*, 109–10.
35. Millett, *Sexual Politics*, 262.

36. Lydia Blanchard, 'Mothers and Daughters in D. H. Lawrence: *The Rainbow* and Selected Shorter Works', in Anne Smith (ed.), *Lawrence and Women* (New York: Barnes & Noble; London: Vision, 1978), 75–100.
37. The letter is less significant for ideological criticism, which rejects Ursula altogether – whether she is single, engaged, or pleading for marriage. Millett, for instance, derides the single Ursula as Lawrence's attempt 'to make the lot of the independent woman repellent', and she despises the engaged Ursula as a subtle reflection of Lawrence's reactionary and 'half derogatory, half vaporous' relation to feminism (*Sexual Politics*, 260–1).
38. Since Lawrence writes that his novel is about 'woman becoming individual, self-responsible, taking her own initiative', it is important to regard the new and exclusive grounds of Ursula's search for a husband within the context of Lawrence's stress on such virtues. Lawrence, *Letters*, II, 165. The marriage she contemplates in her future does not involve escape, easy dependency, or empty conventionality.
39. Lawrence, *Women in Love* (New York: Viking Press, 1960; London: Heinemann, 1984), 305.
40. Moore, *The Priest of Love*, 224. Moore's discussion is a summary of the initial findings of Kinkead-Weekes and a preview of the more detailed corroborations of Ross, both cited above.
41. Lawrence, *Letters*, I, 403.

3

Ursula Brangwen and 'The Essential Criticism': The Female Corrective in *Women in Love*

'But why do you always grip your lips?' he asked, regretful.
'Never mind,' she said swiftly. 'It is my way.'

I

Critics have not been generous to the Ursula of *Women in Love*. Characteristic reactions include the harsh and ideological dismissal of her by Kate Millett and Carolyn Heilbrun, who view her, respectively, as 'Birkin's wife and echo . . . an incomplete creature . . . the epitome of passivity',[1] and as merely the 'satellite to Birkin's star'.[2] Such a common misreading by feminists of Ursula's role is surprising given their frequent calls for woman's active sexual partnership in marriage; for such *is* the status that a persistent Ursula both encourages and achieves with her head-strong and often contradictory husband. There are also the more sober disappointments of consensus Lawrence criticism, which still encourages an approach to the novel that either virtually ignores Ursula or bemoans a purported submissiveness in her relationship with Birkin. Only in some undeveloped remarks by, among others, F. R. Leavis, Frank Kermode, Julian Moynahan,

85

and Charles Ross, is there a significant implication that her function in the work and her attachment to Birkin are other than subsidiary or tangential; even their acknowledgements of her resistance to Birkin's doctrines do not suggest that she provides any compelling counterpoint, any ethos of her own to offer against her lover's more didactic exhortations.[3]

It is my contention that neglected aspects of *Women in Love* are not only the important strengths of Ursula's character, but also how she is used skilfully by Lawrence to fashion a sustained and effective critique of Birkin's most cherished theories; indeed, she holds to an unembroidered view of human conduct, natural energy, and sexual response which is at least as legitimate as the celebrated dialectics about star-equilibrium, corruption, and isolate polarity proposed by Birkin. This matter of legitimacy involves concerns that are more substantive than simply a reader's subjective preference for Ursula's desires over Birkin's directives: the issue becomes related to Lawrence's own adherence to the requirements of his revolutionary art – that is, to that self-imposed set of ambitions about fictional achievement which Lawrence began to formulate and demonstrate during his work on *The Rainbow* and *Women in Love*. Ursula's corrective influence on Birkin is mandated by Lawrence's need to dramatize those aspects of his views on sexuality and great fiction which transcend any predilection of his own for the beliefs of his male hero. Millett and other ideologues scarcely examine the dialectical balance in this novel; they are undermined by a need to find some evidence of sexual politics in *Women in Love* that is in accord with their own preformulated indictment of sexism.[4] Millet states the case with utter confidence: '*Women in Love* presents us with the new man arrived in time to give Ursula her comeuppance and demote her back to wifely subjection.'[5] But it is an odd subjection when Ursula acts as the scrupulous critic and effective 'adjuster' of Birkin's doctrines and sex life. Ursula 'corrects' in the sense that she enables the artist in Lawrence to frame, balance, and ultimately hold in check those apocalyptic notions of Birkin's which, however much Lawrence may parade them in his letters and essays, he must submit to a perspective of doubt in the more tentative fabric of living fiction.

Yet is it reasonable to suppose, it may well be asked, that Lawrence would subject several of his principal ideas, enunciated with committed fanfare by Birkin, to a persuasive counter-attack in the very work which originally was planned as the fictional platform for this novelist's most radical doctrines? I suspect, unfortunately, we have been softer on Birkin than a discriminating reading of *Women in Love* requires. Lawrence's own echoing pronouncement that all 'art is utterly dependent on philosophy'[6] does not preclude the presence in the same novel of a capable argument against that metaphysic; in fact, this pattern of dialectical opposition is urged by Lawrence as the necessary component of any extended fiction which aspires to greatness. He suggests such a texture of antinomy most notably in a passage from his 'Study of Thomas Hardy', which is the seminal work he writes as he completes *The Rainbow* and begins to ponder his ambitions for the novel that would become *Women in Love*:

> Yet every work of art adheres to some system of morality. But if it be really a work of art, it must contain the essential criticism on the morality to which it adheres. . . . The degree to which the system of morality, or the metaphysic, of any work of art is submitted to criticism within the work of art makes the lasting value and satisfaction of that work.[7]

Ursula Brangwen is the primary register of this 'essential criticism' in *Women in Love*. Rupert Birkin's 'system of morality', to which the metaphysical development of the novel (and Lawrence's undisguised commitment) 'adheres', is submitted to the scrutiny of Ursula's sceptical antagonism. It is a scepticism which is rooted in the instinctual essence of her being as a female, and it strikes at the essential vulnerability of Birkin's less instinctive, more mind-centred formulations.

That Ursula's demurral from Birkin's programme often achieves a restraining power over him is not surprising; there is a secondary and correlative level of essential criticism at work in *Women in Love*, a theme of frank self-criticism heightened by a confessional Lawrence in his 'Foreword' to the novel and confirmed by the patches of uncertain rhetoric throughout Birkin's speeches. The Foreword is a warning not to look for consistency or precision in Lawrence's heroic attempt to find the Word for the pioneering themes undertaken in this fiction. It is the glory of the *attempt* at such large topics which the writer stresses: 'Any man of real individuality tries to know and to understand what is happening, even in himself, as he goes along. This struggle for verbal consciousness should not be left out in art. It is a very great part

of life. It is not superimposition of a theory. It is the passionate
struggle into conscious being.'[8] Such lines do yeoman service for
Lawrence, as they call attention to that sense of double perspective
which is a major fascination of this novel: the writer's battle to
bend the form of the novel to suit his visionary goal ultimately
encompasses, and is the frame for, Birkin's struggle to find the
language which can accommodate his doctrine.

In *Women in Love* the stage is often left to Birkin to 'try to know
and understand' this 'passionate struggle', and his accompanying
'struggle for verbal consciousness' is necessarily (for he can only
try) often contradictory, evasive, and inexact. Frequently Ursula
will provide a succinct rejoinder to his verbal outburst, a teasing
and deflating remark by her which reveals his characteristic wordi-
ness and imprecision. But it is also Birkin himself, sometimes
through Lawrence's narrative intrusion, who acknowledges his
own futile attempt to say what he means. Thus we often hear
echoes of the parturition metaphor from the Foreword, as Birkin
also both announces the urgency of his growing metaphysic and
confesses to the impossibility of its satisfactory formulation: 'He
turned in confusion. There was always confusion in speech. Yet
it must be spoken. Whichever way one moved, if one were to
move forwards, one must break a way through . . . as the infant
in labour strives through the walls of the womb' (178). It is usually
a conversation or experience with Ursula which prompts such an
admission of exigency and flawed rhetoric from Birkin. She
becomes not incidental to his verbal catharsis but organically
related to it as part of the relationship they strive to resolve; her
own demands for directness and tangibility enable Ursula to see
through his pomposity and force him to confront the implications,
for them both, of his most revolutionary pronouncements. As if
to confirm the legitimacy of her corrective influence on Birkin,
Lawrence establishes a special stature in Ursula during the first
third of the novel, before her affair with him is well-advanced.
Thus a sense of Ursula's instinctive 'rightness' gradually accumu-
lates, so that when she later expresses the prerogatives of her
'female corrective' before the earnest pleas of Birkin, there is some
context to measure the appropriateness of her fear and disagreement. It is this pattern of impressive authority in Ursula I first
wish to discuss.

II

The Ursula Brangwen whom we meet in the opening pages of *Women in Love* is a cautious woman. Although preoccupied with the issue of marriage, as she was at the conclusion of *The Rainbow*, she bears the scars of her abortive experience with Skrebensky; Ursula also still feels the disappointments of her more recent love life, as she remarks to Gudrun that she has rejected several offers of marriage. But there is no suggestion here by Lawrence of vindictiveness in the Brangwen who was born to the proud optimism of the rainbow vision. In the early scenes of *Women in Love* there is an appealing sense of nurturant affection and energetic striving in her which Lawrence instructively contrasts with the cynical, materialistic outlook of Gudrun. In their initial conversation, for instance, Ursula's main concern about marriage is that it might prove to be 'the end of experience' (1) for her. The fear and the phrasing are nearly identical to those expressed by Isabel Archer in *Portrait of a Lady*; but unlike the unformed and vulnerable James heroine, Ursula already has acquired a seasoned realism which justifies her knowledgeable concerns about a compromised life. She is the young woman who discovered the power of her own freedom in *The Rainbow*, an independence Lawrence tied to her realization of a 'maximum self' in sexual separateness; now a self-sufficient school teacher who has the 'strange brightness of an essential flame' (3), Ursula will not easily accept offers to compromise that hard-earned sense of self through the institution of marriage. Gudrun, however, is characteristically more willing to accept the inevitable drift of the personal life, and she leaves it to her modern and mechanical ethic of survival to see her through; she coldly regards marriage merely as the 'inevitable next step' (3) and, as she takes up the metaphor of *'reculer pour mieux sauter'* which she just introduced, Gudrun confidently claims 'one is bound to land somewhere' (4). It is her announcement of unprincipled adaptability, that poised ability to fix herself for the circumstance which anticipates her manipulative use of Gerald and her decadent partnership with Loerke.

Unlike Gudrun, who is interested in capture and control rather than minute discriminations of her own feelings, Lawrence quickly establishes her sister's different priorities and habits of perception. Throughout the novel Ursula is held almost hypnotically in living touch with her instinctual self, and – as it *must* be the case in

Lawrence's cosmos – such a mode of self-definition also promises the animating exchange with a 'beyond' or 'unknown' which is the hallmark of Lawrencian communion. Already matured by the varied experiences depicted in *The Rainbow*, she retains a child's zest to find out what she feels, and to treat the promptings of her instincts as mandate and birthright: 'Her active living was suspended, but underneath, in the darkness, something was coming to pass. . . . She seemed to try and put her hands out, like an infant in the womb' (3). This need of Ursula's to define herself through what Lawrence calls in the Foreword 'the deep, passional soul' (viii) and then to grope longingly for the transcendent is consistently counterpointed with Gudrun's contented, dispassionate placement in the present. Even minor events point to this contrast, as Lawrence gradually suggests that special sense in Ursula which will later inform her criticism of Birkin's theories. As the two sisters, for example, observe the Crich wedding preparations in the first chapter, Gudrun watches with the icy care of an undertaker and the practised distance of an artist: 'She saw each one as a complete figure, like a character in a book . . . a finished creation. . . . She knew them, they were finished, sealed, and stamped' (8). Here is Ursula's contrasting vantage point, as she typically fits the celebration into a context which is larger and more resonant than the disposable world depicted by Gudrun: 'Now the married pair were coming! The bells were ringing, making the air shake. Ursula wondered if the trees and the flowers could feel the vibration, and what they thought of it, the strange motion in the air' (16). She senses what Lawrence fervently believes about marriage, and what Tom Brangwen in *The Rainbow* came to understand: that it is a rite of passage to the transcendent, which implicates the movements of the earth in its benedictive energies.

It is this alert and responsive Ursula on whom we often shall rely for subtle judgements and touchstone perceptions in the novel, a woman impressively able to interpret the natural signs that prime her instincts. Placed next to the glitter of Gudrun's clothing and conquests, or beside the showy panoply of Gudrun's art, it is easy to underestimate the discerning nature of Ursula's character. Whether she criticizes Birkin's tendency for ambiguity or isolates the false appeal of Gudrun's painting, she has the ability to see through pretence and to epigrammatically sum up the affectation. Although Gudrun is the accomplished artist, Ursula's views about art are more fundamentally wholesome and vital; the expression of her evaluations of various art forms (for example, Gudrun's drawing, Loerke's statues, an old chair) is used by Lawrence to emphasize the limitations of other characters and points of view in the novel. Shortly after she meets Hermione, for instance, the two women converse about Gudrun's painting. To Hermione's affected, inflated praise that Gudrun's work is 'perfectly wonderful – like a flash of instinct . . . perfectly beautiful – full of primitive passion' (32), Ursula replies in a way which anticipates her own aversion to Gudrun's infatuation with Loerke's treatment of the model. She must be diplomatic here (Gudrun *is* her sister), but what emerges is her awareness of Gudrun's predatory vision: 'Isn't it queer that she always likes little things? – she must always work small things, that one can put between one's hands, birds and tiny animals. She likes to look through the wrong end of the opera-glasses and see the world that way – why is it, do you think?' (32) Note the lack of jargon or equivocation in her judgement; she uses a simple metaphor to stress how Gudrun's focus does not *feel* right, how it violates some inner sense in Ursula of the right way to 'see the world'.

When Gudrun and Ursula later watch Gerald diving, Lawrence develops this distinction between the two sisters. As they comment on a related issue about the prerogatives of gender in society, Ursula's instinctive comfort with her own womanhood is played off against Gudrun's vindictive dissatisfaction with her own lot in life:

'God, what it is to be a man!' she cried.
'What?' exclaimed Ursula in surprise.
'The freedom, the liberty, the mobility!' cried Gudrun, strangely flushed and brilliant. 'You're a man, you want to do a thing, you do it. You haven't the *thousand* obstacles a woman has in front of her . . .
'Supposing I want to swim up that water. It is impossible, it is one of the impossibilities of life, for me to take my clothes off now and jump in. But isn't it *ridiculous*, doesn't it simply prevent our living!'
She was so hot, so flushed, so furious, that Ursula was puzzled. (40–1)

Ursula's puzzlement about Gudrun's tirade of sexual politics bespeaks the confidence in her own female self; she is comfortably free from the cynical apologetics which make up her sister's complaint. Where Ursula depends on her own best instincts for guidance and achievement, Gudrun looks toward the organization of society for excuse or motivation. The issue does not turn on the elements of truth in Gudrun's view of discrimination. Lawrence recognizes the institutional reality of her argument, but he insists that the extent of Gudrun's petulance is rooted in her own organic dissatisfaction and not in the social structures of England. Kate Millett is typically irritated by Lawrence's antagonistic depiction of Gudrun, as she wonders why 'Ursula compares very favorably' with her sister 'by accepting their poverty, pointless employment, and close supervision within their father's home'.[9] To this critic Gudrun is all the stronger for envying what Millett describes as Gerald's 'wealth, freedom, mobility, and masculine privilege'.[10] But for Lawrence the issue that divides the sisters is more essential than easy formulations about employment, independence, or social influence. Gudrun's bitterness, that is, is ultimately a declaration of self-contempt, an inverse reflection of Lawrence's mandate in the Foreword to 'let man only approach his own self with a deep respect, even reverence for all that the creative soul, the God-mystery within us, puts forth' (vii). That both women *do* swim naked (in just a few pages and with no difficulty) provides a further comment on the qualities of instability and over-reaction in Gudrun's remarks. No, it does not 'prevent' her 'living', unless her life is lived apart from the meaningful impulses that should direct her.

Ursula's reliance on instinct is neither casual nor easily compromised, as another short conversation with her premeditative sister illustrates. As they ponder the sombre meanings of Gerald's accidental killing of his brother, Ursula anticipates, in effect, Birkin's notions about murder and its victims. She does not develop her idea as a complicated theory but as the inevitable conclusion of her own feelings, of her own sixth sense about hidden motivation: ' "Perhaps there *was* an unconscious will behind it," said Ursula. "This playing at killing has some primitive *desire* for killing in it, don't you think?" ' (43) In response to Gudrun's objection that at bottom it was an accident, Ursula develops her stress on the unconscious to demonstrate her confidence in the messages of instinct, while Gudrun's answer characteristically emphasizes the claims of sexual envy and easy pragmatism:

'No,' said Ursula. 'I couldn't pull the trigger of the emptiest gun in the world, not if someone were looking down the barrel. One instinctively doesn't do it – one can't.

Gudrun was silent for some moments, in sharp disagreement. 'Of course,' she said coldly. 'If one is a woman, and grown up, one's instinct prevents one. But I cannot see how that applies to a couple of boys playing together.' (42)

Gudrun's grudging 'of course' is her tepid acknowledgment of Ursula's confirmation of a guiding, womanly instinct. But Gudrun profoundly misses the lessons which her sister tries to teach. By implicitly rejecting Ursula's belief that such instinct, virtually regardless of age, should prevent one from this perverse playact with a gun, Gudrun reveals her real preoccupation with will and learned response (her arenas, to be sure) rather than with the 'creative, spontaneous' (viii) motivations invoked in the Foreword. Thus develop both Lawrence's judgement that despite Gudrun's more classic beauty, 'Ursula was more physical, more womanly' (75), and Birkin's belief that Ursula is 'like a strange unconscious bud of powerful womanhood' (85).

III

But what happens when Birkin enters her life, a man whose proclaimed doctrines are close to Lawrence's own, a crusading figure who presents Ursula with ideas that do not rest comfortably with her less theoretical perspective? Can she possibly provide any effective 'essential criticism' of Birkin, or must she gradually sacrifice certain instinctive desires for the excitements of his vision? And can the novelist resolve the knotty conflict between two prototypical moulds of Lawrencian character: a woman who submits herself nobly to those promptings of her 'deep, passional soul' (viii), and a man who wages a solitary argument for the principles of commitment and nonconformity that Lawrence had come to espouse?

There seems to be little rhetorical contest when they meet, as Ursula understandably is impressed by the flamboyant school inspector in the classroom scene. She is fascinated by his theory of 'lapsing-out' which she overhears him outline during his argument with Hermione. The version which Birkin outlines (for Ursula's

benefit as well as Hermione's) is an angry, shorthand account of
that liberating idea of 'delivery to the unknown' which he will
develop later with Ursula to include the specific aspects of polarity
and star-equilibrium. Yet even as she listens to his stirring criti-
cisms in the classroom, and contemplates the seductive meaning
of his theories in the context of her disappointing love life, Lawrence also plants the seeds of Ursula's crucial scepticism about
him and his proposals: she undoubtedly recognizes that Birkin's
uncensored, semi-public attack of Hermione here must be read as
an illuminating summary and indictment of his *own* accumulated
habits of loving, for Hermione and Birkin have been a known
'item' for some time. Might there be a split between Birkin's speech
and his ability to enact, or believe in, his programme? What is
Ursula to make of a man who openly assails the mode of love of
his mistress when he offers no convincing indication that their
affair is over? So as Ursula listens to a Birkin who 'sounded as if
he were addressing a meeting' (37), she can both draw back from
his manner even while she 'was concerned now only with solving
her own problems in the light of his words' (36). The chapter ends
with a reverberating hint of that conflicted relation to him that will
preoccupy her for much of the novel, as Ursula is weeping, 'but
whether for misery or joy, she never knew' (38). Do Birkin's words
point the way to her own salvation, or has she merely heard the
pontifications of another life-evader?

The next look in the novel at Birkin's preoccupations occurs on
the train with Gerald, as Birkin sounds a note he will not repeat
again in such uncertain terms. That is, the conversation is notable
for his clear avowal of a desire to 'love' one woman, and he now
is able to use that controversial term without the need to qualify
it with the doctrinal abstractions he will offer Ursula. Indeed, it is
a 'man to man' exchange that has a contradictory relation to the
Birkin who soon expresses a stubborn aversion to *any* protestation
of love with his lover, Ursula Brangwen. We see a different side
of Birkin on the train, a man who appears quite removed from
that inclination to theorize that concludes with his claim to Ursula
at the end of the novel that she is not enough for him. Although
he interrogates Gerald on the train on many of Birkin's pet topics,
there is no attempt to lecture him; what remains is the image of
a relaxed and confiding friend who speaks to Gerald frankly about
his own need to love one woman; it is the most unself-conscious
and the least cerebral Birkin will be in *Women in Love*, as he bears

his instinctive needs without the compulsion to qualify them with elaborate theory. But Birkin is a divided man, split not only over the issue of 'love', but more generally torn apart by an internal struggle between what his instincts require and what his developing doctrines stipulate. Ursula's accumulating doubts about him gradually are seen as legitimate when it becomes evident that he is a brilliant but uncertain man; Ursula's questions about him often are confirmed by Lawrence's depiction of whimsical shifts of vision and attitude in Birkin. For example, after he is hit over the head by Hermione and revived by his naked communion with the forces of nature, his new decision, which rejects his avowal on the train, seems to emerge not from spite or even wounded pride, but as part of a reductive theory of living: 'He did not want a woman – not in the least . . . he wanted nobody and nothing but the lovely, subtle, responsive vegetation, and himself, his own living self' (100–01). My point is not that Birkin's contradictory attitudes and fluctuating views of the world are surprising or debilitating. It is that Ursula listens to him with the keen interest of an alert and serious suitor, and her sceptical responses to his proposals are not to be dismissed as her inability to comprehend radical notions, which some condescending criticism about Ursula suggests.[11] Ursula does have a substantive quarrel with his theories because of her more spontaneous approach to life. In addition, her concerns about Birkin are rooted in a nagging fear that his rhetoric may mask a serious confusion, in *him*, about his real desires, and ultimately may undermine their own affair. Birkin's vision of flowery isolation as he recuperates in the field has a tone of childish absurdity to it, and thus prepares us for a notion which disturbs Ursula enough to inform her accusations to him later in the work; perhaps at bottom Birkin is merely self-involved, perhaps only interested in 'his *own* living self', to the selfish exclusion of social responsibility and nurturant human exchange. That fortunately this proves not to be the case by novel's end is much the result of Ursula's relentless impatience with Birkin's ideas and unresolved personal life, as she forces him to clarify his doctrine and conclude his lingering attachment to Hermione.

When Birkin recovers from Hermione's attack, he adds embarrassing evidence to Ursula's suspicion that he cannot resolve his life. It would seem an opportune time for a final break with his former lover: he has openly indicted her in caustic terms, has survived the fury of her response, and has initiated a promising attachment to Ursula. Yet Birkin's 'resolution' only produces an apologetic letter to Hermione, a cowardly equivocation which even leaves open the possibility of their reunion as lovers. When Ursula and Birkin meet again, after the interlude of their mutual attraction at Breadalby, Birkin has gone through some indefinable illness; he is often ill in *Women in Love*, no doubt a psychosomatic reflection of that organic indecision about his life which agonizes him. His mood here in 'An Island' ranges from despairing cynicism to that overstated truculence about mankind in general which Ursula despises. After she draws him out by impatiently suggesting that he wears his illness too acceptingly ('I think it makes one so ashamed, to be ill . . .', 117), Birkin sounds young and groping, a bit like a frustrated and unformed Paul Morel, as he reveals to Ursula a malaise that is more than depression: 'But it infuriates me that I can't get right, at the really growing part of me. I feel all tangled and messed up, and I *can't* get straight anyhow' (117). So Ursula, who once hoped that his theories might chart a way out for her, begins to sense her more pressing role: she must clarify for Birkin, by untying the knotted strands of his doctrinal commitments, what is really crucial for him.

In the ensuing conversation Ursula is sceptical but entranced as Birkin rages against both humanity and that concept of conventional love he had earlier affirmed in his talk with Gerald on the train; he concludes with a hyperbolic assertion that he 'abhor[s] humanity' (119), which echoes his rhetoric as he lay amid the grass after Hermione's assault. When Ursula wittily reminds him that he has not substituted anything yet for love or humanity ('What do you believe in . . . simply the end of the world, and grass?' (121), Lawrence acknowledges the corrective power of Ursula's verbal jousting against the excesses of Birkin's polemics: 'He was beginning to feel a fool' (121). But soon Birkin's position is momentarily vindicated as wordy conflict melts into Lawrencian communion; here Birkin makes his case in the most ideal way – in short, without saying a word:

Again they looked at each other. She suddenly sprang up, turned her back to him, and walked away. He too rose slowly and went to the water's edge, where, crouching, he began to amuse himself unconsciously. Picking a daisy he dropped it on the pond, so that the stem was a keel, the flower floated like a little water-lily, staring with its open face up to the sky. It turned slowly round, in a slow, slow Dervish dance, as it veered away.

He watched it, then dropped another daisy into the water, and after that another, and sat watching them with bright, absolved eyes, crouching near on the bank. Ursula turned to look. A strange feeling possessed her, as if something were taking place. But it was all intangible. And some sort of control was being put on her. She could not know. She could only watch the brilliant little discs of the daisies veering slowly in travel on the dark, lustrous water. The little flotilla was drifting into the light, a company of white specks in the distance. (122–3)

There is much which is brilliant here: the scene's slow-motion overture, as both Birkin and Ursula are depicted with nearly the identical gestures of the two cats that are about to enter in the 'Mino' chapter; Birkin's happy sense of absolution as he watches the daisies go by, for he finds the confirmation of his theory of lively individuality and communal sanctity dramatically depicted by the flowers' independent yet magically co-ordinated movements and colouration; Ursula's intangible but perceived understanding that she and Birkin share this resonant moment together, and that in some vague way she begins to grasp his objection to that merging which is often called 'Love'. Birkin the preacher, however, will not leave well enough alone, as he seems to agree with his apologetic creator that 'this struggle for verbal consciousness should not be left out in art' (viii): he now persists in baldly stating the symbolic, then scientific, and finally social significance of the luminous and subtle moment they just witnessed. He calls the flowers first 'a convoy of rafts', then 'a perfect little democracy', and finally goaded by Ursula's irritation at his didactic lust for correspondence, he claims 'it's the golden mob of the proletariat' (123). Ursula, who only moments ago was impressed by the magical confirmation of his theory within a natural landscape, warns him that he kills the lesson in his egocentric search for a perfect verbal formulation. Birkin accepts her chastisement and once again grows under the corrective influence of a female who – like Lawrence reading Ben Franklin! – instinctively dislikes the sound of programme:

'How hateful – your hateful social orders!' she cried.
'Quite! It's a daisy – we'll leave it alone.'

'Do. Let it be a dark horse for once,' she said: 'if anything can be a dark horse to you,' she added satirically. (123)

IV

The 'Mino' episode is notable for Birkin's extended enunciation of the principles of star-equilibrium; it would seem, therefore, to be an interlude the least amenable to any persuasive undercutting of Birkin's stature, for his seminal soliloquy on the 'unknown' functions as the doctrinal centre-piece of the novel. But the demands of Lawrence's 'metaphysical' mission must bend to the complicating realities of the fictional characters whose integrity he must uphold. This assertion of priority is signalled at the start of the chapter: although 'Mino' declares, through Birkin, the need for male initiative to direct the female to the required polarization with her mate (in short, 'star-equilibrium'), the chapter begins with a considerable act of independence and courage by a female. That is, Birkin has just taken the easy way out in his perplexing, volatile involvement with Ursula, for he asked her to accompany Gudrun to his room for tea. A gambling Ursula does not reveal the invitation to her sister: in the midst of her own equivocal relation to him she decides to go alone and confront him directly. She undertakes this visit despite Birkin's discouraging gestures towards her, which have fuelled Ursula's worst suspicions about his intentions; he has recently admitted to her that he will let Hermione supervise the decoration of his room, and he has just implied publicly, in the embattled dialogue with her about Gerald and the treatment of horses, that it is the woman's destiny to 'resign her will to the higher being' (132) – the male.

The value of Ursula's instinctive choice to proceed alone is not underestimated by Lawrence. It prompts his first significant use in *Women in Love* of the term 'unknown', which is the code word associated throughout his fiction with a healthy submission to the transcendent 'beyond' required for love communion and other legitimate acts of emotional risk. A few minutes after she arrives at his room Birkin will lecture her on the precise dimensions of this unknown; but as Ursula leaves to see him she demonstrates in the very act of coming what Birkin shall merely outline as dialectic. She seems to embody by deed the sentiments which he celebrates by word: 'She could not consider anymore what anybody would say of her or think about her. People had passed out of her range, she was absolved. She had fallen strange and dim, out of the sheath of the material life, as a berry falls from the only world it has ever known, down out of the sheath on to the real unknown' (135–6).

Birkin's explanation of star-equilibrium after Ursula arrives is conveyed by two rhetorical techniques: a virtual soliloquy on what he calls the 'delivery to the unknown', and a teasingly symbolic dialogue with Ursula about the pantomime between the mino and the stray. Ursula is tense over the issue of female subordination and its possibly central relation to Birkin's impatience with conventional 'love'; she has witnessed his indulgent inability to resolve his affair with Hermione and she has recently heard his degrading diatribe about horses and the surrender of the female will. So Ursula, understandably edgy and wary of his motives, misses the even-handedness in his long and crucial explanation to her; she fails to appreciate the important distinction Birkin now finally makes between female submissiveness (which he does not uphold) and the lovers' mutual 'lapsing out' to an unknown which polarizes the sexes in the courage of their separate surrender of ego. While she quizzically but patiently listens to Birkin's sermon, she pushes him, in effect, for some substantive indication, through his action, of what his theory entails. She is the absolutely instinctual woman, one who will even make the claim, 'I hate people who hurt themselves. I can feel it' (155). She must be made to *feel* the sentiment behind his explanation. From her perspective his doctrine becomes his evasion, his means to avoid honest commitment. Thus she argues her position as the feeling female while she indicts his brand of blindness and conceit: ' "You are very conceited, Monsieur," she mocked. "How do you know what my womanly feelings are, or my thoughts or my ideas. You don't even know what I think of you now".' (139).

When the cats now enact their playful drama, Birkin cannot lose the opportunity to reduce their pantomime to the service of theory; only this time, no doubt piqued by Ursula's persistent scepticism, he overstates his position to wittily conform to the antics of the cats. If his previous remarks appeared to equalize the role of the sexes in their joint responsibility to 'lapse out', he interprets the cats' behaviour to ratify a belief in female subordination. Thus he confirms Ursula's fears about all his earnest speech. Now her critique of him begins to echo more exactly Lawrence's preoccupations with language in the Foreword. She argues again that mere words, because they can camouflage confusion and sugar-coat pretence, might provide Birkin with an easy excuse not to act. She virtually charges that Birkin is a traitor to her, and that his facility with words (which Gerald calls 'his telling way of putting things', 181) is the key to his treason:

> 'I don't trust you when you drag in the stars,' she said. 'If you were quite true, it wouldn't be necessary to be so far-fetched.'
>
> 'Don't trust me then,' he said, angry. 'It is enough that I trust myself.'
>
> 'And that is where you make another mistake,' she replied. 'You *don't* trust yourself. You don't fully believe yourself what you are saying. You don't really want this conjunction, other-wise you wouldn't talk so much about it, you'd get it.'
>
> He was suspended for a moment, arrested.
>
> 'How?' he said.
>
> 'By just loving,' she retorted in defiance. (144)

What is it that Ursula wants? There are hints in the phrasing of her indictment, 'by just loving', of the intimate frustrations in her displeasure. For all their talk of versions of love there has been no sex, not a bit; when Birkin concludes the 'Mino' chapter with his tired, capitulatory plea, 'let love be enough then, I love you . . . I'm bored by the rest' (146), he speaks of a fatigue with passion as well as with iterations of theory. When they finally do make love, in that stark and desperate atmosphere after the drowning, their sex is lustful, consummating, and devoid of the doctrinal significance just preached by Birkin. But the immediate release of libido gratifies him even if he cannot square its reductive quality with his ideal of star-equilibrium. Thus this unsure visionary is now tempted to an apostatic reversal because of his sex in the mud; he considers abandoning his doctrine for the future promise of unproblematic one-night stands: 'What did it matter, what did anything matter save this ultimate and triumphant experience of physical passion, that had blazed up anew like a new spell of life. "I was becoming quite dead-alive, nothing but a word-bag", he said in triumph, scorning his other self' (180). If Birkin is uncertain about what he really wants, Ursula senses the mere instrumen-tality for them both of their groping passion on the dark road.

That is small comfort to her now. Neither sufficiently committed to Birkin, nor free from his potent influence, she feels adrift towards death, in a limbo of irresolution accelerated by their deathly sex and his inconsistent treatment of her.

After he returns to her house she is in no mood to hear more theory from him. He responds to her irritable query about his wretched appearance with the absurd claim that he doesn't know how he feels or looks; Ursula listens to this admission of his complete divorce from his own instinctive life, and she breaks out with marvellous vindictiveness: 'Don't you know whether you are unwell or not, without thinking about it? . . . I think it's *criminal* to have so little connection with your own body that you don't even know when you are ill' (188). Her rage suggests that more is at stake here than Birkin's nonchalance about illness. Indeed, her response sums up fundamental issues of gender distinction which have informed the conflict between them. This flashpoint for Ursula, for example, about his non-relation to his own body had come up before in the novel, when she assailed him in 'An Island' about his lack of shame in becoming ill so often. The issue of illness does not develop in the novel; it merely repeats itself because we are meant to feel that Birkin must be the way he is on this subject. He will not alter the uncomfortable relation to his own body any more than Ursula will depart from her secure connection to the physical and instinctual. In his 'Study of Thomas Hardy' Lawrence clarifies this sense of both representativeness and inevitability which contributes to the portrait of intractable differences between the lovers in *Women in Love*:

> A real 'man' takes no heed for his body, which is the more female part of him. He considers himself only as an instrument, to be used in the service of some idea. The true female, on the other hand, will eternally hold herself superior to any idea, will hold life in the body to be the real happiness. The male exists in doing, the female in being. The male lives in the satisfaction of some purpose achieved, the female in the satisfaction of some purpose contained.[12]

Lawrence's stated antinomy suggests what has been felt in the novel and speculated about his life: that this conflict between the 'real man' and 'true female' in *Women in Love* is not amenable to final resolution, and that Ursula's and Birkin's struggle with each

other depicts both the rudiments of Lawrence's visionary arche-
types as well as significant strains of discord in his relations with
Frieda. Certainly Ursula and Birkin invariably return to the same
patterns of tension between them, with Birkin mired in nympho-
leptic anxiety and Ursula vainly trying to calm and correct:

'I don't know what really to *do*. One must do something
somewhere.'
'Why should you always be *doing*?' she retorted. 'It is so
plebian. I think it is much better to be really patrician, and to
do nothing but just be oneself, like a walking flower.' (117–18)

The sound of 'really patrician', spoken from Ursula's plebian
family background in *The Rainbow*, suggests by contrast the image
of Frieda von Richthofen; it is not unwarranted, in this regard, to
consider briefly the complementary context of Lawrence's
strenuous marriage to Frieda during the period he was writing
The Rainbow and *Women in Love*. His biographers are in agreement
on the fact of an unusually heated struggle between them, despite
the extraordinary success of Lawrence's creative efforts.[13] Their
difficulties may originate in the understandable tension between
a deracinated Frieda's need for at least a minimum of engaged
attention from Lawrence, which would require him to get beyond
his work, and Lawrence's need to follow his writing obsessions
into longer periods of self-involved productivity, which often
would not allow for unhampered consideration of his wife. It is
not unlikely that Lawrence understood these tensions with Frieda
sufficiently to reflect on them in his fiction. Indeed, it is known
that when Lawrence first created his Ursula for *The Rainbow*, he
writes about her: 'It came of trying to graft on to the character of
Louie the character, more or less, of Frieda.'[14] Given Louie
Burrows's vaunted feminine demeanour, she seems closer than
Frieda to the physical bearing and quiet assurance which is
Ursula's way. The more aggressive Frieda is generally accepted,
of course, as the model for much of Ursula's doctrinal dispute
with Birkin, and I have no major quarrel with such a probability.[15]
When Frieda writes the following letter during Lawrence's initial
work on the character of Ursula, the possibilities become more
intriguing. Is an enlisted Frieda here picking up the precise
wording and thrust of Lawrence's preoccupations in his fiction
and his 'Study of Thomas Hardy', or is she helping to lay the

foundations for his convictions, or is she writing out of a calm moment in the marriage when their vision was fused, their purpose joined: 'I think women should be satisfied to be and let the men *do*. We can *do* so much more *that* way – I hate the women for not having enough *pride* to be themselves just their own natural selves. . . '[16]

V

That Ursula Brangwen seems fated to act as a corrective influence on Birkin – that is, as a woman who both must clarify Birkin to himself as well as untangle her own relation to him, is summed up in her conclusion: 'She saw him as a clear stroke of uttermost contradiction, a strange gem-like being whose existence defined her own non-existence' (190). The accuracy of her perception of his paradoxical nature is illustrated in his hampered attitude towards sex; he is easily roused to passion but tends to retreat because of the interference of his mind:

> She cleaved to him, and he could feel his blood changing like quicksilver.
> 'But we'll be still, shall we?' he said.
> 'Yes,' she said, as if submissively . . .
> He kissed her many times. But he too had his idea and his will. He wanted only gentle communion . . . no passion now. (244–45)

Thus the sexual tension here is again resolved on his idiosyncratic terms. Lawrence immediately affirms the basis of Ursula's suspicion all along that there is a conflict in Birkin between what he instinctively feels and what his theories dictate to him: 'The next day, however, he felt wistful and yearning. . . . Perhaps he had been wrong to go to her with an idea of what he wanted. Was it really only an idea, or was it the interpretation of a profound yearning?' (245) After the skirmish between the lovers caused by Birkin's boorishness when he proposes at her house, Ursula is temporarily reconciled with him ironically through a conversation with Hermione; when Birkin's former mistress tirades against Birkin's suitability as a husband, maintaining that he only wants a slave, Ursula correctly realizes that Hermione merely projects her own need to be enslaved. Ursula concludes with the most fundamental criticism she can make: 'Hermione now betrayed herself as a woman. Hermione was like a man, she believed only in men's things. She betrayed the woman in herself' (287). The battle in the 'Excurse' chapter between Birkin and Ursula occurs because Ursula realizes, amid all of Birkin's protestations of unconventionality, that his inane need to say goodbye to Hermione is further proof of his inclination to contemplate rather than make final decisions. Although there is some legitimacy to Birkin's counter-charge of jealousy in Ursula, Lawrence knows who delivers the more essential criticism: 'A clearer look had come over Birkin's face. He knew she was in the main right' (300). It is significant that after this sincere acknowledgment of his own blame, it is only then that Ursula feels confident enough to submit herself to the particulars of Birkin's sexual vision – in short, both to that elusive quiet passion he professes, and then to that probing sex, 'deeper than the phallic source' (306), which seals their betrothal.

Yet if such reconciliation brings them to marriage, it cannot erase that archetypal tension between them which Lawrence dramatizes in the novel and summarizes in passages from the 'Study of Thomas Hardy'. There is a resonant illustration of the characteristic tension which may come with their married life, when they stop to purchase a chair. After a short squabble about its value they give it to an indigent young couple. Although Lawrence catalogues the 'rat like' qualities of this husband, Ursula is attracted to the 'aloof furtive youth' (349) because he offers what Birkin cannot – sex without theory. For an Ursula who is to be married tomorrow, who supposedly has just discovered the 'palpable, real otherness' (312) of her lover, this is not the once-over from a satisfied woman: 'She was attracted by the young man. . . . He would be a dreadful, but wonderful lover to a woman, so marvellously constituted. His legs would be marvellously subtle and alive . . . under the shapeless trousers' (350). Might I presume to wonder if we also have witnessed a moment which has bearing on the quality of frustration in Frieda's marriage to Lawrence? Furthermore, are Ursula's frequent charges against Birkin that his penchant for theory is a camouflage for self-involvement a clue to the sort of argument Frieda might make to Lawrence about the cause of her own dissatisfactions? In December of 1915, just as he completes *The Rainbow*, Lawrence writes intimately to

Lady Ottoline Morrel (yes, she of the Hermione caste!) in a way which precisely anticipates Ursula's charge that Birkin permits theory to betray her real needs: 'We had some fine hours, all of us together, didn't we. But there comes the inevitable friction. Frieda hates me because she says I am a *favourite*, which is ignominious (she says), also she says I am a traitor to her. But let it be – it is a bore.'[17] The last words recall the nearly identical language by Birkin about his increasing fatigue with sex, love, and conflict with Ursula; the correspondence between life and fiction reappears in another letter by Lawrence of August 1915, as he echoes that optimism in Ursula which would try to correct Birkin's overstated desire that humanity be swept away: 'Frieda says things are not so bad as I pretend, that people are good, that life is also good.'[18] Millett's discussion of this novel demeans Ursula and the allegedly 'docile'[19] questions she asks of Birkin; her dismissal of this woman amounts to not only a misreading of Ursula's strenuous interrogation of her lover, but also an ignorance of Frieda's less than timid influence on her brilliant but often erratic husband. She also claims that Ursula suffers because 'Laurentian marriage resembles a plunge into another sleep, even a death', as 'Ursula resigns her position' and is now ready for enslavement to a Svengali.[20] But Millett neglects to add that Birkin resigns his own position just as quickly, and it is Birkin who is tired at novel's end and half in love with the oblivion of death.

There is no persuasive sense in any of Lawrence's correspondence, or in the reliable reports of his contemporaries, that this 'inevitable friction' he mentions in his letter and analyzes in the Hardy essay was not fully relevant to his marriage with Frieda. The friction is certainly a fundamental aspect of the relations between Birkin and Ursula in *Women in Love*; even its last page documents the *instinctive* feeling by Ursula that she is enough for him in unresolvable conflict with Birkin's *theory* that he can also have eternal union with a man. In his art, and perhaps in his life, Lawrence searched for some final reconciliation between the male and female principles. In his 'Study of Thomas Hardy' he declares the magnitude of his ambition:

> there shall be the art which knows the struggle between the two conflicting laws [of male and female], and knows the final reconciliation, where both are equal, two in one, complete. This is the supreme art, which yet remains to be done. Some men

have attempted it, and left us the results of efforts. But it remains
to be fully done.[21]

No, he did not 'do' it in his art and he could not do it in his life.
But in *Women in Love* he provides a glimpse of those 'conflicting
laws' in action. In the process of his art he has been fair to the
principles of a female corrective which often contest his own
doctrines and modify his phallic imagination with the claims of
a woman's instinct. Such aesthetic catharsis was hard work for
Lawrence, and he describes a 'terribly weary' (470) Birkin at the
end of the novel. Norman Mailer's summary of D. H. Lawrence
as novelist may hold the key to Birkin's fatigue as well as to the
remarkable achievement of *Women in Love*:

> he never forgets that he is writing novels, and so his ideas
> cannot simply triumph, they have to be tried and heated and
> forged, and finally be beaten into shapelessness against the anvil
> of his profound British scepticism which would not buy his
> ideas, not outright, for even his own characters seem to wear
> out in them.[22]

Notes

1. Kate Millett, *Sexual Politics* (Garden City: Doubleday, 1970; London:
   Virago, 1977), 263–5.
2. Carolyn Heilbrun, *Towards a Recognition of Androgyny* (New York:
   Harper & Row, 1974), 102.
3. While Leavis urges wisely that Ursula is to be seen 'as opposing plain
   and profound truth to shallow sophistication and sophistry', and that
   'she offers a natural and femininely tenacious resistance', he does not
   nearly establish either the quality or significance of her 'truth', and
   he does not indicate how her 'resistance' functions as part of a corrective ethic in the novel. *D. H. Lawrence: Novelist* (New York: Simon &
   Schuster, 1969; Harmondsworth: Penguin, 1970), 171, 178. Despite
   Moynahan's suggestion that 'Ursula's task is to persuade Birkin to
   abandon his fatalism', and that occasionally 'Ursula argues him and
   his theories into the ground', he still regards Birkin's doctrine as
   exempt from serious scrutiny; he sees as Birkin's primary achievement
   his ability to 'train Ursula in the principles of star-equilibrium', but I
   argue that she has some training ambitions of her own for Birkin.
   The Deed of Life (Princeton: Princeton University Press, 1963), 75, 81.
   Kermode recognizes that 'one of the achievements of the novel is to
   criticize the metaphysic', yet he does not discuss the seminal role of

Ursula in such criticism; although Kermode states that Ursula 'instinctively rejects the apocalyptic excesses of Birkin', he does not see the interrelated pattern of her rejections, or develop her instinctual reliance into the counter-metaphysic which she proposes. *D. H. Lawrence* (New York: Viking, 1973; London: Fontana, 1985), 66, 69. In his comprehensive introduction to the Seltzer text version of *Women in Love*, Charles Ross perhaps comes the closest to formulating a role for Ursula that praises her substantive disagreement with Birkin. While Ross gives 'thanks to Ursula's opposition', as it permits us to 'see the sympathetic, "quick" side of Birkin which otherwise would have been obscured by his inflexibility and priggishness', Ross does not acknowledge sufficiently the value, in its own right, of Ursula's ethical stance. *Women in Love* (Harmondsworth and New York: Penguin, 1982), 39.

4. For a welcome departure from this trend in feminist criticism, note Hilary Simpson's more balanced verdict: 'Even in, say, *Women in Love* . . . the notion of male supremacy is only one of a whole range of controversial subjects discussed, often in a spirit of intellectual play, by the central characters. Ultimately, the reader of *Women in Love* feels that Lawrence has no one axe to grind.' *D. H. Lawrence and Feminism* (Dekalb: Northern Illinois University Press; London: Croom Helm, 1982), 65.

5. Millett, *Sexual Politics*, 262.

6. *Fantasia of the Unconscious* (New York: Viking, 1960; Harmondsworth: Penguin, 1971), xv.

7. 'Study of Thomas Hardy' (Cambridge: Cambridge University Press, 1985) and in Edward D. McDonald (ed.), *Phoenix: The Posthumous Papers of D. H. Lawrence* (New York: Viking 1972), 476.

8. From the Foreword to *Women in Love* (New York: Viking, 1960; London: Heinemann, 1984), viii. Page numbers in my text refer to the Viking edition.

9. Millett, *Sexual Politics*, 268.

10. Ibid.

11. David Cavitch writes with particular condescension about Ursula, as he stresses the way Birkin's doctrine 'disappoints her expectations of more romantic language', 'On *Women in Love*', from Leo Hamalian (ed.), *D. H. Lawrence: A Collection of Criticism* (New York: McGraw-Hill, 1973), 55.

12. 'Study of Thomas Hardy', 481. H. M. Daleski, in *The Forked Flame: A Study of D. H. Lawrence* (Evanston: Northwestern University Press, 1965), discusses several relevant contradictions in Birkin's explanation of his metaphysic and employs the Hardy essay to speculate on 'male' and 'female' elements in the novel. But Daleski disregards the active, directive function of Ursula's own criticism of Birkin, and he fails to relate Lawrence's idea of 'female being' in the 'Study of Thomas Hardy' to either an instinctual mode of living or to Ursula's affirmation of such a response to life.

13. For a relevant sense of the Lawrences' life during this period, see especially Harry T. Moore, *The Priest of Love: A Life of D. H. Lawrence*,

rev. edn (New York: Farrar, Straus & Giroux, 1974; Harmondsworth: Penguin, 1980), 191–365, and Keith Sagar, *The Life of D. H. Lawrence* (New York: Pantheon, 1980; Harmondsworth: Penguin, 1985), 85–103.

14. George J. Zytaruk and James T. Boulton (eds), *The Letters of D. H. Lawrence*, II (Cambridge and New York: Cambridge University Press, 1981), 142.

15. Harry T. Moore concludes as much in his biography, when he discusses a personal letter he received from Frieda in 1952: 'Frieda further pointed out that although Louie Burrows may have been the model for Ursula outwardly, "the inner relationship is Lawrence's and mine, like the ring scene in *Women in Love*, where I throw the ring at him".' *The Priest of Love*, 224.

16. *Letters*, II, 97.

17. *Letters*, II, 462.

18. *Letters*, II, 380.

19. Millett, *Sexual Politics*, 264.

20. Ibid.

21. 'Study of Thomas Hardy', 515–16.

22. Mailer, *The Prisoner of Sex* (New York: New American Library, 1971), 101.

4

Snake's Eye and Obsidian Knife: Art, Ideology, and 'The Woman Who Rode Away'

For now we see through a glass darkly; but then face to face.
I Corinthians 13:12

And flickered his tongue like a forked night on the air, so black.
D. H. Lawrence, 'Snake'

I

For several years it has been difficult to find a good word written about 'The Woman Who Rode Away'. Today's established opinion might date from Julian Moynahan's belief in *The Deed of Life* (1963) that it is 'a heartless tale *au fond*', its central action 'neither excusable nor interesting'.[1] Frank Kermode, in *D. H. Lawrence* (1973), virtually dismisses the story entirely, claiming that 'the end of the tale is naked doctrine, racial mastery'.[2] Still, Kermode's dismissal at least follows *some* treatment of 'The Woman Who Rode Away'; if his concern only amounts to a short paragraph, several critical studies of Lawrence's fiction bypass any discussion of this tale on the implicit understanding that it is an embarrassment not worthy of extended analysis.[3] Feminist criticism is virtually unanimous in condemning the alleged doctrine in the work. Perhaps the most outspoken attack on the story is expressed through Kate Millett's vituperations in *Sexual Politics* (1970), when she closes her chapter on Lawrence with a roll-call assault on the reputed 'ethics' in 'The Woman Who Rode Away'; she concludes with the charge that the work is merely 'pandering to pornographic dream', and that it 'would reward a careful comparative reading with *The Story of O*; in a number of ways it resembles commercial hard-core'.[4] More recently, Sandra Gilbert and Susan Gubar openly affirm Millett's allegation of vindictive participation by Lawrence in the violent murder of the Woman; they see no humane perspective by him on the brutal sacrifice in the story, as Gilbert and Gubar argue both that the tale 'mythologizes and mystifies masculinism', and that 'almost pornographically', Lawrence convinces himself of her own desire for the theatrical death and sexual horror.[5]

That such a disturbing fable about atavistic religious practice and sexual sacrifice might produce impassioned critical response is not surprising in this era of women's liberation and heightened political consciousness. What is unfortunate, however, is the extent to which reasoned discussion of this tale seems to have ceased, as if a new generation of readers no longer knows how to distinguish what happens in a story from the ironies, symbols, and mythic structures that Lawrence uses to frame and balance the discomforting plot. There is scarcely a sustained reference to this work today that does not imply both that Lawrence's creativity in this story has been undermined by a lack of a humane, civilizing conscience, and that the ethos of 'The Woman Who Rode Away' dogmatically depicts versions of his purported racism, sexism, and unrestrained cruelty. That the treatment of the Woman appears to many readers as the embodiment of Lawrence's supposed death wish for Mabel Luhan, and that the story appears in that Lawrencian period often dismissed as his 'fascistic phase', such *ad hominem* reasoning only strengthens the adamance of those who assert a belief in the unwholesome character of the work.

This preponderance of negative response rarely makes reference to two of the earliest full-length studies of D. H. Lawrence, both of which look favourably on 'The Woman Who Rode Away', and both of which appeared in the 1950s before the wave of assaults on that short story began: Graham Hough's *The Dark Sun* and F. R. Leavis's *D. H. Lawrence: Novelist*. Hough concludes his admiring remarks with the statement that it is Lawrence's 'completest artistic achievement', and 'his profoundest comment on the world of his time'.[6] Similarly, F. R. Leavis praises the tale for demonstrating 'the intensity and profound seriousness of Lawrence's interest in human life', and he salutes its 'earnestness and profundity of response to the problems of modern civilization'.[7] Despite their enthusiastic response, neither Leavis nor Hough sufficiently examines Lawrence's careful perspective on the Woman and Chilchui Indians of the story; such an examination of point of view is necessary to discourage the frantic readings of this work which now predominate. Leavis is characteristically content to quote generously from 'The Woman Who Rode Away' to illustrate how the 'spell worked by the tale' is related to aspects of Indian life that 'are evoked with irresistible actuality'.[8] Hough, who deals with the work more extensively, does provide two seminal but undeveloped clues to a more fruitful interpretive approach. First, he properly suggests that an understanding of Lawrence's view of Mexican Indian religion is essential before any meaning can be determined, as 'to see it for what it is, as he does here, is an important step towards turning away from it'.[9] Second, he uses one timely reference to another Lawrence work, the non-fictional *Mornings in Mexico*, to buttress his belief that in the tale Lawrence depicts a largely antagonistic judgement of the Mexican Indian society. In the expressions of anger in the last thirty years over Lawrence's putative treatment of the Woman, the logic of Hough's initiative has been ignored. I wish to build on his insight in order to demonstrate that Lawrence's depressing short story offers a more sensible understanding of inter-cultural conflict than his irate critics acknowledge.

II

Shortly after Lawrence completes 'The Woman Who Rode Away' in the late summer and early fall of 1924, he writes the long essay, 'The Mozo', that is later collected by his publisher, Martin Secker, in a 1927 volume of related pieces, *Mornings in Mexico*. This outspoken essay is notable for its nearly contemporaneous clarification of that negative attitude towards the Mexican Indians he expresses in the short story. It also echoes the themes and terminology of the recently completed tale with a precision that is more than coincidental; the shared preoccupations of both works may reveal an intense need by Lawrence in the second half of 1924 to reach a more deliberate appraisal of that primitive culture he so lavishly praised early in his first visit to Mexico in March 1923.[10] On one level there is nothing unusual in his ruminations in 'The Mozo' on the life patterns and myths of the Indians he encounters now in his role as a more seasoned observer of Mexico; with typical Lawrencian exuberance and confidence he builds on those sequences of antinomian distinctions he has outlined in such earlier non-fictional work as 'The Crown', the 'Study of Thomas Hardy', his travel-articles and books, his essays on American literature, and his two volumes on the unconscious. That is, 'The Mozo' – and the other essays in *Mornings in Mexico* – present theme and variation on Lawrence's favourite topic: the contrast between modern, mechanical man, who is mired in thought and racked with inhibition, and representatives of some darker, more subterranean way of life, who appear directed by feelings and are geared for spontaneous action.

In *Mornings in Mexico* the clash, more exactly, is between the traditional, colonial, and materialistic white man, and the instinctual, primitive, and ritualized Indian tribes. As might be expected from his previous preoccupations with these contending polarities, Lawrence does criticize the intrinsic softness and wilfulness of a comfortable white race, as he contrasts in 'The Mozo' the 'white monkeys forever mechanically bossing'[11] with the organic passions of the native tribes. The Indian survives in what amounts to a fiercely existential relation to such disparate, bedrock elements in life as time, money, distance, and honesty. He lives in that state where 'there is even no midday, and no evening', where 'two miles are as good as twenty to him, for he goes exactly by his feelings'.[12] Lawrence bemoans the white man for his 'horrible, truly horrible monkey-like passion for invisible exactitudes', [13] while the Indian remains content merely to consult his senses for any reliable guidance.

But Lawrence is wary of the danger in any society that so totematically celebrates a doctrine of 'if it feels good, it is good'. For instance, in his short but trenchant review of Ernest Hemingway's *In Our Time*, a 1925 fictional work by one of the coming exponents of what Norman Mailer later would call the 'burning consciousness of the present', Lawrence's most adamant praise is for Hemingway's ability to avoid sentimentality and excess in both the depiction and evaluation of a character's emotion;[14] similarly, in his

Mexican essays Lawrence keeps a sharply judgemental eye on where this uncerebral Indian life may lead. In fact, there is no sense in *Mornings in Mexico* that the Aztec way – a life built on the categorical imperative of instinct – is a proper alternative to the mind-conscious narrowness of the Western white man. Lawrence even warns the reader not to 'fool [your]self and others into believing that the befeathered and bedaubed darling is nearer to the true ideal gods, than we are'.[15] As he describes Rosalino, who is the quirky, temperamental 'mozo' (that is, servant) of the essay's title, Lawrence shows how this representative Indian, who seems balanced on some precarious edge of stability, is ultimately committed not to the freedom of the instinctual, but to the uncompromising demands and routines of a mythologized religion. The pressures in him to conform to the rituals of his tribe and the habits of its generations of hatred are evident in the enraged gods he worships as well as in the moodiness of his behaviour: 'The Aztec gods are . . . an unlovely and unlovable lot. In their myths there is no grace or charm, no poetry. Only this perpetual grudge, grudge, grudging, one god grudging another, the gods grudging men their existence, and men grudging the animals'.[16]

While Lawrence ponders these vengeful idols he tries to fathom the riddle of Rosalino. He wishes to discover what the mozo's cryptic and persistently ebony stare portends; even this servant, who is a more educated Aztec than his fellow Indians, cannot prevent Lawrence's discovery of a larger truth that emerges like a horrid gleam from Rosalino's face: 'And now the reaction. The flint knife . . . his heart was an obsidian knife. He hated us, and gave off a black steam of hate . . . a glare of pure, reptilian hate from his black eyes'.[17] The textured symbolic connections among volcanic emission, a serpent's eyes, the sharp threat of violence, and the pressure of instinctive hate comprise a familiar rubric in Lawrence's work through the years. Even the framing image of a snake emerging from a primeval source in the bowels of a volcano echoes the use of a similar embodiment of unharnessed passion in his poem 'Snake'. In *Mornings in Mexico* Lawrence further clarifies his penchant for this group of metaphors, and he conveniently adds a special sun as the luminous origin for such underground energies: 'The snakes lie nearer to the source of potency, the dark, lurking, intense sun at the centre of the earth. For to the cultural animist . . . the earth's dark centre holds its dark sun, our source of isolated being round which our world coils its folds like a great snake. The snake is nearer the dark sun, and cunning of it.'[18] It is a composite statement of Lawrencian belief, for the crux of his credo always turns on the paradoxical interrelation of dark and light, of inner and outer; the vision insists that the true, life-giving sun burns in the core of the earth to irradiate the world's surface, just as our potent and fertile warmth, as individual men and women on earth, is only nurtured by the dark instincts deep in our stomach canals.

Recall in the 'Snake' poem that there is a portion of distaste in Lawrence that qualifies his basic affirmation of the reptile: he is willing to admit that its slinking, primordial manner disgusts even the 'uneducated' sensitivities in himself. There is little doubt, however, on the issue of blame for the pettiness that causes Lawrence's unprovoked attack with the water pitcher. In the poem it is the modern world (both embodied in himself and 'out there') that irritates the poet more than the encroaching, dirty snake. Lawrence regards his own conditioned prejudices as the culprit, as a strange animal escapes from one Western man to that earth tunnel from which it emerged. In Italy and Sicily in 1921, where Lawrence essentially begins his decade of international pilgrimage, he has only recently escaped from the various persecutions he endured in England; a newly arrived Lawrence, in comfortable Mediterranean exile, may well have envisaged his former plight in his native land as evidence of how a modern technologized state can assault the dark messages of its visionary serpents. Indeed, in the sensuous warmth of his southern exile – where he will shortly encounter his snake – his letters do confirm Lawrence's belief that his experience in England, a place about which he writes 'is so depressing and uneasy and unpleasant in its temper', [19] should be seen as symptomatic of the mentalized world's attitude toward all prophets of the instinctual.

But as is suggested by the resonant words 'cunning' and 'reptilian hate' in the above passages from *Mornings in Mexico*, there now begins to emerge in Lawrence's work – near the end of his second Mexican trip and at least two years after he sees the snake in a Sicilian July – a significant change in emphasis in his already conflicted attitude towards unremitting primitivism. By late 1924 Rosalino is seen as the unkempt and unpredictable snake in the garden of *Lawrence's own* white world. Those hating snake eyes in the mozo bespeak a brutal and inhumane motivation, and they also suggest a developing reaction by Lawrence against both his underground snake image and the primitive houseboy. Such a change in Lawrence's point of view is not surprising. For years critics and biographers have documented the shifting roles of the themes of educated consciousness and dark instinct in Lawrence's work. In writing about the poem 'Snake', Harry T. Moore provides a relevant summary: 'This division of the consciousness, here split between admiration and repulsion, again reveals Lawrence's essential polarization, of the kind found in Birkin in *Women in Love*, who sees both the flower and the mud it is rooted in. The "Snake" poem is also reminiscent of the two opposing forces in Lawrence's 1915 essay "The Crown;" and there is always in Lawrence the battle between darkness and light.'[20]

Darkness may now lose a considerable edge. The mornings have dawned on two trips to darkest Mexico and it is 1924. His utopian vision of Rananim, still alive for him in Southern Italy only eighteen months ago, is now faded: he has watched the Mexican primitives and he is no longer impressed. In fact, Lawrence now may be sufficiently realistic about the consequences of a 'snake's eye' perspective to be terrified. There is a sense in 'The Mozo', gleaned from Lawrence's frequently transfixed comments about Rosalino's eyes, that the Indians' extreme reliance on instinct, and their alternately embattled and slavish relation to their Aztec Gods, may push them into dangerous excesses of hatred, and finally into a ceremonial violence that Lawrence deplores. He insists in *Mornings in Mexico* that this unqualified commitment by the tribes to a literal enactment of their deepest feelings represents a direct and ongoing threat to D. H. Lawrence and other Western whites. In this painfully deterministic view both Indian and white must fight each other as part of their destiny, for the Indian, 'in all his atrocity is true to his own creative mystery. And as such, he must be fought'.[21] Thus Lawrence's mandate for an embattled stance against the embodiments of 'creative mystery' marks a significant recasting of his dialectic; in his summary of an inevitable conflict in Mexico between the radically primitive and the civilized modern, Lawrence announces that he will join and cheerlead the latter.

But just as *Mornings in Mexico* is rarely read today, so is 'The Woman Who Rode Away' often misunderstood. Because the Woman offers so little resistance to the atrocities directed at her, and because of her purportedly negative characterization, critics assume that 'her side' in the conflict is unreported in the tale, and that she is somehow sacrificed with Lawrence's bloodthirsty approval; they often refer to Lawrence's strained relations with Mabel Luhan to provide a logical justification for his supposedly violent attitude toward the Woman. For instance, in a recent discussion of Mabel Luhan, Lois P. Rudnick argues that the root of the unwholesomeness of the tale is that Lawrence holds the Woman 'ultimately responsible for the fact that the phallus is transformed into a murder weapon', and – as the ideological resonance of her tone indicates – Rudnick refers approvingly to Kate Millett's comparable view of the major action.[22] Similarly, Gilbert and Gubar write how 'Lawrence exults' over the white woman's destruction, as if he displays the same attitude towards her as those of her racist killers.[23] I believe that such a reading misses the ample evidence of an antagonistic attitude toward the primitive 'darkness' in the story. It also fails to catch the subtle suggestions of *strength* in the Woman – that is, of her impressive quality of judgement, primarily evident in her perspective on both the modern life she leaves and on the atavistic death that is forced upon her. It is to her journey and the meaning of her terrible fate that I wish to turn.

III

In 'The Woman Who Rode Away' it is ultimately not the Woman whom Lawrence despises, nor is it the Chilchui Indians. It is her husband for whom he reserves his greatest irony and contempt. In Lawrence's vision of the ongoing war between the insistencies of will (as in the spoiled Woman) and the passionate excesses of the instinctual (as in the Indians), it is the technocratic husband who safely oversees and is insulated from the struggle. It is he who lacks the desperate imagination of his wife, an initiative that ultimately prompts her departure, and the primitive fires of the Chilchui, an inflamed resentment that enables them to kill. He is the mechanical lever made animate, the human equivalent (as in Gerald Crich and Clifford Chatterley) of what Lawrence in *Mornings in Mexico* calls 'the great white monkey' who 'has got hold of the keys of the world'.[24] In the first two pages of the tale 'wiry' is used four times to describe him, and that functional repetition sets up the Lawrencian oxymoron 'dynamo of energy',[25] a term that properly locates the husband's force not in any organic source but in the entrails of a puffing generator. As early as the second paragraph there is the kind of layered pictorial tableau admired by Leavis, as in the following description of a mining hell on earth; the metaphors progressively reveal that ugly violation of countryside that Lawrence bemoans throughout his career: 'When she actually *saw* what he had accomplished, her heart quailed. Great green-covered, unbroken mountain-hills, and in the midst of the lifeless isolation, the sharp pinkish mounds of the dried mud from the silver works' (546). What can be overlooked through such a graphic description of machine blight is the realization that the understanding eye belongs to the Woman. No dull lady here, for her incisive view of both the power and detritus of industry is part of a fundamentally reliable vision she displays throughout the tale. Yes, her escape to the mountains has its element of 'foolish romanticism' (549), and her personal history is no doubt filled with instances of wilful pride. But it is she who has the quailing heart at 'what he had accomplished', and it is her sensibility that picks up the depressing irony of pink slime amid the pastoral greenery.

In this despoiled environment death is not only common, it becomes a redundant aspect of the landscape, a familiar waste product. Thus the opportunity for the Woman to embark on a scenic tour with her husband becomes for her a visit to a village that resembles a rustic mortuary: 'And in his battered Ford car her husband would take her into the dead, thrice-dead little Spanish town. . . . The great, sun-dried dead church, the dead portales . . . a dead dog lying between the meat-stalls' (546). We learn of the husband's immature sexual passion for her, as 'she was to him always the rather dazzling Californian girl from Berkeley' (547). His adolescent affection helps explain why he is described as 'dimmed', as if 'by some curious inaccessibility on his wife's part' (547). Later, on the trail with the Indians and undergoing the pain of her encampment with them, Lawrence similarly writes that the Chilchui 'were inaccessible' to her and 'they could not see her as a woman at all' (557). Thus the sense of her alienation gradually assumes an archetypal relation – further buttressed by her anonymous title – to Lawrence's prediction in so much of his fiction, prose, and poetry of a modern world increasingly inhospitable to the prospect of revivifying passion and love; she is understandably neither comfortable with her machine-boy mate nor attractive to the avatars of the primitive. When Lawrence writes ironically that her husband 'admired his wife to extinction' (547), his admiration is seen as a further extension of the tapestry of morbidity that frames this blasted country.

The Woman does not fight against her domestic enslavement because she endures it in a trance; her alonenes, her sense of private female self, is never sufficiently jostled by her husband to awaken her. He scarcely exists for her and is hardly worth the trouble to rebel against. A bit like Addie Bundren in Faulkner's novel of death and female will, the Woman drifts in limbo because no-one from without violates her prison. She simply has ceased to care: 'Her husband had never become real to her, neither mentally nor physically. In spite of his late sort of passion for her, he never meant anything to her, physically' (547). It is only when she hears about the isolated Chilchui Indians that an alternative occurs to her; her 'vague enthusiasm for unknown Indians' (549) is described as sophomoric, for it is not the result of any self-analysis or seriously contemplated future. But it remains the only 'unknown' she can possibly enter at this time; she correctly senses her relation to the tribe as part of some fabled, irresistible fate – an alternative, at least, to the death-in-life she now experiences: 'She felt it was her destiny to wander into the secret haunts of these timeless, mysterious, marvellous Indians of the mountains' (549).

Yet it is not my intention, nor is it Lawrence's, to make her into an existential heroine. She is spoiled, white, and the wealthy, passively wilful wife of a captain of destructive industry. Although she is demonstratively capable of judging the horrors of her environment, she is not depicted as embarking on any profound search for a grail of ultimate meaning in her life.[26] Just before she leaves on her journey, but after she makes up her mind to go, Lawrence is careful to highlight her self-involved temperament; he uses several lines as an elliptical transition to suggest the extent of her narrow and selfish concern:

> But she had her own horse, and she dreamed of being free as she had been as a girl, among the hills of California.
> Her daughter, nine years old, was now in a tiny convent in the little half-deserted Spanish mining-town five miles away. (550)

Thus the imprisoned plight of her daughter – with which the mother ought to empathize – is merely appropriated as part of the

Woman's plan to assert her own freedom; she concocts the story of a convent visit to fool the protective servants. She is able to leave without any guilt for abandoning her child to a harsher version of the enclosed life from which she now escapes. When a servant objects to her unaccompanied trip through the mountains, she summons up her will one last time and abruptly silences him. Although dulled by a ravaged country and muted by the moral domination of her husband, she still relies on the successful administration of whatever orders she gives. Her inability later to respond on the trail to the Indians' disregard of her commands is as much a product of her shock at their ridicule as it is of her already benumbed state. No doubt she usually finds a strategy to get what she wants, and she is unaccustomed to any opposition.

The Woman's vulnerability to easy subordination by the Chilchui is advertised by the inappropriately decorous clothes she wears on the journey: 'a riding suit of coarse linen, a riding-skirt over her linen breeches, a scarlet neck-tie over her white blouse, and a black felt hat on her head' (551). Perhaps she even reveals to the three Indians, through the sparse provisions she carries, her unconscious desire for only a one-way excursion to the tribe; she does not leave her home with nearly the proper support equipment for what is at least a six-day trip in rough terrain. Indeed, it is as if she openly declares, by way of her solitary state, inappropriate dress, and willing demeanour (for example, 'she did not care', 551), that she is fated to be the perfect victim of the Aztecs: she is to be the Woman who enters as easily as from a fairy tale into the savage convenience of the Chilchui mythology. As she moves through the predatory land, she is dazed enough to ignore the coded scenery that warns her of the murder beyond the hills: 'Curiously she was not afraid, although it was a frightening country, the silent, fatal-seeming mountain slopes, the occasional distant, suspicious, elusive natives among the trees, the great carrion birds occasionally hovering' (551). Although hungry and thirsty, 'a strange elation sustained her from within' (552), and it results from this new experience of a self-defined rhythm in her life. For whatever reason, and at whatever cost, she is finally acting on her own impulse, on what *she* feels she must do.

In *Mornings in Mexico* Lawrence elaborates on this sense of self-definition as he relates the instinctual mode of living to its umbilical origin. He writes of Indians who 'are giving themselves again to the pulsing, incalculable fall of the blood, which forever

seeks to fall to the centre of the earth'.[27] The Woman's elation now
connects with the same symbolic source, but Lawrence ominously
suggests that *her* yielding to the intimate urging of her blood is to
be associated with her death: 'She was not sure that she had not
heard, during the night, a great crash at the centre of herself,
which was the crash of her own death. Or else, it was a crash at
the centre of the earth, and meant something big and mysterious'
(552). Lawrence's use of distracting negatives here, that renders
the fact of the 'crash' fuzzy and akin to fantasy, is not bad prose
but a symptom of the bending, tentative realism of this tale. The
Woman who now has 'no will of her own' (553) has abandoned
civilized certainties and emerged into a fable as her final active
gesture on earth. A prominent element in this fabulous effect is her
penchant for coincidentally providing answers to the Chilchui's
questions that are most likely to alert the myth-hungry tribe to the
parable of sacrifice she soon will embody. Her first response about
her destination, 'To the Chilchui Indians', is followed by her fore-
boding assertion that she wishes 'to know their gods' (554). It is
a frightening reply, as the Chilchui for years have predicted the
coming of a woman to fill the stipulations of their gods for a
cosmic revenge.

On the trail with the Indians, the Woman is not frightened, for
she has the 'assurance of her own womanhood' (554). Yet it is
precisely such a female confidence that this patriarchal Chilchui
culture assaults and degrades even within its own tribes; it utterly
despises the female who is Western and white, with her more
developed will and civilized bearing. There are virtually no Indian
women evident in the village to which the Woman is taken, and
their invisibility is caused by tribal custom rather than Lawrence's
oversight. In *Mornings in Mexico* he decries the function of women
in Chilchui society as more biological than participatory; the
manipulated squaw gradually appears as an inevitable extension
of the male's relation to anthropomorphized Aztec gods: 'The
goddess of love is goddess of dirt and prostitution, a dirt-eater, a
horror, without a touch of tenderness. If the god wants to make
love to her, she has to sprawl down in front of him, blatant and
accessible.'[28] Sure enough, the eyes of the Chilchui soon reveal to
the Woman, through that familiar nexus of Lawrencian symbols,
that her sexual appeal is meaningless to them: 'The man's eyes
were not human to her, and they did not see her as a beautiful
white woman. He looked at her with a black, bright inhuman

look, and saw no woman in her at all. . . . She met the eyes of
the young man, and in their bright black inscrutability she saw a
fine spark, as in a snake's eye, of derision' (555). The 'snake's eye'
and the 'bright black inscrutability' bespeak the Indians' connection to the subterranean impulse, to that volcanic centre of the
earth wherein lies for Lawrence the energy source of primal
motivation.

Thus the Woman attempts to make the Aztecs scrutable through
conventional formulae of female will and sexuality that she has
learned in her own world. When they easily rebuff what little will
remains in her by hitting her horse and ignoring her pleas, the
story's perspective once more slowly becomes the Woman's. There
is now a sense that her evaluation of the Indians as dangerous
creatures is shared by Lawrence, who is willing to choose the
'educated' antagonism of the Woman over the barbarism and coldness of the Chilchui: 'Through the twigs of spruce she could see
the three men squatting round the fire on their hams, chewing
the tortillas they picked from the ashes with their dark fingers. . . .
And they showed no more sign of interest in her than if she had
been a piece of venison they were bringing home from the hunt,
and had hung inside a shelter' (557). The impression is not only
that the Indians ignore her as a female, but that the extent of their
contempt for her illustrates the cultural gap between Indian and
white that Lawrence explores in *Mornings in Mexico*: 'Usually, these
people have no correspondence with one at all. To them a white
man or white woman is a sort of phenomenon, just as a monkey
is a sort of phenomenon; something to watch, wonder at, and
laugh at, but not to be taken on one's plane.'[29] As she prepares
for sleep in an isolated mountain camp, she has traded in the
pathetic attentions of a husband for the enigmatic insults of a trio
of Indians.

IV

The images used to describe the Chilchui become increasingly
associated with a dark, devilish underworld as the plight of the
Woman becomes more desperate. The next morning she hears the
'click of flint and steel' of a 'man crouching like a dog over a bone'
(557), and at the village the old chief's eyes are described as
'black and of extraordinary piercing strength, without a qualm of

misgiving in the demonish, dauntless power' (559). That sense of
the tale as a destined fable reappears when she is urged to be
more precise about why she has sought out their tribe; her answer
neatly serves the needs of her interrogators: 'I came to look for the
God of the Chilchui' (560). Confident that her coming is wedded to
the stipulations of their ancient rituals, the Indians now risk the
ultimate question. When she is asked by the Indian with a face
'like dark glass', who has 'black eyes' emerging from 'a glassy
dark face', whether she 'bring[s] her heart to the Chilchui', her
affirmative response commits her to the sacrifice (563). As she is
stripped naked and then impersonally touched by the old man,
not the least of the scene's terror – 'as if Death itself were touching
her' (564) – is its semblance to an oddly casual and almost necro-
philic examination. Here the efficient knife, the Indian obliviousness of her living self, and the compulsive manner of the disrobing
are all directed at ignoring rather than abusing her female sexual
identity:

> Then two of the old men came, and with curious skill slit her
> boots down with keen knives, and drew them off, and slit her
> clothing so that it came away from her. . . . The white-haired,
> glassy-dark old man moistened his finger-tips at his mouth, and
> most delicately touched her on the breasts and on the body,
> then on the back. . . . And she wondered, almost sadly, why
> she did not feel shamed in her nakedness. She only felt sad and
> lost. (564). . . . It must have been almost December, for the days
> were short when she was taken again before the aged man, and
> stripped of her clothing, and touched with the old finger-tips.
> (573)

'Delicately' adds a disturbing note and makes it easy to overlook
the chief's intention to treat her as a species of inanimate object.
Thus Lawrence dramatizes how an obsessed and insulated culture
unself-consciously accomplishes its purpose through an
expeditious combination of asexual violence and strategic
gentleness.

Her violation is even more significant in light of Lawrence's
essays. In a resonant passage from Mornings in Mexico, he sums
up the rhythm and perspective of Indian primitivism; in this
description we see the stark nudity of the Woman, hear the rip of

her torn clothing, and feel, at last, the deadly meaning of her tormentors' attentions:

> Strip, strip, strip away the past and the future, leave the moment, stark and sharp and without consciousness like the obsidian knife. The before and after are the stuff of consciousness. The instant moment is forever keen with a razor-edge of oblivion, like the knife of sacrifice.[30]

The obsidian knife, with its razor sharpness and bright, glaring blackness, becomes Lawrence's perfect metaphor to depict both the origin and excess of their murderous energy. Obsidian stone, with its smooth glassy texture and scalpel edge, is a congealed mass of forged rock emitted from an earth core that has become too hot. In the more clinical terms of geologic definition, a prominent quality of obsidian is its 'unindividualized' consistency,[31] and thus there is even more precision in its use as symbol: Lawrence insists throughout both 'The Woman Who Rode Away' and *Mornings in Mexico* that there is scarcely a sense in these Indians of non-communitarian, personalized emotion or of nonconformist behaviour. They invariably act not as individuals but as robots who are tied to the dogma of a fanatic, vengeful relation to their gods.

As her imprisonment and drug-induced stupor continue, Lawrence leaves no doubt about his disenchantment with the Mexican Indians. It is a function of the ideological passion in Kate Millett's lengthy attack on this story that she can miss so profoundly the simple truth of a dramatized situation: it is the Chilchui who kill the Woman, not D. H. Lawrence, and – most surprising of all, perhaps, to strident dismissers of the tale – the murder does not even have his blessing.[32] Lawrence scatters symbolic fragments of a dark and sharp obsidian glass throughout the work to chart his horror of a tribe's passion that has gone wild. For instance, even when the Chilchui occasionally smile at the Woman, the obsidian glare gives them away; it is as if the black is too deep in colour and too deeply rooted to hide its infernal ray: 'Yet their dark eyes, brooding over her, had something away in their depths that was awesomely ferocious and relentless. They would cover it with a smile, at once, if they felt her looking' (566). On the next page she sees beyond the calm exterior of the young Indian: 'And he, feeling her watching him, would glance up at her swiftly with a dark luring look in his eyes, which immediately he veiled with that half-sad smile' (567). So D. H. Lawrence, although disgusted with aspects of the hyper-conscious, materialistic world represented by the Woman, is willing to admit that her enemies are composed of killers; they are killers born of tribal women whose essential female function is to produce those dangerous boys who grow to be the adversary of Lawrence, the Woman, and all of Western man. He says no less in *Mornings in Mexico*: 'And to this day, most of the Mexican Indian women seem to bring forth stone knives. Look at them, these sons of incomprehensible mothers with their black eyes like flints and their stiff little bodies as taut and as keen as knives of obsidian. Take care they don't rip you up.'[33] After the young Indian in the tale is further described as hiding 'a soft, strange malignancy' (570) behind a smile, there occurs an important exchange that stresses the duplicity of the Chilchui:

'But,' she faltered, 'why do you hate us so? Why do you hate me?'

He looked up suddenly with a light on his face, and a startling flame of a smile.

'No, we don't hate,' he said softly, looking with a curious glitter into her face.

'You do,' she said, forlorn and hopeless.

And after a moment's silence, he rose and went away.

The Indian has learned the strategy of subterfuge, and such is all he can offer in return: a speaking silence that confirms her awful recognition.

Certainly there are aspects of the Chilchui commitment to instinctual darkness that Lawrence admires; he has celebrated similar energies in other peoples throughout his earlier travel books and essays – most memorably, perhaps, in his youthful rhapsodizing on the earthy Italians in his 1916 volume, *Twilight in Italy*. By 1924 Lawrence has grown to be more leery of the unadulterated primitivism in a particular race or ethnic tribe. From approximately the time of *Aaron's Rod*, through 'The Woman Who Rode Away' and the reworking of *The Plumed Serpent*, and beyond to his frankly critical view of the dark miners in *Lady Chatterley's Lover* in 1928, Lawrence grows recognizably circumspect about that support of social atavism he dramatizes in his works during and immediately after the first world war.[34] Admittedly, much of this growth in 1924 is related to the dialectical momentum of his 'leadership phase', as his developing distrust of democracy carries with it a caution about the ascribing of utopian passions to large categories of people. In essence, in the early 1920s he has more confidence in a 'leader' than in the best intentions of any group. If there is a positive aspect to this largely discomforting, anti-democratic phase in Lawrence's career, it is its inheritance of scepticism for a *'people* darkness' and its developing preference for a celebration of individual passion that will culminate in *Lady Chatterley's Lover*.

Is Mabel Luhan to be the sacrificial pawn for Lawrence to torture in this transitional period in his writing? Perhaps Lawrence *did* begin 'The Woman Who Rode Away' with the vengeful desire to eliminate his New Mexican benefactor, who herself was reported to have described the story as the one where 'Lorenzo thought he finished me up'.[35] Yet Lawrence always understood the real dangers of the intentional fallacy, and that awareness bears on Mabel Luhan's possible relation to the work. If Lawrence did have Mabel in mind as he began a fiction that ultimately will hand her to the Chilchui, his 'art sense' may have prevailed over his personal need to one-sidedly settle the score with her. In short, Lawrence knows that 'art must give a deeper satisfaction. It must give fair play all around.'[36] Fair play in the tale in 1924 compels him as artist to make his own dislike of Mabel–Woman retreat behind a sobering and terrified view of her polar antagonists. Lawrence even writes a warning letter to Mabel that alerts her to this fated antagonism in the Indians even as it warns her to keep her famous will at home: 'I tell you, leave the Indians to their own dark destiny. And leave *yourself* to the same.'[37]

Although the Woman comes to know 'she was a victim' (577), she at least retains the freedom of a final knowledge: she sees through the communal gestures of the tribe to the murder in their obsidian eyes. She comes to understand – again the perspective insists it is her perception as well as Lawrence's – that the Chilchui are the practitioners of an underworld devotion so intense as to simulate the gyrations of a devil's mass; they seem riveted to notions of some parable they are programmed to enact: 'She watched their faces bending over her. . . . And in this weird, luminous-dark mask of living face, the eyes were fixed with an unchanging steadfast gleam, and the purplish-pigmented lips were closed in a full, sinister, sad grimness' (577). As Lawrence

126   *D. H. Lawrence and the Phallic Imagination*

completes 'The Woman Who Rode Away' he writes another letter
to Mabel, this time cautioning her about 'the collective self' and
'the mass self' in her own being.[38] If the Woman is meant to be
Mabel, there results a pertinent irony from Lawrence's fictional
inversion of the elements in his cautionary note to her: the Woman
is killed by a 'collectivity' from *without* – that is, by a social hysteria,
by an organized mass self that destroys the ratified self she finally
achieves (by way of her poised understanding of her killers) in
the few hours before her death.

It is not only the grotesque murder or the pathos of the Woman's
final recognition that makes the final scene so painful. Lawrence
purposefully enhances the brutality with a scrupulously impersonal tone of narration; any melodramatic reaction to the event
by the reader is stifled, rendered inappropriate by a journalistic
perspective that prefers to observe with accuracy rather than react
with horror. As Lawrence employs all his familiar symbology,
man, cosmos, and unwilling subject come together for the ritualized killing: 'Behind him came another robeless priest, with two
flint knives. When she was fumigated, they laid her on a large
flat stone, the four powerful men holding her by the outstretched
arms and legs. Behind stood the aged man, like a skeleton covered
with dark glass, holding a knife and transfixedly watching the
sun, and behind him again was another naked priest, with a knife'
(580). In *Mornings in Mexico* Lawrence unambiguously relates the
Mexican Indians to the use of this executioner's knife. In the
process he reveals his attitude towards a primitivism he believes
will degenerate to such savagery. Lawrence has just asked about
the Aztec God, 'What is the infant-god she tenderly bears?' He
answers with the bitter explanation he coolly dramatizes in the
tale:

It is a stone knife.
It is a razor-edged knife of a blackish-green flint, the knife of
all knives, the veritable Paraclete of knives. It is the sacrificial
knife with which the priest makes a gash in his victim's breast,
before he tears out the heart, to hold it smoking to the sun.
And the Sun, the Sun behind the sun, is supposed to suck the
smoking heart greedily with insatiable appetite.
This, then, is a pretty Christmas Eve.[39]

But if his contempt is evident in this essay, why merely the reportorial stance in the tale to describe so ghastly an act? The depiction of the murder in 'The Woman Who Rode Away' does agitate many critics, as if its impersonal tone in some way suggests a ratification of the act, or as if 'the mastery that man must hold and that passes from race to race' (581) is the bloody signature by Lawrence of his need to uphold, *in extremis*, some ancient patriarchal mandate.

Feminist critics despise the tale, but they disagree about how to read its tone and intent. When Rudnick, for instance, argues 'that the death of Woman is eroticized as the ultimate religio-sexual experience is most horrible of all', she shuts her eyes to an enforced tone in the story's last moments so coldly unerotic as to make me wonder if she read the same scene. Eroticized it is not.[40] Millett, however, who is even angrier, argues that 'by sterilizing the story – removing all traces of overt sexual activity', Lawrence merely sets up a transparent veneer for his own imperialistic designs over dark people. It is difficult, of course, to picture the savagery of the Indians in the tale or in *Mornings in Mexico* colonialized by the likes of weakened Westerners for whom Lawrence has such contempt.[41] Judith Ruderman's recent study similarly distorts Lawrence's intention and mocks his humanity, as she virtually argues that there is a cruel Benthamism in the story, a 'glorification of the savage element' by Lawrence that ends up with 'the American protagonist about to be stabbed in the heart for the good of society'.[42]

Let me first address the issue of the story's last lines, for the full burden of their meaning bears on this question of tone in the sacrifice scene. Surely it is clear by now that such a 'mastery' refers to the Chilchui's reading of a destiny in which they *must* prevail. That mastery is part of the bequest of a ruthlessly directive religion; their mastery suggests that compulsive requirement of the Indians to assert their primacy as a people (that is, 'man') by directly engaging the myths they have inherited (that is, 'race to race') through the generations from their gods. As Lawrence further explains in *Mornings in Mexico*, such a life lived amid intense metaphors requires of the Indians a periodic purging of the undiluted poison they bring with them from that underworld sun; it is as if the 'snake's eye' that the Woman once saw in the young Chilchui can bring him peace only when he commits the kind of purgative atrocity with the obsidian knife that concludes the tale: 'In the core of the first of suns, whence man draws his vitality, lies poison as bitter as the rattlesnake's. This poison man must overcome, he must be master of its issue'.[43]

The story concludes with a description of hypnotic absorption by the Chilchui as they prepare to kill the Woman. That paragraph of rapt concentration precedes the one-line coda, as the final words establish – as I have illustrated – the ongoing nature of such acts in the vision of life embodied by these Indians. The transitional effect is critical and worth quoting in full:

> Only the eyes of the oldest man were not anxious. Black, and fixed, and as if sightless, they watched the sun, seeing beyond the sun. And in their black, empty concentration there was power, power intensely abstract and remote, but deep, deep to the heart of the earth, and the heart of the sun. In absolute motionlessness he watched till the red sun should send his ray through the column of ice. Then the old man would strike, and strike home, accomplish the sacrifice and achieve the power.
>
> The mastery that man must hold, and that passes from race to race. (581)

A significant passage from 'Indians and Entertainment' is relevant here; it is the essay, later collected in *Mornings in Mexico*, that is exactly contemporaneous with Lawrence's writing of 'The Woman Who Rode Away'. As he writes the following lines from that most psychologically speculative of his Mexican essays, Lawrence reveals the reason for the disconcerting and unemotional tone that ends the tale: 'The Indian is completely embedded in the wonder of his own drama. It is a drama that has no beginning and no end, it is all-inclusive. It can't be judged, because there is nothing outside it, to judge it.'[44] So Lawrence lets the rhythm of the fiction's lines precisely embody the vision of Indian experience. It may not have been his intention 'to judge it'. But how well he taught us to trust the tale and not the artist. That sense of Indian relentlessness, of Chilchui life lived beyond the appeal of civilized scruple, may enable Lawrence to evade any intrusive statement in the narrative of his own final judgement. As readers we cannot afford the same evasion. From a snake's eye to an obsidian knife, the artist gives us much to judge.

Notes

1. Julian Moynahan, *The Deed of Life* (Princeton: Princeton University Press, 1963), 178.

2. Frank Kermode, *D. H. Lawrence* (New York: Viking Press, 1973; London: Fontana, 1985), 119.

3. See this peculiar lack of concern for one of Lawrence's most lengthy short stories in two seminal critical studies of his work that appeared in the 1960s: H. M. Daleski's *The Forked Flame: A Study of D. H. Lawrence* (Evanston: Northwestern University Press, 1965) and Colin Clark's *River of Dissolution: D. H. Lawrence and English Romanticism* (New York: Barnes & Noble, 1969). While both studies are primarily on the novels, each also discusses several shorter fictions that have significant bearing on Lawrence's career and/or the thesis of the respective critic. It is notable that Clark does not even mention 'The Woman Who Rode Away', and Daleski – who might have employed the 'sun' images in the tale to great advantage in his argument – merely relegates it to a small footnote citation. Similarly, three of the most recent examinations of the full range of Lawrence's fiction either ignore the story or miss entirely the crucial perspective in it that Lawrence establishes. There is not a word about 'The Woman Who Rode Away' (although there is much on other tales) in Graham Holderness's *D. H. Lawrence: History, Ideology, and Fiction* (Dublin: Gill and Macmillan, 1982), or in Gamini Salgado's *A Preface to D. H. Lawrence* (London and New York: Longman, 1983); in an otherwise excellent and comprehensive study, *D. H. Lawrence: The Artist as Psychologist* (Lawrence: University Press of Kansas, 1984), Daniel Schneider's only comment on the tale is the wrong-headed assertion that the Indians 'command the sympathetic response and credibility that Lawrence means them to have' (97). As my analysis of this story will insist, the Chilchui do not command such response, and Lawrence does not intend that they should.

4. Kate Millett, *Sexual Politics* (Garden City: Doubleday, 1970; London: Virago, 1977), 287.

5. Sandra Gilbert and Susan Gubar, 'Introduction: The female imagination and the modernist aesthetic', *Women's Studies*, 13 (1986), 5, 6.

6. Graham Hough, *The Dark Sun* (New York: Capricorn Books, 1956; London: Duckworth, 1970), 146.

7. F. R. Leavis, *D. H. Lawrence: Novelist* (New York: Simon Schuster, 1969; Harmondsworth: Penguin, 1970), 275.

8. Ibid.

9. Hough, *The Dark Sun*, 139. Hough also makes the important point – quite relevant for my own use of Lawrence's dialectic in *Mornings in Mexico* – that Lawrence regards 'the religion of the present-day pueblo Indian as a legitimate descendant of that of the Aztecs . . . he had always seen the Aztecs and the Indians as one' (140). It is this perception by Hough that informs an occasional use, in my analysis of the Chilchui tribe in 'The Woman Who Rode Away', of observations

about Indians that Lawrence makes in *Mornings in Mexico* about primitive American tribes.

10. For an incisive and well-documented study of the development of Lawrence's attitude toward Mexico through his three visits there, see Charles Rossman's 'D. H. Lawrence and Mexico', in Peter Balbert and Phillip L. Marcus (eds), *D. H. Lawrence: A Centenary Consideration* (Ithaca: Cornell University Press, 1985), 180–209.

11. D. H. Lawrence, *Mornings in Mexico* (Salt Lake City: Gibbs M. Smith, 1982; London: Heinemann, 1956), 62. Ross Parmenter's introduction to this edition provides a useful dating of the composition and first publication of each of the essays in *Mornings in Mexico*, as well as an informative summary of the origin of the volume's appearance in 1927. His more recent book on Lawrence's experience in Mexico, *Lawrence in Oaxaca* (Salt Lake City: Gibbs M. Smith, 1984), is primarily an analysis of four months just after Lawrence completes 'The Woman Who Rode Away', when he lived with Frieda in Oaxaca; Parmenter's attention to Lawrence's reworking of *The Plumed Serpent* in this period and to the apparent influence on his prescriptions for an innovative religion in Mexico, confirm the conflicted feelings about primitivism that Lawrence charts throughout *Mornings in Mexico*.

12. Ibid., 57.

13. Ibid., 58.

14. Norman Mailer, 'The White Negro', in *Advertisements for Myself* (New York: Putnam, 1959), 342. Lawrence's review, '*In Our Time*: A Review', is collected in Edward D. McDonald (ed.), *Phoenix: Posthumous Papers of D. H. Lawrence* (New York: Viking; 1972; London: Panther, 1970), 366.

15. Lawrence, *Mornings in Mexico*, 104. On this issue of Lawrence's ultimate judgement of the Mexican Indians in this story, Kingsley Widmer is incisive. Widmer asserts the notion (which he develops more fully in relation to other tales) that 'Lawrence writes primitivistic art but he is not a *primitivist* in the sense of making a moral affirmation of a past or less civilized culture.' *The Art of Perversity: D. H. Lawrence's Shorter Fiction* (Seattle: University of Washington Press, 1962), 33.

16. Lawrence, *Mornings in Mexico*, 53–4.

17. Ibid., 69–70.

18. Ibid., 154–5.

19. James T. Boulton and Andrew Robertson (eds), *The Letters of D. H. Lawrence*, III (Cambridge: Cambridge University Press, 1984), 475. Periodic letters from page 416 in this volume (November 1919) to page 581 (July 1920) unequivocally illustrate this negative estimation by Lawrence of his homeland.

20. Harry T. Moore, *The Priest of Love: A Life of D. H. Lawrence*, rev. edn (New York: Farrar, Straus & Giroux, 1974; Harmondsworth: Penguin, 1980), 319–20.

21. Lawrence, *Mornings in Mexico*, 120.

22. Lois P. Rudnick, 'D. H. Lawrence's New World Heroine: Mabel Dodge Luhan', *The D. H. Lawrence Review*, 14 (1981), 99.

23. Gilbert and Gubar, 'Introduction: The female imagination and the modernist aesthetic', 5.
24. Lawrence, *Mornings in Mexico*, 59–60.
25. D. H. Lawrence, 'The Woman Who Rode Away', *The Complete Short Stories*, III (New York: Penguin, 1976), 546. Page numbers in my text refer to this edition.
26. James C. Cowan includes a fine summary of many of the mythological and archetypal patterns that inform Lawrence's symbols in the story. He is also provocative on the precise relevance of the Christian symbolism, and he explains its relation to the 'monomyth' at the heart of the tale. *D. H. Lawrence's American Journey* (Cleveland: The Press of Case Western Reserve University, 1970), 70–8.
27. Lawrence, *Mornings in Mexico*, 110.
28. Ibid., 54.
29. Ibid., 56.
30. Ibid., 59.
31. Obsidian: 'A glassy volcanic rock, usually black and having a conchoidal fracture without individualized crystals.' *Funk and Wagnalls Standard College Dictionary* (New York: Harcourt, Brace, & World, 1963), 933.
32. Millett is intent on claiming a felony. She argues that Lawrence 'relish[es] the beauty of the dark-skinned males', and that his murderous sexism is evident in 'leaving the emancipated woman to the "savage" to kill', *Sexual Politics*, 286. Even Kermode appears to regard the killing as Lawrence's personal gift for the Woman, as he sees *no* 'internal criticism of the fiction itself', *D. H. Lawrence*, 119. In a more reasonable approach, Kingsley Widmer understands Lawrence's disgust at the ritual killing, and he intelligently argues that for Lawrence 'when the primitive is taken in itself, or as an actuality of life, it is found to be repulsive', *The Art of Perversity*, 29. Similarly, David Cavitch wisely does not indict Lawrence for the murder, as the critic develops several compelling notions about the sexual problematics of Lawrence's relation to the Indians. He concludes that 'the ambiguity of tone indicates the author's own feelings of anticipation and revulsion over the meaning of the symbolic act', *D. H. Lawrence and the New World* (New York: Oxford University Press, 1969), 168.
33. Lawrence, *Mornings in Mexico*, 55.
34. Although more uncertain than I am about this issue, Widmer provides relevant background material on Lawrence and his paradoxical primitivist streak. Widmer concludes that 'probably Lawrence in some ways wanted to be a moral primitivist, but both personal ambivalence and an amoral aesthetic lucidity did not allow any such simple affirmation.' *The Art of Perversity*, 29.
35. Mabel Dodge Luhan, *Lorenzo in Taos* (New York: Knopf, 1932), 238.
36. Lawrence, 'Study of Thomas Hardy', in *Phoenix*, 476.
37. Harry T. Moore (ed.), *The Collected Letters of D. H. Lawrence*, II (New York: Viking, 1962), 761.
38. Ibid., 809.
39. Lawrence, *Mornings in Mexico*, 54–5.

40. Rudnick, 'D. H. Lawrence's New World Heroine: Mabel Dodge Luhan', 99.
41. Millett, *Sexual Politics*, 286.
42. Judith Ruderman, *D. H. Lawrence and the Devouring Mother* (Durham: Duke University Press, 1984), 135, 14.
43. *Mornings in Mexico*, 173–4.
44. Ibid., 119.

5

Feminist Displeasure and the Loving of Lady Chatterley: Lawrence, Hemingway, Mailer, and the Dialectic of 'Sex-with-Guilt'

'A woman has no glamour for a man any more.'

'Kiss me!' she murmured.
'Nay, wait a bit! Let me simmer down,' he said.
That amused her.

I

The antagonism many feminists feel about Lawrence's portrait of Ursula Brangwen in *Women in Love* is exceeded by their anger at his claims for the sexual rebirth of Connie Chatterley. And just as these critics undervalue the essential criticism Ursula supplies for Birkin's cherished beliefs, so do they often not admire – or even acknowledge – the real target that informs Lawrence's characterization of Lady Chatterley: her gradual acceptance and ultimate understanding of Mellors's brand of loving suggests the full extent of Lawrence's disgust with what he disparagingly calls the 'modern' notions of sexuality and commitment popular in the 1920s. By the time of *Lady Chatterley's Lover*, Lawrence dogmatically associates his culture's more liberal, post-war attitudes towards passion, gender roles, courtship, and marriage with a deadening mechanization (a 'mentalizing', as he often puts it) of the instinctive sexual impulse: 'The body of men and women today is just a trained dog. And of no one is this more true than of the free and emancipated young. Above all, their bodies are the bodies of trained dogs.'[1] Thus not surprisingly today, considerable feminist displeasure often is directed at the structure, premises, and ethics of Lawrence's most phallic novel; other aspects of recent ideological attacks variously are levelled at Mellors and/or Connie and the purported sexism of their characterizations.

Such negative perspectives on the work range from the archly aesthetic stance of Carolyn Heilbrun, who oddly berates the novel for its alleged 'demeaning of the female figure',[2] to the trendy formulations of social science, as Anne Smith smugly writes of the 'elements of adolescent fantasy' that she deems evident in 'Lawrence's inability to come to terms with women as full human beings'.[3] She writes such feminist buzz-words without any sense of a pertinent irony: Smith indicts Lawrence through a utopian tone of evasive platitude (what *is* a 'full human being' filled with, we want to ask) that is also articulated without much meaning by the emasculated wags at Wragby; they inhabit the Chatterley estate as a collection of representatively modern thinkers who unendingly babble about the sex 'connection' as a limiting facet of 'the full life'. Indeed, there is a sense in similar expressions of resentment over this novel that for Lawrence to focus so intensely on the sexual education of a female in some way suggests a short-changing of her potential as a – their jargon insists on one word here – 'person'. It is the response Lawrence would expect from his antagonists. He writes *Lady Chatterley's Lover*, in part, to dramatize his contempt for the society that scorns his work.[4]

In his last full-length novel Lawrence did not write his greatest fiction, but he may have created his most integrated piece of literature. *Lady Chatterley's Lover* uses the whole form of the novel the way Lawrence speaks of his need to catch the 'whole hog' of 'man alive';[5] he writes the work as simultaneously a method, justification, and metaphor for the intimate process of sexual discovery that he charts through Connie and Mellors. As if to complete the daring implications of such unity in one novel, Lawrence states his case for the pursuit of this aesthetic integration in a few seminal lines in the work itself. It is rare for such an explanation of narrative form to link so organically with stated theme, as Lawrence explains both his topic and its treatment:

> It is the way our sympathy flows and recoils that really determines our lives. And here lies the vast importance of the novel, properly handled. It can inform and lead into new places the flow of our sympathetic consciousness, and it can lead our sympathy away in recoil from things gone dead. Therefore, the novel, properly handled, can reveal the most secret places of life: for it is in the *passional* secret places of life, above all, that the tide of sensitive awareness needs to ebb and flow, cleansing and freshening.[6]

This is the announcement of the phallic theme of the novel, related intrinsically to the language of literary analysis, to the developing affair of Connie and Mellors, and to our experience of reading the work. For *Lady Chatterley's Lover* will 'inform' us about the loving of its titled Lady; it will 'lead us', as it also teaches Connie, to recoil 'from a thing gone dead' called Clifford, and from the deathly life he represents. The novel is so archetypally phallic because of the probing and penetrating ethic of discovery that is the major structuring design in this fiction. The 'passional secret places' of *Lady Chatterley's Lover* have a complex literal and figurative significance that Lawrence must intend. Whether the 'places' connote the largely unexamined areas of sexual life that Lawrence will battle to portray against both the restrictions of censorship and the casual concerns of his detested modern love, or whether they become the actual openings to Connie's body that Mellors will explore, Lawrence announces in those resonant lines of Chapter Nine a large ambition: he makes the declared doctrinal responsibilities of his art into metaphoric extensions of its plot, preoccupations, and stylistic rhythms.

Yet Lawrence's crusading ambitions and his radical formulations do not meet the agenda of today's interpreters of female freedom. The dismissive comments by Heilbrun and Smith suggest that feminist criticism of this novel often remains content to ignore the work's organic unity in favour of a narrowly partisan effort to isolate Lawrence as cruel and reactionary towards women. For instance, there are the predictably severe and orthodox denunciations by Kate Millett, who is compelled to berate the novel as merely a chauvinistic illustration of Lawrence's alleged belief that 'sex is for the man'.[7] As her indictments continue – with their distinct reminder of de Beauvoir's earlier complaints – they begin to anticipate the revisionism of an unsympathetic and fashionable Lawrence critic like Robert Scholes a decade later; his semiotic manhandling of *Lady Chatterley's Lover* in 1982 will echo the following assertions by Millett in 1970 about the godfather analyst and those parts of the female body purportedly overlooked by Freudian theory and Lawrence's novel:

> The sexual mystery to which the novel is dedicated is scarcely a reciprocal or co-operative event – it is simply phallic . . . no reference to a description of the female genitals: they are hidden, shameful, and subject. . . . The scenes of sexual intercourse in the novel are written according to the 'female is passive, male is active' directions laid down by Sigmund Freud.[8]

This pattern of accusations about male favouritism is strange on many counts, not the least being the clear evidence of an adamantly *directive* participation by Connie in her sex with Mellors beginning with their second meeting. Also, Millett's facile summary of Freud's principles becomes even less helpful in its simplistic application to a delicate dialectic of risk and shared exchange that develops between the lovers as their affair continues. I shall anatomize aspects of such courage and reciprocity in my later discussion of the basic sexual ethics in the novel. For now I will merely suggest that Juliet Mitchell, in her interesting study of psychoanalysis and feminism, capably demonstrates the inadequacy of Millett's easy dismissal of several seminal Freudian distinctions that operate in *Lady Chatterley's Lover*.[9]

Millett's charge nearly two decades ago that this novel is merely a celebration of 'male ascendency'[10] is the totalitarian reformulation of de Beauvoir's more measured conclusion that Lawrence's work is occasionally flawed because he 'believes passionately in the supremacy of the male'.[11] But de Beauvoir, while she never fully justifies her assertions or demonstrates their destructive influence on Lawrence's art, always supplies a sympathetic and clarifying context for the discussion of his fiction; she consistently recognizes his fundamental, non-sexist ethic that insists, in her balanced

reading of the Lawrence mandate, 'male or female, one should
never seek in erotic relations the triumph of one's pride or the
exaltation of one's ego'.[12] De Beauvoir does not provide, however,
the available examples of such a doctrinal imperative in Lawrence's
work, and her silence raises for me an important question in
relation to the demeaning of *Lady Chatterley's Lover*. Where is the
feminist criticism that is willing to confront, much less quote, the
clear implications of a series of resonant moments in this novel –
phrases and incidents that are established as warning lights to
slow up those angry critics who voyage through the land of Tevershall with eyes only for Millett's bill of accusations? For instance,
as Connie presumptuously asks Mellors for a key to the hut,
and he too gruffly responds to her attempt at some diplomacy,
Lawrence writes with impressive equity of the sexual electricity in
the air: 'He saluted and turned abruptly away. She had wakened
the sleeping dogs of old voracious anger in him, anger against the
self-willed female. And he was powerless, powerless. He knew it.
And she was angry against the self-willed male' (134). Later
Connie questions Mellors about whether he's 'always been right'
with the women he battled in intimate dispute, and he responds
with frank, reasoned judgement: 'God, no! I let my wife get to
what she was: my fault a good deal. I spoilt her. And I'm very
mistrustful' (264); even Mrs Bolton, amid her crucial discussion
with Connie on the need to 'give in' to the man, concludes with
this tantalizing confession so ripe with poignant ambiguity: 'But I
must say, Ted 'ud give in to me sometimes, when I was set on a
thing, and in the wrong. So I suppose it cuts both ways' (300);
and more famously, here is that lively exchange between Mellors
and Connie on the penalties to be levelled on those who violate
the most basic Lawrencian dictum:

> 'When a woman gets absolutely possessed by her own will,
> her own will set against everything, then it's fearful, and she
> should be shot at last.'
> 'And shouldn't men be shot at last, if they get possessed by
> their own will?'
> 'Aye! – the same!' (349)

Thus despite her lack of sufficient substantiation, de Beauvoir's
essential understanding about Lawrence's insistence on shared
gender responsibility for the tyrannies of ego, sadly appears

forgotten in the din of harsh revisionist attacks on *Lady Chatterley's Lover*. Scholes, for instance, asserts that Mellors's expressed contempt for a woman's desire for clitoral stimulation amounts to nothing more than 'the bare bones of a Freudian scenario', in which Lawrence, in effect, asks women to give up a legitimate source of erotic excitement and – in Scholes's reading – 'to become less sexual in the process'.[13] There remains not the vaguest effort by this critic to discover how Mellors's abhorrence is neither sexist nor fastidious but ultimately an organic expression of a dialectic more mystical and more culturally conservative than the easy Freudianism that Scholes pretends is Lawrence's inheritance. Lawrence wishes to indict society's penchant for sexual thrills that do not entail both the suspension of ego and the willingness to seek transcendence in the act of love. Scholes fails to recognize that Freud's discussions of a woman's possible inability to move beyond clitoral focus, and Freud's related categorizing of the ideal stages of her sexual response and development, has little to do with Lawrence's visionary, nearly theologic view of the imperatives of intercourse.

Mailer's devastating response in *The Prisoner of Sex* to Millett's undisguised clitormania is equally relevant as a response to Scholes's semiotic simplification of *Lady Chatterley's Lover*. Like Lawrence, Mailer believes that a tolerant attitude towards a generation's marketable sexologists is often a touchstone indication of an acceptance of a dangerous, developing alliance this century among bureaucrats, technologists, and the proponents of radical innovations in procreative techniques, sexual stimulation, and gender styles. Both novelists feel that the privacy of erotic relations and its ideal capacity for self-definition are increasingly adulterated by those triple pressures of advancing science, improving technology, and a climate of contemporary scepticism about traditional sexual roles. Scholes's naive, uncritical remarks on the current practitioners of bedroom investigation and behaviouristic tolerance ('perhaps Masters and Johnson, Shere Hite, and others have brought us closer to some kinds of truth about the body at last'[14]) suggest why he does not submit Mellors's indictment of Bertha's sexual habits to the scrutiny of the Lawrencian doctrines that fuel the gamekeeper's anger. As they push the standard feminist line about the rights of the female and the tyranny of male notions about women, both Millett and Scholes conveniently forget that the scope of Lawrence's disapproval in *Lady Chatterley's Lover* also extends to the male; he depicts obsessive clitoral friction as the unholy complement to the patently masturbatory sexuality of Michaelis and the other defaulting denizens of Wragby.

Lawrence fears that onanistic sexuality has become a primary mode of erotic expression in the liberalized atmosphere of the 1920s. A recent book, Hilary Simpson's *D. H. Lawrence and Feminism*, examines the historical context of Lawrence's relation to his culture with greater precision. Her criticism provides a relevant example in its sections on *Lady Chatterley's Lover* of what happens when a competent feminist critic in a generally capable study pushes an ideological assumption too far. Simpson is correct to note that the novel castigates the premises and programmes of much that was espoused by women's rights advocates after the first world war. Yet she is wrong to imply that Lawrence's discomfort with liberationist ideas on sexuality and 'freedom' is sufficient proof of his faulty vision and lack of human sympathy. As Simpson accurately writes, for example, of the increasing lack of excitement by Lawrence for aspects of women's recent achievements in the area of sexual rights and vocational opportunity, she then openly declares that women had entered 'the man's world with a vengeance, and Lawrence's writing betrays his unease at this development'.[15] But where is her analysis of the relevant fiction that Lawrence uses to dramatize and clarify the larger context of his fears? 'Betrays', of course, is the word that gives Simpson away, the term that betrays her own admirable commitment in most of her work to non-partisan investigation rather than party propaganda. It suggests that she is not hospitable to a Lawrencian dialectic about sex roles and gender responsibilities that regards new sexual freedoms and increased options for work as not automatically a boon to culture, the economy, or the passionate potentials of love. Such inhospitability is her right, but only if she records the full burden of Lawrence's vision as he carefully delineates it in his fiction.

More exactly, Simpson's occasional failure in the second half of her study is not that she describes the post-war Lawrence as in some ways a sexual reactionary – a fair enough epithet, if clarified, for her to employ; it is that she remains manifestly unprobing of the compelling targets of his reactionism which he illustrates in *Lady Chatterley's Lover*. When Simpson touches on that work, she is content to quote Millett and anticipate Scholes's argument about the absurdity of Lawrence's antagonism to clitoral orgasm. She

evidences the same disinclination as Millett and Scholes to broaden
her analysis with any complementary examination of the various
male modes of masturbatory sex that Lawrence also denigrates in
the novel. Simpson never really looks with balance at Lawrence's
'phallocentricity' once she begins to indict him for 'his own
consciously misogynist attitudes'.[16] She is unusually insensitive
to the bedrock values of nurturance and tenderness gradually
embodied by Mellors; she peculiarly argues that Connie's plight
in the novel 'is really a Hobson's choice between Clifford and
Mellors'.[17] In such a levelling summary, a simplification that
reduces Mellors to the status of Clifford is the crux of Simpson's
error and those of her feminist colleagues: there is little understanding or sympathy for the courage and energy demonstrated
by Connie and Mellors in their profound and elemental attraction
to each other. It is this interrelated group of issues – the dramatized
sexual ethics in the novel, the legitimacies of Lawrence's scathing
criticism of the world his lovers inhabit, and the existential
education in 'loving' which Connie gets from Mellors – that I
wish to consider before the conclusion of this chapter. The sexual
treatment of Lady Chatterley (by Michaelis, Clifford, and
especially by Mellors) is carefully integrated by Lawrence's
theories on language, sex, and the 'machine'. Feminists must at
least confront such a dialectic before they seek to dismiss the novel
as sexist and demeaning to women. Such a Lawrencian pocket
of doctrine and artistic drama in *Lady Chatterley's Lover* is best
illuminated at the start through the literary concerns of echo and
influence, and precisely through various works and statements by
D. H. Lawrence, Ernest Hemingway, and Norman Mailer. A look
at one of Hemingway's early novels may provide a helpful context
to view the loving of Lady Chatterley and to appreciate the texture
of Connie and Mellors's achievement.

II

Several months after the publication in Italy of *Lady Chatterley's
Lover*, Hemingway's *A Farewell to Arms* is published in the United
States. The novels are linked by more than their contemporaneous
publication, as there is also a provocative resemblance in their
themes and sexual preoccupations. Both works depict, with diff-
ering emphasis, the struggle of an emotionally scarred man and

woman to renew their sexual selves during and shortly after the
first world war. Although the novels are set in different countries
and several years apart, there remains a similarity of essential plot
elements: Henry's knee injury and Mellors's pneumonia; Henry's
divorce from the society of his time (his avowed 'separate peace'[18]),
and Mellors's willing isolation in the woods followed later – in his
self-imposed, separate exile from Connie – by his own 'peace that
comes of fucking' (374); Catherine's sexual frustration after the
death of her fiancé in the war before they ever make love, and
Connie's lack of sex with Clifford after his injury in the war. Each
love affair also soon develops as a species of pastoral retreat (on
the mountains and in the woods) amid the industrial blight
represented by the unharnessed technologies occasioned by international conflict and by coal production.

It is interesting to note that such a late 1920s shared wave-length
by an established, dying British novelist and a younger luminary
in America was casually confirmed a few years earlier, when Lawrence reviewed Hemingway's first full-length work, *In Our Time*
(1925). Lawrence's short piece not only isolates the predominant
tone of that short story collection, but it also displays Lawrence's
critical prescience, as he delineates a fundamental ethic in Hemingway's writing that the American soon will display again in his first
two novels. Thus Lawrence's praise here of *In Our Time* becomes
the announcement of his own allegiance to a rising writer's unmis-
takable credo in fiction – that is, to Hemingway's consistent devotion to instinctual truths over the temptations offered by codified,
bourgeois morality and conventional inhibitions: 'It is really
honest. And it explains a great deal of sentimentality. When a
thing has gone to hell inside you, your sentimentalism tries to
pretend it hasn't. But Mr. Hemingway is through with sentimentalism.'[19] The 'sentimental' failure of people to address their real
organic needs, and their inability to unflinchingly act on them at
whatever personal or social risk is required – such notions are
understandably on Lawrence's mind as he takes a valedictory look
at the embattled unconventionality of his own life and begins to
write *Lady Chatterley's Lover*. Indeed, lines from his important
essay, 'A Propos of *Lady Chatterley's Lover*', more directly declare,
in effect, his own kinship with the thrust of Hemingway's fiction
even as Lawrence defends the central motivations for his own
most controversial novel: 'Never was an age more sentimental,

more devoid of real feeling, more exaggerated in fake feeling than our own.'[20]

It is not surprising that the author of *Lady Chatterley's Lover*, who himself both endured and portrayed the damaging effects of cultural barbarism on the organic self, should express an appreciation of the quality of emotional honesty in Hemingway's work. *Lady Chatterley's Lover* is so free from sentimental bias that it confidently requires its readers not only to understand the needs of Connie Chatterley, but also to condone a woman's abandonment of a crippled husband for the love of her spouse's gamekeeper. And like Hemingway's ethically charged atmosphere of destruction and rebirth in *A Farewell to Arms*, Lawrence's novelistic depiction in *Lady Chatterley's Lover* of the rights and obligations of sexual wholeness stresses both the devastation of libidinal energy occasioned by the first world war, and the consequent emergence of the machine as the potent force of modern life. In essence, what Lawrence really anticipates in Hemingway's future work is the unsentimental notion that the younger novelist will celebrate so famously in *The Sun Also Rises* and *A Farewell to Arms*: that a man and a woman may have to pay a large price to live and love their own way in the real world, and sentimentality only occurs – in Mailer's words – when you try to 'cut a corner, tr[ied] to cheat the heart of life, tr[ied] not to face our uneasy sense that pleasure comes best to those who are brave'.[21]

To be sentimental about sex is a seductive option for a man, and especially when he must carry the scar of a phallic wound. As that poignant casualty so common in the post-war twenties, it is then a particular temptation for him to renounce the claims of courage and assertion in favour of an appeal to necessary compromise and inevitable accommodation in his life; he comes to assume that the injury in the groin somehow frees him from the requirements of real discipline and ambition. For years critics have charted the significance of the 'wound motif' in Hemingway's work. I only wish to demonstrate that this pattern of preoccupation in his first two novels provides a helpful context to view Lawrence's criticism of the mawkish sentiment and industrial cant expressed by the phallic evaders who inhabit and visit the Chatterley estate. For example, in Hemingway's first novel, *The Sun Also Rises* (1926), an impotent, impatient, but admirably self-disciplined Jake Barnes divorces himself from society and establishes the private code of values that his creator will reproduce for thirty-five years. Nick

Adams's back injury, in the work Lawrence reviewed so favourably, moves unsentimentally in *The Sun Also Rises* to the male's
genitals; Hemingway is thus even more direct as he isolates the
representative assault on men unleashed by the psychic and
physical devastation of the War. As the impotent male who is not
a castrato, Jake's only hope in the living hell that is his life is to
play it honestly through a delicate balance of instinct and self-
discipline. Thus he develops a recognizable and unalterable
working code of conduct to make his life manageable, passionate,
and dignified within the limits of his incapacity. In that archetypal
vignette in the cab, Georgette sympathizes with his excuse and is
not without understanding of the limbo in which he lives. When
she first obligingly reaches for him where it hurts, and he 'put her
hand away',[22] she is not surprised to learn that he is sick in the
manner of so many of her potential clients: variously injured, war-
weary, confused, and despairing, the men of the 1920s appear to
lack phallic imagination as well as sexual ability.

Jake Barnes, however, is impressively different than most emasculated casualties of the war, primarily because he resolutely stays
on the sexual stage of life, as it were, although he can never
perform the final act. Immediately after the scene with Georgette,
as he kisses Brett Ashley in a counterpointed taxi ride through
Paris, he mournfully asks the woman he loves, 'isn't there
anything we can do about it?'[23] It is a rhetorical, not a sentimental
question, as it is not meant to shield Jake from the obvious answer.
It further suggests the irony that Jake Barnes, who cannot 'do'
anything, admirably does what he can, while his friends in Paris
(or the defaulting men at Lawrence's Wragby) do little more than
rationalize and evade. Connie Chatterley's ultimate contempt for
Clifford comes when she recognizes that he *is* to be blamed for
the desiccation of those human wellsprings of warmth and sensu-
ality of which he alone is responsible even in his paralysis. Jake
Barnes cannot make love, but his blood tells him to stay in intense
connection with Brett and (as the occasions arise) even in close,
confiding contact with a harlot. Jake's instincts remain his fiercely
reliable guide, and he will go where he must and suffer how he
may as he listens to their mandates.

In this regard Mailer's witty appropriation in *The Prisoner of Sex*
of a popular Hemingway phrase to help him describe the moral
imperatives that can influence a man's erotic nature – 'the phallus
erect is nothing less than grace under pressure'[24] – is more than

a pun about the possibility of sexual transcendence poised beneath the tumescent weight of engorged semen and blood; in relation to my concern with *The Sun Also Rises*, it suggests an even more admirable grace embodied by Jake, a man who never avoids the pressure despite the impossibility of release. Similarly, recall the Hemingwayesque language resonantly employed in *Lady Chatterley's Lover*, when Mellors is tempted to use the personal devastations of his past as an excuse to avoid any entanglement with a woman who is slowly entering the erotic orbit of his life: 'Especially he did not want to come into contact with a woman again. He feared it; for he had a big wound from old contacts' (131). Unlike Jake, Mellors can begin to heal in the very process of his sexual re-engagement, and he will manifest that quality Connie calls so appropriately 'the courage of your own tenderness' (346) as he surmounts the inhibitions prompted by his experiences during and shortly after the war.

In Hemingway's next novel, *A Farewell to Arms*, the hero is potent but also is gradually alienated from the values and compromises of his generation. It is evident early in this work that he too must fight to retain his phallic imagination within a war that too easily makes passion a pastime just for the decadently diligent or the indolently despairing. The only sex Henry can manage amid the machines and armaments of war is that easy brand purchased from whomever is available during his leave from the frontlines. For instance, before he first meets Catherine, he just returns from a holiday with the lowland prostitutes. As his friends predictably tease him about this recently concluded leave, his suggestive ruminations about the cars he must drive during the war become a painful reminder to him of the sordid affairs from which he has just returned:

> I left them working, the car looking disgraced and empty with the engine open and parts spread on the workbench, and went in under the shed and looked at each of the cars. They were moderately clean. . . . Everything seemed in good condition. It evidently made no difference whether I was there to look after things or not.[25]

Henry's feeling of disgrace and powerlessness is revealed in his sexual description of the violated cars; like his used and dirty town whores, the cars can be serviced without him. Henry is not

necessary for the greasing of street love or for the oiling of the
war machine. His sex life has become as inert and unimaginative
as the machines, with the clear implication that this derogation of
his phallic force is tied to the current lack of meaning and commitment in his working life. But at least Henry begins to sense the
tyrannies of technology and its ability to mechanize the soul and
passion of man. This moment of Henry's increasing disgust near
the machines that regulate his life is in sharp contrast to Clifford
Chatterley and his cronies' enthusiastic endorsement of the inorganic life of machines over the vagaries of human instinct and the
unpredictability of love.

The compulsive speed with which Henry's affair with Catherine
accelerates is initially a result of those special qualities of nurturance and sex appeal that she embodies even in a military environment so unencouraging to their expression. It does not take long
for Henry to feel a complementary self-definition from her love, a
feeling in Henry not unrelated to the confidence that enables him
to desert the war and all its habits of institutional authority. But
his willingness to rebel, to defy conventions, really begins with
his ability to feel and express uninhibited sexual desire for a real
woman; as with Jake Barnes and Oliver Mellors, there is a sense
in these post-war fictions that often the mere expression of pure
phallic urgency itself is a species of male achievement amid the
fragmentations of war and technological rampage. So Henry's
spirits perceptibly rise along with his lust when he meets
Catherine; he quickly senses that the sexual stakes for him are to
be changed. He is willing now to take a chance with passion
beyond the empty security of the easy flesh he just purchased
during his leave. In a resonant moment near the frontlines early
in his relationship with Catherine, Henry makes a futile plea that
sounds both like Barnes's rhetorical question to Brett in the cab
and like Mellors's frustrated comment to Connie, 'let's have it, an'
damn the rest' (173). Here is Henry's simple appeal:

> 'I wish there was some place we could go,' I said. I was
> experiencing the masculine difficulty of making love very long
> standing up.
> 'There isn't any place,' she said.[26]

As with Connie and Mellors's sensual trysts virtually under the
eyes of the paralyzed industrial magnate, Henry and Catherine

must take their love where they find it, even if near a battlefield. Henry's stand-up, comic, and honest confession of his 'masculine difficulty' has symbolic relevance in any comparison of the developing visions of sexual ethics in *Lady Chatterley's Lover* and *A Farewell to Arms*. This scene of Henry's inconvenient priapic posture virtually between the machines of war, sets off the counterpointed pathos of Clifford's phallic failure and absolute reliance on his mechanized wheelchair. Henry will stand and strive while Clifford will sit and adapt. Although frantically and awkwardly, Catherine and Henry have made a start towards real engagement and emotional health. Admittedly Henry is still a predator here, and his erection – amid the smell of gunpowder, tires and polished steel, and the gaze of soldiers – is no doubt as humiliating as it is daring.

III

The tone of the sex early in the affair between Henry and Catherine – of compulsive need combined with degrading awkwardness – is similar to the atmosphere during those first uncomfortable and coldly passionate moments experienced by Mellors and Connie, when the gamekeeper and titled Lady couple on the floor of the hut on a 'brown soldier's blanket' (163) that Mellors saved from the war. Through the years many critics have demeaned on several counts this quick-fix-sex by both couples, with the most usual displeasure reserved by feminists like Kate Millett and Vivian Gornick, who charge the males with sexist opportunism and coldly manipulative lust.[27] This kind of criticism not only indicts Henry and Mellors for their seduction of such allegedly vulnerable and naive women, but it also implies a correlative censure of Catherine and Connie for being such easy and capitulative prey. In my view such a reading of these preliminary episodes undervalues the participatory rationale of both women's involvement in the sex; each woman appears to balance for several pages, and often unconsciously, the risk of their yielding against the nothingness of the status quo. The implications in the accusations about male over-insistence and irresponsibility do not square with the special claims about erotic engagement that both novelists dramatize in their novels. That is, Lawrence and Hemingway each insist, albeit in different ways, that the fulfilment of sexual desire by these wounded couples, and especially within the devastated lands they inhabit, is a significant gesture of rebellious courage as well as a natural affirming way to transcend the limitations of their informing culture.

In a discussion in *The Prisoner of Sex* on the technological significance of contemporary 'sexual-liberation' politics, Mailer may have uncovered a clue about the extent of recent antagonism to the characterizations of Connie Chatterley and Catherine Barkley. He writes that he 'did not know if there was any journey more difficult in a technologized world than a woman reaching the deeps of femininity'.[28] Mailer's comment may suggest what is also wrong about the frequently adverse critical reaction to Connie's first sex with Mellors: critics fail to locate the function of such sex as a necessary and valiant step in that existential journey she takes with Mellors to love him fully and to be properly loved in return. Mailer's corresponding assertion about the male imperative has relevance to the decisions by Henry and Mellors to begin their affairs with Catherine and Connie: 'He was never to encounter any comprehension among female writers that a firm erection on a delicate fellow was the adventurous juncture of ego and courage.'[29]

Millett naively confirms Mailer's charge with her glib statement about Mellors's first loving of Lady Chatterley, as Millett conveniently ignores the complex inheritance of the gamekeeper's painful past: 'Of course Mellors is irreproachably competent and sexuality comes naturally to him.'[30] So the critic misses the anxieties of Mellors in her haste to dismiss him as a stud. She takes for granted a minor sexual performance that he cannot be sure is even in him; he must summon up his phallic imagination from the recollections of his buried instincts. Oliver Mellors has not made love in a long time. This 'delicate fellow', with his frail frame, weakened lung condition, hermetic existence, and tense suspicion of women, is rather different than Frederick Henry, who expresses through his robust body the more hardy habits of war and frantic copulation. But recall that when he meets Catherine his self-image is sufficiently low ('it evidently made no difference whether I was there . . . or not') to suggest that the 'juncture of ego and courage' that he requires for Catherine is also an 'adventurous' achievement.

Catherine's deceptively wise and succinct response – 'there isn't any place' – to Henry's desire for a posture of graceful lovemaking, reminds both Hemingway lovers of their limited options in an exploding world. They grope for a kiss in *A Farewell to Arms* between the sounds of shrapnel because they feel uncompromising urgings of passion in their blood. Quite simply, they are at the only 'place' to which they can go. Similarly, when Mellors and Connie meet secretly on Clifford's property, it is always with the eyes of Mrs Bolton on them and with the threat of legal action by Clifford always a looming possibility. But from that first casual yet significant meeting in *Lady Chatterley's Lover* between Connie and Mellors in the woods, there is no real sense that they can ignore the need to meet again: 'he had frightened Connie, he seemed to emerge with such a swift menace . . . like a sudden rush of a threat out of nowhere' (84). It is the relentless demand of the 'logic of the soul' that urges them together against all odds, the same instinctual demand that Lawrence dramatized in *The Rainbow* and that Mellors inimitably calls 'life' (165).

Thus early in *Lady Chatterley's Lover* and *A Farewell to Arms* the male protagonists affirm their ability to act on what they feel when they feel it. They ratify that bottom-line power of the existential self to dictate action without succumbing to abstract warnings about propriety or convention. Norman Mailer, in a 1959 work that 'derives' himself and his own Manichean view of existence, both states the consequences of such instinctive behaviour, and emphasizes a useful connection between Lawrence and Hemingway:

> If the intellectual antecedents of this generation can be traced to such separate influences as D. H. Lawrence, Henry Miller, and Wilhelm Reich, the viable philosophy of Hemingway fit most of the facts. . . . What fitted the need of the adventurer even more precisely was Hemingway's categorical imperative that what made him feel good became therefore the Good.[31]

The 'good' for Mellors and Henry soon becomes associated – and nearly exclusively – with their female lovers; Mellors may occasionally ponder the pastoral beauty of the isolate woods and Henry may think of magic mountains like the Abruzzi, but it is these women who, by their mere presence, manifest for the men a sacred ability to transform the dull rooms of a hut, hotel, or hospital into a private sanctuary for love. In each novel Mellors and Henry follow the instincts of their phallic imagination to a developing realization of this 'good', and they act on this blood knowledge despite the considerable risks from civil and military law. Mellors and Henry thus abandon the relative security of institutions and jobs for dangerously open-ended love affairs that are opposed by all manner of social and governmental convention. Yet there is evidence that both men fear the consequences of their 'categorical imperative' even as they pursue this good passion. For as Henry gets involved with Catherine long before his necessary desertion, he thinks with scarcely concealed concern: 'Nobody had mentioned what the stakes were. It was all right with me.'[32] Similarly, after his first sex with Connie, Mellors asks her, 'Don't you care about a' the risk?' (173), and to her ensuing question of whether he is afraid, Mellors answers with a redundant emphasis that judges their affair and summarizes his perspective since the war: 'Ay . . . I am. I'm afraid. I'm afraid. I'm afraid o'things' (173).

In this atmosphere of antagonistic pressures – summarized memorably by Mellors as 'things. Everybody! The lot of 'em' (173) – the greatest danger for those who trust instinct is either to misread their own emotion or to permit empty, deadened, and abstract words to confuse the empirical guidance they receive from their own *perceived* fact and *felt* emotion. They must not trust slogans or institutions; they cannot make a conventional mistake when their self-definition is so intensely allied with the dictates of a private demon who rules about 'the good'. For such existential romantics as Mellors and Connie, or Henry and Catherine, to name an object or emotion incorrectly is to tamper with their belief in a faith that has become the signpost of their daily life; it is to undermine that confidence in their own instinct and sense perception and to extinguish what Mailer in 'The White Negro' calls 'the burning consciousness of the present'.[33] To confirm Mailer's reading of influences on the modern temper, note the shared preoccupations of Lawrence and Hemingway in passages written only months apart, from *Lady Chatterley's Lover* and *A Farewell to Arms*, respectively, as they reveal a divorce between the word and the word-made-flesh:

All the great words, it seemed to Connie, were cancelled for her generation: love, joy, happiness, home, mother, father, husband, all these great dynamic words were half dead now, and dying from day to day. . . . As for sex, the last of the great words, it was just a cocktail term for an excitement that bucked you up for a while, then left you more raggy than ever. (102)

I was always embarrassed by the words sacred, glorious, and sacrifice and the expression in vain. . . . There were many words that you could not stand to hear and finally only the names of places had dignity. Certain numbers were the same way and certain dates, and these with the names of the places were all you could say and have them mean anything. Abstract words such as glory, honor, courage, or hallow were obscene beside the concrete names of villages, the numbers of roads, the names of rivers, the numbers of regiments and the dates.[34]

Both Lawrence and Hemingway portray the post-war disillusion of a whole generation. The 'words' in the above passages have lost value for Connie Chatterley and Frederick Henry because the sustaining values that these abstract words should reflect have been dismissed or adulterated. Sex and love, for instance, have been rendered dispensable and mechanical by the cynical intellectualizing of the men at Wragby. Courage and honour, as the social conventions lazily interpret them, are deemed irrelevant by Henry to his concrete, immediate need for survival in a war in which he neither believes nor belongs. But the comparison goes further. Both Connie and Henry – each the central consciousness of the lines quoted above – become passionately involved in love affairs that ultimately energize for them with meaning, by branding anew in the crucible of their own experience the abstract words they disparage. Before I turn with particular attention to Mellors's brand of loving Lady Chatterley, I wish to pursue a related notion about language and experience; its genesis is still via the Lawrence-Hemingway-Mailer connection, and its implications are useful to explain the dialectic responsible for Connie's changing attitudes toward sex and commitment that she learns from her wounded and courageous gamekeeper. A passing comment by Mailer on a renowned Hemingway story provides the telling clue that eventually will lead us back to Connie.

IV

In Mailer's *The Prisoner of Sex*, within his discussion of the feminists' inability to acknowledge the special fragilities of men, he writes that 'not for nothing had he long considered the first of Hemingway stories to be "The Short Happy Life of Francis Macomber".'[35] Such praise suggests an unexamined aspect of the existential theory that both links Hemingway to Mailer and ultimately explains a significant quality in Lawrence's sexual doctrine. Lawrence, of course, makes the notorious observation in his essay on *The Scarlet Letter* in *Studies in Classic American Literature* that the American man's tendency toward moral weakness before his woman is a symptom of the male's disastrous and total abandonment of any 'ithyphallic' authority;[36] that analysis seems especially relevant to Macomber's pattern of failures on his safari. His cowardly relations with his wife and his panic during the hunt are dramatized by Hemingway as the interrelated symptoms of a contemporary, post-war disease at the root of Francis's being: he permits himself to be conditioned by the easy tonics and mechanized bromides of a society that values the rote prescriptions of mind over the uncertainties of instinct; he learns to fear any open-ended scenarios in sex, war, and occupational competition, for the story insists that Macomber's anxiety attacks about the jungle hunt are extensions of his fears and inhibitions at home, in his world of money, court games, marital insecurity, and horses. Macomber has come to depend on the familiarity of routines and the insulating security of his wealth to protect him from failure. He goes through life like a perpetually cramming student, a boyish man who relies on predetermined formulae and endless practice to limit the uncertainty he must encounter.

What Hemingway carefully highlights about the habits of Macomber and the age in which he lives is crucial in the depiction of Macomber's typical failures and short-lived success in the tale. It appears, in effect, that Macomber's need for mentalized preparation even extends to his bedroom rites of passage, as Hemingway writes with caustic irony about the salient qualities of Macomber's very modern, pragmatic approach to life: 'He knew about . . . sex in books, many books, too many books.'[37] In short, this masturbatory penchant for closed-ended titillations and self-protecting aphorisms becomes his way of shielding himself from unpremeditated, instinctual behaviour – that is, from what Lawrence calls throughout his work 'blood knowledge'. To vary the wording of Mailer's passage about the influence of Hemingway on modern generations, what Macomber *thinks* should make him feel good becomes 'the good' for him.

Hemingway's disgust at Francis's cowardly, reading relation to sex emphasizes this weak husband's preference for the directives of mind and the confirmations of language over the mandates of instinct. No doubt Francis's usual pattern is to try for an inner security before a coming event through a strenuous combination of book learning and nagging questions to knowledgeable authorities. But as with his safari journey, all his crammed education characteristically ties him in knots; apparently he never even researched the proper questions about necessary hunting amenities. Margot's irritable reaction, the night before his disgrace, to his persistent, futile verbalizing of the issue of fear, indicates that she is familiar with his neurotic paroxysms of over-preparation. Francis becomes the 1920s version of a man Emerson assailed in 'The American Scholar' more than a century ago: such a man cannot appreciate experience unless he studies for it before and speaks about it after. Whether his precious words are the 'abstractions' that Frederick Henry abhors or 'the great words' that Connie Chatterley distrusts, Francis Macomber depends on such language rather than the rush of his sensations to get his guidance. For instance, his unexpected and precipitous redemption with the buffalo is unmistakably tied to a set of lucky circumstances in the morning that call forth his better instincts. He did not have time to worry or prepare or verbalize before the encounter – no time, for once, for his very modern mind to inhibit him: 'It had taken a strange chance of hunting, a sudden precipitation into action without opportunity for worrying beforehand. . . . Beggar had probably been afraid all his life.'[38]

Predictably, however, the full lesson of instinctual primacy remains difficult for Francis to absorb. Immediately after his effective actions with the buffalo, Macomber backslides momentarily to the level of insecure, over-mentalized man: he demonstrates that he cannot accept his own elation unless he can announce the feeling and thus find the equivalent in language for the emotion he experiences. He is at the peak of inner satisfaction over his act, and he still needs to ask Wilson the gratuitous question: ' "But you have a feeling of happiness about action to come?" '[39] In response the great white hunter warns him to abide by the terms of his newly discovered existential wealth, as Wilson recommends to Macomber that the American permit the feeling to grow rather than look for words to circumscribe it: ' "Yes," said Wilson. "There's that. Doesn't do to talk too much about all this. Talk the whole thing away. No pleasure in anything if you mouth it up too much." '[40] Thus Wilson enunciates Hemingway's seminal mandate about language and experience, and its restrictive advice applies to the height of elation as well as to the depths of despair. Frederick Henry's famous reticence by the bedside of a dead Catherine and Wilson's warning to an ecstatic Macomber reflect Hemingway's profound impatience with the tendency to articulate abstractions rather than to silently absorb the emotion.

Mailer does not fully explain his preference for 'The Short Happy Life of Francis Macomber', but his interest in this short story makes sense in the terms both of Mailer's own developing dialectic and his existential reading of the fiction of D. H. Lawrence. Three years before *The Prisoner of Sex*, Mailer writes this tantalizing passage in *The Armies of the Night*:

> For guilt was the existential edge of sex. Without guilt, sex was meaningless. One advanced into sex against one's sense of guilt, and each time guilt was successfully defied, one had learned a little more about the contractual nature of one's own existence to the unheard thunders of the deep – each time guilt herded one back with its authority, some primitive awe – hence some creative clue to the rages of the deep – was left to brood about.[41]

It is the clarion call of Mailer's sexual aesthetics: sex as potentially the one pure act of self-definition, which is what he writes in a more casual, anecdotal manner about Marilyn Monroe in *Marilyn*: 'Once after going to bed with Marlon Brando she said next morning to Milton Green, "I don't know if I do it the right way," but then which of us does know. . . . Sooner or later we all reveal our innocence about sex in a candid remark.'[42] It is also what Mailer formulates later, as I suggested in my discussions of Lawrence's earlier major novels, in his reading of the transcendental imperative that informs the sexual encounters of characters in Lawrence's fiction: 'They have to deliver themselves "over to the unknown." No more existential statement of love exists, for it is a way of saying we do not know how the love will turn out.'[43]

Such interrelated passages by Mailer embody that paradoxical synthesis of the prophetic and conservative which he shares with Lawrence; their visionary impulses amount to a mystical, almost priestly insistence on the need to keep sexual encounters open-ended and unadulterated by conditioned response, easy adaptation, or deprivatizing language. In *The Deer Park*, for instance, as Eitel ponders the complexity of his sexual relations to Elena, he concludes: 'But he knew that he would marry her, that he could not give her up, for there was that law of life so cruel and so just which demanded that one must grow or else pay more for remaining the same.'[44] Mailer clearly wishes to preserve all potential for self-definition in intercourse, and to encourage that 'lapsing-out' that also is at the core of erotic communion in Lawrence's own fiction. When sex is not relieved of this self-defining guilt that each person possesses, when sex is confronted silently with all the fears, doubts, and anxieties that comprise the inevitable baggage of one's personal history, when it is faced directly and without preparation, practice, or affectation, then it becomes (in Mailer's dialectic and in Lawrence's fiction) the polarized equilibrium of isolate selves. Lawrence and Mailer dislike their respective generations' tendency to promote the many slogans and aids that are geared to delimit the jarring but pure delivery 'over to the unknown' that Birkin describes to Ursula. Courtship confessions between lovers, post-coital analysis of orgasm in group therapy, the self-indulgent use of abortion and contraception – they are all, to these existential romantics, similar versions of the increasingly sophisticated resources of a hypochondriacal and indolent civilization.

Thus Lawrence and Mailer consistently indict a technocratic culture that is willing to enclose the revelatory potential of sex in favour of the 'cold-hearted fucking' that Mellors describes as 'death and idiocy' (266) to the spirit of humanity. In 'A Propos of *Lady Chatterley's Lover*', Lawrence outspokenly assails the artificial feelings of his age. In the process of his attack, he unknowingly anticipates the power and production levels of a later generation's cameras and computers; he provocatively sets the stage for a 1980s when people will buy masturbatory leisure through the easy sex offered on television and VCRs:

> Sentimentality and counterfeit feeling have become a sort of game, everybody trying to outdo his neighbor. The radio and the film are mere counterfeit emotion all the time, the current press and literature the same. People wallow in emotion: counterfeit emotion. They lap it up: they live in it and on it. They ooze with it.[45]

Lawrence could not foresee with precision the extent to which the modern machine would adulterate the pure and engaged sexual instinct that is at the heart of his self-proclaimed 'pollyanalytics'. But *Lady Chatterley's Lover* remains brilliant for the accuracy of its essential prediction that technology would continue to ravage the land of England and the soul and body of its people. Mailer has a half-century more evidence to absorb into his reading of the dangerous direction of Western culture, as his perceptions pick up the metaphors and fears of that earlier novelist from Nottingham: 'One cannot buy a Polaroid in a drugstore without announcing to the world, one chance in two, the camera will be used to record a copulation of family or friends. Everything technological now has the impulse to enter the act of creation, as much as art used to.'[46]

Lawrence and Mailer's antagonism to popular notions of sexual freedom and gender liberation appear even more similar when the socio-cultural context of their disapproval is examined more closely. Amid the furor over sexual explicitness in literature aroused by the publication in 1928 of *Lady Chatterley's Lover*, Lawrence writes the essay 'Pornography and Obscenity'. It is a spirited work that functions not only as a lively defence and explanation of the ethics of his novel, but also as a fundamental, non-fictional indictment of the reigning trends in middle-class sexual ethics and sociological preoccupations. Lawrence's essay appears in a post-war decade that is increasingly tolerant of the crusading notions of several liberal sexologists, most of whom encourage the public to adopt a more frank and clinical discussion of sex, procreation, and birth control. One of Lawrence's targets for his censure in 'Pornography and Obscenity' is Dr Marie Stopes, an articulate, outspoken, and well-publicized darling of the women's movement. Stopes's front-page reputation at the time was the result of a series of publications that explained her unequivocal belief that sex was a medical and reproductive matter, and in no way a mystical or sacred subject. Her most popular work, *Married Love* (1918), often described by historians as in many ways a welcome Bible to those impatient children of restrictive, late Victorian parents, advocated family planning, government attention to the intricacies of female sexuality and motherhood, sex education, and state child care.[47] An innocent enough, if controversial agenda by today's standards, and even reasonable to many in England just after the dislocations of the war. Lawrence, however, baulks at the demystifying and crass marketing aspects of such a programme, as he argues that this lust to 'purify' sex is really an attempt by 'the idealists along the Marie Stopes line' to 'kill the dirty little secret of sex' with 'the vicious circle of masturbation and self-consciousness'.[48]

Throughout her discussion of Lawrence's contempt both for Stopes's reforms and for her publicized appeal to the educated classes, Hilary Simpson's feminist displeasure with Lawrence carries with it a largely tacit assumption: it is Simpson's belief that Lawrence's disagreement with progressive sexual movements must be petty and ultimately destructive. Simpson writes of Stopes's feelings about sex often with undisguised advocacy, and both women appear to have D. H. Lawrence in mind when they chide the opposition: 'To those who suggested that such matters could be safely left to instinct, she replied that "instinct is not enough." '[49]. While there are several aspects of Stopes's agenda that Lawrence might accept, the tone of his essay remains angry and belittling; Lawrence consistently asserts those visionary convictions about the sexual impulse that he regards as more urgent than the specific facets of her programme. He argues that Stopes's well-meaning, clinically detached, and conscientiously pragmatic handling of the post-Victorian inheritance of a 'sex problem' ultimately sacrifices the communal potential of sexual relations by submitting lovemaking to public scrutiny, trendy social discussion, and casual verbal description. Indeed, Stopes might be the articulate pragmatist whom Francis Macomber studied during his voracious reading of 'sex in books, many books, too many books', for in Lawrence's view she remains too talkative, too tolerant, and too scientific:

You can't do it by being wise and scientific about it, like Dr. Marie Stopes: though to be wise and scientific like Dr. Marie Stopes is better than to be utterly hypocritical, like the grey ones. But by being wise and scientific in the serious and earnest manner you only tend to disinfect the dirty little secret, and either kill sex altogether with too much seriousness and intellect, or else leave it a miserable disinfected secret. The unhappy 'free and pure' love of so many people who have taken out the dirty little secret and thoroughly disinfected it with scientific words is apt to be more pathetic even than the common run of dirty-little-secret love. The danger is that in killing the dirty little

version his forward to Woman in Love

secret, you kill dynamic sex altogether, and leave only the scientific and deliberate mechanism.

This is what happens to many of those who become seriously 'free' in their sex, free and pure. They have mentalized sex till it is nothing at all, nothing at all but a mental quantity. And the final result is disaster, every time.[50]

Thus in the terms of Mailer's seminal formulations about 'sex with guilt' from *The Armies of the Night*, Dr Stopes must be regarded as society's dangerous sanitizer, and Lawrence castigates her, in effect, for removing the necessarily 'dirty' guilt that must be appropriated by lovers for existential definition in the sexual act. In the same work Mailer also describes an antagonist whose function for Mailer is similar to Dr Stopes's for Lawrence. He is Paul Goodman, a popular writer whose views on the inhibited modern condition of man are antithetical to Mailer's unrelenting mandates about pure instinct and polarized sexual force. He summarizes Goodman's work with metaphors that catch the texture of Mailer's contempt for a 1960s philosopher-guru: 'The super-hygiene of all this mental prophylaxis offended [Mailer] profoundly. Super-hygiene impregnated the air with medicated vaseline – there was nothing dirty in the damn stuff.'[51] Goodman's impeccably tolerant and liberal notions about sexual freedom, onanism, gender roles, and homosexuality – notions that are often enunciated by Chatterley's guests at Wragby – contradict Mailer's categorical imperative that 'sex was better off dirty, damned, even slavish! than clean and without guilt.'[52] Perhaps the most compelling way to illustrate Lawrence and Mailer's attack on society's preference for the erotic hygiene of 'sex-without-guilt' is to examine the loving of Lady Chatterley. It is to the developmental pattern in the novel of such a dialectic that I wish to turn. *I don't see guilt as a major (even minor) aspect of Connie or Mellors.*

V

The sexual love experienced by Connie Reid, before she meets Clifford Chatterley, offers a practical and theoretical example of what Lawrence hates about the 'modern love' he describes in 'Pornography and Obscenity', that brand of erotics Mailer calls 'sex-without-guilt'. Connie's social life as a young woman on the continent provides a cultural conditioning that makes her vulnerable for the mentalized life she must endure at Wragby. As a single, attractive, and intelligent woman in Europe, and armed with the most fashionable notions about women's liberation and the rights of the female, she accepts her Fabian indoctrination that the mind is more important than any instinctual or sexual self-knowledge. So her first affairs become predictable, almost standardized rites of passage, diversions undertaken through boredom and peer pressure; such liaisons require uninvolving and undramatic offerings of her body to emasculated 'humble and craving' men, who conveniently never demand a Lawrencian singling-out into 'otherness' from her, and who give her the security of interesting discussions:

> It was the talk that mattered supremely. Love was only a minor accompaniment. . . . So they had given the gift of them-selves . . . each to the youth with whom she had the most subtle and intimate arguments . . . the love-making and connection were only a sort of primitive reversion and a bit of anti-climax. (39)

Lawrence's interwoven puns here, arranged around the meta-phors of tea-set amenity, melodramatic theatre, and popular socio-logical jargon, suggest a woeful absence of passion in her life. She indulges in a prototypical copulation that is without a shred of guilt, as Lawrence's 'little flame brilliant and yellow' (374) or Mailer's 'unheard thunders of the deep' are not generated or desired by Connie; the visionary element in her lovemaking is replaced by a sectarian need to articulate spurious concepts of will and independence even amid the sweat of sex. Indeed, on these terms the bed becomes her wilful kingdom, where she can rule easily with new transactions of mastery over an unvarying inferi-ority in her lover:

> Rather she could use this sex thing to have power over him. For she had only to hold herself back in sexual intercourse, and let him finish and expend himself without herself coming to the crisis: and then she could prolong the connection and achieve her orgasm and her crisis while he was merely her tool. (40)

Lawrence sees Connie's need for this adolescent manipulation as doubly cruel: first, it is openly sanctioned by the contract Lawrence criticizes between the lust for political power and the feminist claims for sexual liberation; second, it deprives Connie – who gets a mild masturbatory excitement from the affair – of any belief that sex can be deeper than this Machiavellian romp.

Such an illustration of Connie's dominant mode of loving tends to confirm Michaelis's later complaints about her sexual gamesmanship; yet the obsequious playwright never acknowledges in that tirade his own willingness to enter this contest of ego and evasion on the bed with Connie. In short, he approves this modern erotics of will and ambition because the adulterated sex shields him from the Lawrencian 'lapsing out' that he fears and Connie cannot as yet imagine. Lawrence's summary of her early sex life also permits him to mock the political idealism of the Fabians and the supposedly enlightened opinions on love of men like Bertrand Russell, H. G. Wells, and Bernard Shaw. He suggests that the basis of their publicized agitations for social, economic, and sexual equality is the familiar dimension of counterfeit love and mechanized lust; Lawrence further asserts – the irony that his feminist detractors never notice – that those early twentieth-century crusaders for liberation often imprison their vulnerable wives and mistresses in modern versions of sexual servitude and emotional frustration. Lawrence believes that little frightens the proud rationalism of the socialists more than ineradicable differences between people, and thus gender polarities become the real and often unconscious target of Fabian supporters. The post-war world is a willing captive to their political claims, as a wounded legion of men and women appear increasingly tempted by the seductive talk of equal lovemaking and shared sexual responsibility.

Soon Connie Reid dispenses with that continental, soul-sucking brand of sexuality to marry Clifford Chatterley, who later returns home as a paralyzed mine owner in no condition to initiate her to any deeper secrets of the flesh. But his impotence, unlike that of Jake Barnes, reflects a failure of the phallic imagination as well as the phallus; he reveals before his injury a wilting absence of any grace under the pressure of courtship:

> He had been a virgin when he married: and the sex part did not mean much to him. They were so close, he and she, apart from that. And Connie exulted a little in this intimacy which was beyond a man's 'satisfaction'. Clifford anyhow was not just

keen on his 'satisfaction', as so many men seemed to be. No, the intimacy was deeper, more personal than that. (46)

Clifford thus affirms so much of what Lawrence despises about the lack of manhood in modern male lovers, that lack of what Mailer calls an 'existential edge'. The term 'personal' in the passage above is the inevitable signature of an insecure ego involvement that Clifford characteristically masquerades as an informed and selfless tolerance. There is no thought in him of the enriching submission to Paul Morel's 'great hunger and *impersonality* of passion', or to Tom Brangwen's 'scalding peace' of sexual otherness. Clifford is content with the cosy smugness of dispassionate compromise, as his real satisfaction (which we glimpse now and then with Mrs Bolton) insists on a child's intimacy of filthy little secrets.

Connie's necessary adjustment to Clifford's impotence is helped initially by her own history of this programmatic, uninspired sex as a young woman in Europe; his injury fits in with the established rhythms of her already dispassionate connections with Clifford and her former lovers. But her celibate frustrations at Wragby gradually build, and soon she merely tolerates her crippled husband through the long, talky hours of uneventful days; she wastes away listening to tired, bruised, and pretentious men denigrate sex with their self-serving and escapist discussions. The more these pseudo-intellectuals seek to trivialize sensual impulses through their incessant word play, the more they both welcome the increasing popularity in the 1920s of an androgynization of the sexes, and belittle the pre-war habits of gender distinction and 'love at first sight'. In addition, as Clifford and his friends continue to derogate the importance of unharnessed, romantic passion in lovemaking, they also manifest a tone of celebration about the intrusion of technology into the texture of sexual relations.

On this issue of the modern world's gradual receptivity to the machine's encroachment on daily life, Lawrence and Mailer share an obsessive and nighmarish fear. At Wragby, for instance, note the cowardly lack of perspective offered by Olive Strangeways as she revealingly endorses a link between test-tube conception and the prerogatives of women's rights: 'Olive was reading a book about the future, when babies would be bred in bottles, and women would be immunized: "Jolly good thing, too!" she said. "Then a woman can live her own life" ' (115). 'Live her own life' is the same jargon used by the feminist critic Anne Smith, who accused Lawrence of a failure to depict women as 'full human beings'; both phrases imply a peculiar discomfort with the existential *feel* of womanhood, and Lawrence illustrates the biological self-contempt that underlies such complaints when Olive exults at the thought of a future when 'a woman needn't be dragged down by her *functions*', and when Lady Bennerley maintains that the coming civilization 'has to help us forget out bodies' (115,116).

The medical technology predicted by Mrs Strangeways, of course, is Lawrence's 1920s guess about a future that is now a reality, that is now a contemporary reflection of Mailer's greatest fear, his 'most pessimistic belief – that the spirit of the twentieth century was to convert man to a machine. If that were so, then the liberation of women might be a trap.'[53] As Mailer insists throughout *The Prisoner of Sex*, the inevitable and enthusiastic support for scientific advances in reproduction by an educated and highly articulate class, carries with it the strong possibility of 'a logic that will not stop'[54] short of a radical restructuring of fundamental polarities between the sexes. The following recent rumination (that Mailer quotes with horror) by a feminist theoretician, reads no more apocalyptically *today* than did Lawrence's 1929 depiction, through the words of Olive Strangeways, of the test-tubes and machines that wait around the corner:

> The first step that would have to be taken before we could see exactly what the status of sexual intercourse is as a practice is surely to remove all its institutional aspects. We would have to eliminate the functional aspect. Sexual intercourse would have to cease to be Society's means to population renewal. This change is beginning to be within our grasp with the work now being done on extra-uterine conception and incubation. But the possibilities of this research for the women's movement have been barely suggested and there would have to be very concentrated research to perfect as quickly as possible this extra-uterine method of pre-natal development so that this could be a truly optional method, at the very least.[55]

'Eliminate the functional aspect' describes the same hackneyed sound and cynical outlook as Strangeways's prospect of a woman 'dragged down by her functions'. In both cases there is an expression of disgust by a woman for organic desires that she cannot control and that require of her a suspension of ego so essential to Lawrence's vision of human possibility.

Before Lady Chatterley can understand the wilful motivations and cravings for power that fuel such female disgust, she must submit herself to an unhappy affair with Michaelis, a man who embodies the notions of masturbatory love affirmed by the denizens on her husband's estate. She is quite desperate when she meets him, as even the apologetics and witticisms of Wragby conversation do not compensate for the total lack of emotional or sexual connection in her life. Her move to him is a predictable turn for a woman so inexperienced in the demands of a deeper Lawrencian love; her depressed state makes her quite willing to settle for sex that requires so little risk or self-definition from her. He is an available, submissive, and adoring lover, whose physical love for Connie is so ego-enclosed and so obsessively expressed that he is often described as an adolescent, a man 'working his hands furiously in his trouser pockets' (93) just before their tryst. He remains so narcissistic and uncaring that he becomes furious when Connie – who at least *knows* she makes manipulative love with him – requires him to hold on longer so she can reach her clitoral orgasm. Their sex thus precisely reflects that frictive self-abasement Mellors rails against during his speech to Connie about Bertha; it is this meek, recreational sex that Mellors and Connie will transcend as their affair progresses through various stages of passion.

The major difference between Michaelis and Connie during their fling is that she always acknowledges the onanistic nature of their copulations; she is shocked for him to use his outburst to pretend that deep needs were being served. Lawrence is explicit in his essays, fiction, and letters on how he feels contempt for a male who comes to the female for anything less than the transcendence of full sexual satisfaction. That mandate for love describes no easy achievement, and in one letter he writes with poignant candour: 'It is the hardest thing in life to get one's soul and body satisfied from a woman so that one is free from oneself.'[56] Michaelis is a wealthy and insecure intellectual who is unable to make the attempt at such freedom. As he desperately clutches his trousers and ego, his loving of Lady Chatterley illustrates a profound failure of phallic responsibility. Here is Michaelis when he first makes love to her, characteristically unable to 'lapse out', and with a disillusioned and frustrated woman who could not care less

about intimations of the 'unknown': 'He was a curious and very
gentle lover, very gentle with the woman, trembling uncontroll-
ably, and yet at the same time detached, aware, aware of every
sound outside. To her it meant nothing except that she gave
herself to him' (61–2). It is such 'awareness' in Michaelis that
bespeaks the merely functional aspect of his use of intercourse, as
if he is the casual player who glances at the weather as he prepares
to serve.

As Lawrence and Mailer maintain in 'Pornography and
Obscenity' and *The Prisoner of Sex*, and as W. D. Snodgrass
suggests in his important essay on 'The Rocking Horse Winner',
masturbatory sex and worship of the machine are related perver-
sions of passion;[57] erotic desires brought back to oneself or subli-
mated by a devotion to the inanimate are similar evasions of
Lawrence's dictum that sexual energy must seek for the transcendent *through* the very process of self-knowledge it provides. The
following passages are written by Lawrence and Mailer, respectively, and rarely have two novelists been willing to stake out so
forcefully (and in such similar terms!) an unpopular position in
the service of their framing vision of human exchange:

> The great danger in masturbation lies in its merely exhaustive
> nature. In sexual intercourse, there is give and take. A new
> stimulus enters as the native stimulus departs. Something quite
> new is added as the old surcharge is removed. . . . But in
> masturbation there is nothing but loss. There is no reciprocity.
> There is merely the spending away of a certain force, and no
> return. . . . There is no change.[58]

> Masturbation is bombing. It's bombing oneself. . . . When you
> make love, whatever is good in you or bad in you, goes out
> into someone else. I mean this literally. I'm not interested in the
> bio-chemistry of it. . . . All I know is that when one makes
> love, one changes a woman slightly and a woman changes
> you slightly. . . . But if one masturbates all that happens is,
> everything that's beautiful and good in one, goes up the hand,
> goes into the air, is lost.[59]

During the stalled chair scene, Lawrence memorably dramatizes
the role of the machine in onanistic sexuality. The episode is
significant because it combines the poignancy of romantic drama

with the bitterness conveyed by double-entendre and an unadorned phallic symbology. A generation ago Mark Spilka provocatively explained that by the time of this scene we have learned to hate Clifford, that 'thing gone dead', as much as Connie does.[60] By then the affair between Connie and Mellors is well-advanced. Recall Lawrence's line in Chapter Nine extolling the form of a novel, as he maintains that when it is 'properly handled', the novel can 'inform and lead into new places the flow of our sympathetic consciousness'. His confidence of the proper place for reader 'sympathy' is so great in *Lady Chatterley's Lover* that even his radical reordering of the most basic gestures of social convention appears easily justified in the work. That is, we clearly side with the adulterous wife of the paralyzed husband when she warmly touches the hand of her adulterous lover, and she supplies that embrace while her lover pushes the woman's unknowing and cuckolded husband up a hill. The whole scene reads as a species of novelistic dare, with Lawrence tweaking the bourgeois complacencies of his age's morality with the clear evidence of the more irresistible claims of instinctual life.

Clifford's motorized wheelchair, into which (as Spilka wisely indicates) he has sunk the roots of his moral being, is his only means of feeling erect and potent. The chair stalls going up a hill, and Clifford refuses to call for help. He is wedded to his machine for support; he treats it with all the cruel excesses of displaced libido, as he hysterically insists that the chair can make it. After repeated efforts to start an obviously 'improperly handled' engine, Clifford must call on Mellors. Thus the functioning lover is asked by the broken husband to fix the unfixable motor. Clifford is child enough to want the impossible. He wants Mellors to miraculously make potent the impotent props of industrial support – in short, he wants the gamekeeper to add power to an inorganic failure. But Oliver Mellors knows more about ignored women than he does about modern machines, and he cannot fix the motor of Lady Chatterley's husband. After an exasperated Clifford guns the engine several times, he climaxes his frustrations and his masturbatory evasions over the source of real energy by 'putting her in gear with a jerk, having jerked off his brake' (246). Now that Clifford has so brutally reached his climax, the lover of his real woman peers under Clifford's mechanical lady for a little peek, as 'the keeper lay on his stomach again' (247). Connie watches with concern the exertions of her lover, who is as confused and ineffective with her husband's machine as he is proud and nurturant with her. The multiple ironies and puns about the perverse distortion of the phallic imagination in this scene all begin with the realization that Lawrence does not make easy sport of Clifford or his paralysis. Rather, he criticizes the extent to which Clifford permits his own incapacity to blind him to what is sustaining, unmechanized, and eternal. It is only through the twin props of the machines and Mrs Bolton that Clifford 'got his pecker up' (153), but the machine breaks and Mrs Bolton is nowhere in sight. Lawrence argues that 'the great danger in masturbation lies in its merely exhaustive nature . . . there is merely the spending away of a certain force'. His claim is confirmed by the persistent screech of the gunned motor-chair, a noise that Lawrence so deftly merges with the spent sputterings of Clifford's pale face that the two sounds become nearly indistinguishable.

VI

Into this environment of onanistic desire and fraudulent love comes Mellors. Connie's attraction to him, which is developed over a few short meetings before their first sexual encounter, is not just the result of her vulnerable, frustrated state. She comes to admire the appealing privacy of his endurance, and she recognizes the authority of his silent and primitive life, especially when he manifests such independence adjacent to the coterie of weak, communal spirits who frequent her husband's house. He may be poor, coarse, and often undiplomatically direct, but he also may be the first man she meets who is legitimately self-sufficient and unapologetic. Mellors's first loving of Lady Chatterley is understandably abrupt and unfulfilling for both of them, and it is further hampered by Connie's old casebook need to have sex-without-guilt. So she plays examining and doctrinaire liberationist; she becomes more involved in formulating epistemological questions than in feeling her connection with a man. Just like a naive and over-conditioned Francis Macomber, Connie cannot wait to reduce the event to the verbal service of some manageable category. After she first makes love with Mellors, listen to her thoughts appropriate a standard feminist catechism to shield herself from the unknown, from that special ecstasy beyond the constraints of ego: 'Was it real? Her tormented modern-woman's brain still had no rest. Was it real? And she knew, if she gave herself to the man it was real. But if she kept herself for herself, it was nothing' (164).

Recall Mailer's existentialist praise of the 'primitive awe' with which 'one was left to brood about' *after* sex. For when Connie reaches her room and thinks more intensely about Mellors, she begins to feel a real stirring in her, an incipient sense of an attachment to a man different than she has ever experienced. In a blunt and beautiful passage, clearly written from her own educable and sensitive perspective, she manages to make all the right observations about her affair with Mellors and about the inadequacy of her former admirers. But note how Lady Chatterley provocatively stops just short of that fundamental appreciation about her loving by Mellors that she will only reach later in the novel:

> It really wasn't personal. She was only really a female to him. But perhaps that was better. And after all, he was kind to the female in her, which no man had ever been. Men were very kind to the *person* she was, but rather cruel to the female, despising her or ignoring her altogether. Men were awfully kind to Constance Reid or to Lady Chatterley, but not to her womb they weren't kind. And he took no notice of Constance or of Lady Chatterley; he just softly stroked her loins or her breasts. (169)

In such a passage Connie is sufficiently prescient to anticipate the precise topics of sexual politics a few generations ahead. Her linguistic preoccupations sound familiar – shades of 'Ms' and 'chairperson' in the petty ideological wars of the 1970s. It is not difficult to sense how Lawrence would feel about such silly issues of title, salutation, and demeanour, whether those name-games are casually contemplated by Connie in this novel, or examined with the formality of manifesto so recently in our cultural history. For as Connie ponders, she almost concludes what Mellors already knows: she nearly understands that the titles and slogans are easy social indices, and they properly have no relation to Mellors's perception of her real being – that is, to Mellors's uncompromising, basic recognition of her sexual 'otherness' as a woman. Such a recognition by him is not 'personal', it is fundamental and relentless. Thus Connie is almost ready to accept ('perhaps' conveys her lingering doubt) what oddly sounds offensive to many people more than a half century after Lawrence's death: that her 'female' identity is the most important element of her being, and that she knows men and women before she knows the jargon of 'persons'. Easy for the ineffectual men at Wragby to be 'kind to Constance Reid or to Lady Chatterley', so kind that they treat her as one of the guys. Such is the sexual distortion implicit in their veneer of gender egalitarianism; they enact and demand a set of empty gestures and verbal trifles that Lawrence sees as the socially acceptable form of their indolent androgyny.

The conclusion that Connie begins to feel, but not yet fully affirm, is that Mellors's eminently 'male' appreciation of her womb (which he constantly verbalizes), or her own acceptance of such essential homage, is not common, not to be taken for granted, and not to be dismissed as chauvinism. Mellors's kindness to Connie's womb is both his ultimate tribute to her as a woman, and – the rich paradox that today's ideologues refuse to accept – the place from which any honest communication between the sexes always begins. When Mailer argues that 'one attitude in Women's Lib remained therefore repellent', he explains it as 'precisely the dull assumption that the sexual force of a man was the luck of his birth, rather than his finest moral product'.[61] Clifford Chatterley expresses the dominant views of his Wragby cronies that such force is invariably a genetic gift of breeding and inherited blood (thus he never suspects Mellors), and at bottom crucial not to the character of a man but only to the pedigree of his fatherhood (thus he minimizes his own incapacity). Clifford's enthusiastic willingness to let Connie be impregnated by another man is an indication of his contempt for the moral signature implicit in either the 'phallic imagination' or in 'womb knowledge'. He believes in no visionary claims that take him beyond the pragmatics of authority and power, and his only expectation is that Connie should know her suitor's bloodlines as she picks the right 'sort of fellow' (83). Clifford's cynical attitude towards the magic of procreation between lovers becomes again Lawrence's pained prediction of what Mailer more explicitly fears: a mechanized and unerotic future that moves even beyond extra-uterine conception to a credit-card world of sexual reproduction, in a coming civilization that advertises the easy availability of surrogate mothers, categorized sperm banks, and Dr Ruth Westheimer's branch offices.

Throughout *Lady Chatterley's Lover* Lawrence locates this developing sense of Connie's 'female' element unequivocally in her womb; he emphasizes that organ through both the precise phrasing of Mellors's admiration and through Lawrence's association of the uterus in a female with the source of her instinctual passions. This archetypal pattern of appreciation of woman by Lawrence begins to suggest the error in Millett's angry disappointment that there is 'no reference to or description of the female genitals: they are hidden, shameful, and subject'.[62] Repeatedly in the novel the mystery of the changeable shape of the phallus is counterpointed not to the vagina but to the shifting and unpredictable yearnings of Connie's womb; it is her womb, the magical and paradoxical internal organ of both desire and enclosure, that was not reached by the erotic exertions of her previous lovers – that is, not reached either by their semen or their sexual presence. Before Mellors her orgasms were always located (as in her affair with Michaelis) at her clitoris and never engaged her organic, female self; that history of limited focus in her sexual sensation speaks of both the limitations of her men as well as the constrained lovemaking Connie is willing to accept. Mailer's resonant comment about the phallus seems particularly appropriate to *Lady Chatterley's Lover*, and it may also suggest some related phrasing for Lawrence's special depiction of the womb: 'The phallus was the perfect symbol of man, since no matter how powerful a habit was its full presence, it was the one habit which was always ready to desert a man'.[63] It is in a comparably exclusive and representational sense that the womb becomes the appropriate metaphor for Connie, since no matter how many lovers she has exhausted at Wragby or on the continent, it was the one place apparently closed to all lovers but one.

The term 'womb' in this novel gradually takes on the meaning that Lawrence begins to derive for it first in *The Rainbow* and the 'Study of Thomas Hardy', and later in *Fantasia of the Unconscious*: it begins to embody the full force, the secrets, and the source of Connie's instinctual self as a woman. Repeatedly it is described in *Lady Chatterley's Lover* as both her most sensitive place of sensual response, and as an opening reserved for Mellors's special affection: 'That touched Connie's womb. . . .' (132) 'that almost opened her womb to him' . . . (164) 'when all her womb was open and soft' (183) . . . 'her womb that had been shut' (185). Mellors's glib and bawdy praise of Connie, 'best bit o' cunt left on earth', is his frank expression of praise not for the surface beauty of her vagina, but for the passion he can feel through those labial entrances, when – as he slyly tells her – 'th'art willing' (233). Only a few months after his completion of this novel, Lawrence describes the famous Etruscan dance in such a way as to counterpoint again his dualistic metaphors about sexual passion and the human body. It is unfortunate that Millett, Simpson, and other feminists continue to ignore evidence of such a fascinating and equitable symbology:

> There it is, the delightful quality of the Etruscan dance. They are neither making love to music, to avoid copulation, nor are they bouncing toward copulation with a brass band of accompaniment. They are just dancing a dance with the elixir of life. And if they have made a little offering to the stone phallus at the door, it is because when one is full of life one is full of possibilities, and the phallus gives life. And if they made an offering also to the queer ark of the female symbol, at the door of a woman's womb, it is because the womb too is the source of life, and a great fountain of dance movements.[64]

The investment by Lawrence of this species of visionary magic in Connie's womb is not to be interpreted as a statement that sex has no meaning for him outside procreation. Lawrence insists that the pure 'delivery to the unknown' is the one essential mandate for sexual communion; Lawrence's freeze-frame description of a moment of orgasm between Connie and Mellors tells more about metaphysical faith than it does about the clinical fact of conception: 'as the seed sprang in her, his soul sprang toward her too, in the creative act that is far more than procreative' (348).

Thus Lawrence believes in some mystical polarized meeting of souls here, an embrace that resonates with the ingredients of the future. Mailer's karmic interpretation of orgasm is quite similar: 'The come was the mirror to the character of the soul as the soul went over the hill into the next becoming.'[65] Thus in the terms both of Lawrence's dialectic and his metaphoric representations of the female body, Connie's instinctual sexual desire is reached *through* the vagina and is felt and embodied by her in the womb. In effect, she must break the self-involved habits of clitoral stimulation if she is to achieve the isolate singleness of being that Birkin outlined to Ursula. Her 'womb needs' are not only for children, but also to be alternately stimulated and calmed by the admiring love of a man like Mellors. Late in the novel Connie confidently defines the rare qualities of a phallic imagination in Mellors:

'Shall I tell you?' she said, looking into his face. 'Shall I tell you what you have that other men don't have, and that will make the future? Shall I tell you?'

'Tell me, then,' he replied.

'It's the courage of your own tenderness, that's what it is, like when you put your hand on my tail and say I've got a pretty tail.'

The grin came flickering on his face.

'That!' he said.

Then he sat thinking.

'Ay!' he said. 'You're right. It's that really. It's that all the way through.' (346)[66]

There is no insistence here by Connie or Lawrence that Mellors is any sexual athlete. It is simply that he loves to love her, and his unself-conscious manner of loving declares his warm appreciation for the intrinsic beauty of Connie as 'female'.

Feminist critics such as Millett, Scholes, de Beauvoir and Simpson will all variously assail Lawrence for his opposition to a woman's willingness to settle for sexual excitement primarily achieved through clitoral orgasm; as I suggested earlier, Millett and Scholes point with emphatic anger to Mellors's tirade about the orgasmic habits of his wife as a prime example of Lawrence's alleged misogyny. In Simpson's generally more sober evaluation of this issue, she at least shows an awareness of aspects of Lawrence's dualistic symbology about the phallus and womb pattern in the novel; Simpson also does make an effort to demonstrate how Lawrence develops 'the phallus into a symbol adequate to represent the full complexity of maleness'.[67] Yet she unfortunately concludes that Millett's and de Beauvoir's charges are correct about Lawrence's lack of celebration over female sexuality, as she confidently writes that their serious accusations are 'of course justified'.[68] Similarly, Scholes's openly enthusiastic endorsement of Millett's indictment of Lawrence sounds as ideological and trendy as Millett's open demand in *Sexual Politics* for 'a single permissive standard of sexual freedom'.[69] These critics seem offended by Lawrence's imposition of a visionary morality that seeks to judge the reigning sexual habits of a culture or a gender. Neither Millett nor Scholes bothers to relate Lawrence's doctrines on sexuality to the existential imperatives that fuel his conservative dialectic. Lawrence is neither cruelly sexist nor dangerously reactionary; he does not want clitoral stimulation outlawed any more than he wants masturbators put in jail. But he wishes to announce that Bertha Coutts's habits of labial friction embody an onanism that is the dominant mode of modern love in the 'liberated' decade in which Lawrence writes *Lady Chatterley's Lover*. Sex for Lawrence must strive for deeper levels of meaning, stimulation, and singling out, for he does believe in the quintessential dream of a romantic, that – in the words of Mailer's own credo – 'a man can become more male and a woman more female by coming together in the full vigors of the fuck'.[70] Those lines suggest a significance beyond the needs of Mailer's participial pun, for 'full vigors of the fuck' tells us more about the necessary quality of the sex than of the luck of simultaneous orgasm. Here is Lawrence's own expression of a similar faith, as he permits Mellors to describe it with the downright language of a wise gamekeeper: 'I believe in being warm-hearted in love, in fucking with a warm heart. I believe if men could fuck with warm hearts, and the women take it warm-heartedly everything would come all right. It's all this cold-hearted fucking that is death and idiocy' (266).

VII

Sexual gamesmanship remains an established facet of the 'bitch goddess success' described by the men at Wragby; they willingly prostitute themselves on her altar, hold tightly to their egoistic defences, and engage in the mechanical sexuality they describe as a 'connection'. In Lawrence's novel and Mailer's *The Prisoner of Sex* there is a depressing prediction by both writers that the institutions of culture will become increasingly antagonistic to rebellious and romantic men like Mellors. Because the ongoing androgynization of society is a transformation consistent with the goals of technocrats and economists – ponder the probable advantages for future computer terminals and job opportunities when the sexes are ever more indistinguishable! – the unadorned phallic imagination of a gamekeeper can strangely threaten the uniform workings of industry even as it inspires the envy of emasculated lovers. On this issue of passion-versus-the-machine in *Lady Chatterley's Lover*, Mrs Bolton is marvellously sensitive to the underlying horrors. As an enduring widow of a once sensual collier, she knows firsthand how the machine eats its human workers and grinds up the legitimate claims of privacy and conjugal love. Here she speaks with poignant Lawrencian insight, not sentimental paranoia, about the ruthless demands of technology and the tragedy of an overwhelmed marriage:

> 'Oh, my lady! And that's what makes you feel so bitter. You feel folks *wanted* him killed. You feel the pit fair *wanted* to kill him. Oh, I felt, if it hadn't been for the pit, an' them as runs the pit, there'd have been no leaving me. But they all *want* to separate a woman and a man, if they're together.'
> 'If they're physically together,' said Connie.
> 'That's right, my Lady! there's a lot of hard-hearted folks in the world. And every morning when he got up and went to th' pit, I felt it was wrong, wrong. But what else could he do? What can a man do?' (218)

But this Lawrencian 'togetherness' of a man and woman, justifiably commemorated by Mrs Bolton's remarks, is not easy for the gamekeeper to accept. A hurt and disillusioned Mellors must battle against his own temptation to avoid any entanglement with Connie: part of him wishes to stay alone and undisturbed in the separate peace of his lovely, dark, and deep woods. When Connie bends before the chicken coop, her tears that emerge 'in all the anguish of her generation's forlornness' (163) convey both an indictment of the men with whom she fraternizes and a statement on the urgent nature of her sexual frustration. A scarred Mellors struggles to stay uninvolved, struggles to deny the passionate urge in him that is unleashed by an awareness of the appealing 'otherness' of Connie. His phallic imagination makes demands on him, as if he is summoned by the god of fire *against his will*. That summoning suggests the central point of Lawrence, Hemingway, and Mailer about the men and women who still trust the emotional dictates of instinct. The cowardly 'will' of modern man does not stand a chance when the real and consuming heat arrives; it is the fire that Paul Morel described to Miriam fifteen years earlier in *Sons and Lovers* with the metaphor of forging, and now Mellors feels its power: 'And he stood up, and stood away, moving to the other coop. For suddenly he was aware of the old flame shooting and leaping up in his loins, that he had hoped was quiescent for ever. He fought against it, turning his back to her. But it leapt, and leapt downward, circling in his knees' (162).

The full fascination of this baptismal scene, and of the sex that immediately follows, is often misunderstood by feminist critics as either an example of Mellors's pity for Connie or of his manipulative use of her obvious vulnerability. As for the former criticism, only the most weather-beaten and insensitive stud (which Mellors clearly is not!) can make love for charity and stay reasonably sane. Millett charges, however, that he merely 'concedes one kiss on the navel and then gets to business'.[71] As I noted in an earlier chapter, Millett's characteristic tactic in her reading of Lawrence of insensitive analysis and meretricious quotation is exposed memorably by Norman Mailer in *The Prisoner of Sex*, and in effective summary fashion by Patricia Meyer Spacks in *The Female Imagination*.[72] In addition, Millett's card-carrying accusation of male sexism in the scene is patently foolish on the most elementary level: Connie's primitive unconscious helps *her* take all but the very final initiative with him. Mellors before, during, and after their first sex is racked with an unmacho concern not about his performance, or Connie's perception of him, but about the 'complications' (165) that such an act must bring upon them. He knows that after their passion they cannot merely enjoy the easy clean-up and quick good-bye of a one-night stand. Mellors significantly refers to their lovemaking here as 'life', as if the sex was inevitable and not really theirs to turn down. In short, Mellors in no way treats the encounter as if it were simply the hot passion of an afternoon's seduction – although that indulgent option, given Connie's critical state at the coop, certainly was open to him.

Sex remains sacramental for Lawrence. Thus Oliver Mellors, from the very start of his affair with Lady Chatterley, has a resolute inability to envisage the act of love divorced from the potential of a longer and more complicated connection with her. During their second sexual episode Mellors begins to accept the likelihood of their deepening involvement. As if to attest to the growing nature of his affection, he becomes progressively more tender and worshipful during their sex, as his phallic imagination moves from the phallus to a gentle caressing by voice and hand. But Connie is new to all this selfless admiration from a man. She persists in having her sex-without-guilt in a manner reminiscent of Miriam Leivers and recently learned, no doubt, from the ground rules of her masturbatory affair with Michaelis. So she watches Mellors's every move, distractedly observes her own reactions as he enters her, and misses her accustomed clitoral orgasm, as 'she knew partly, it was her own fault' (174). Indeed, even after her happiness over simultaneous orgasm with Mellors in a later scene, she is still a victim of the conditioned need to find the verbal counterpart for her sexual excitement. Like Francis Macomber after his rebirth in the jungle, Connie looks for praise and explanation through the Word; just like Wilson's gentle admonition to the ecstatic American, she is warned by Mellors to let the instincts, not the words, confirm the experience:

> 'Are you glad?'
> He looked back into her eyes. 'Glad,' he said.
> 'Ay, but never mind.' He did not want to talk. . . .
> 'Don't people often come off together?' she asked with naive curiosity.
> 'A good many of them never'. . . . He spoke unwittingly, regretting he had begun. (184)

When Connie fully learns to experience egoless sexual excitements with Mellors ('She dared to let go everything, all herself. . . . and closer and closer plunged the palpable unknown' (229)), she confirms the reason that this 'consummation was upon her'; she has absorbed the value of the special *silence* that is the result of instinctual satisfaction:

> He held her close, but he said nothing. He would never say anything. She crept nearer to him, nearer, only to be near the sensual wonder of him. . . . And her heart melted out with a kind of awe.
> And this time his being within her was all soft and iridescent, purely soft and iridescent, such as no consciousness could seize. Her whole self quivered unconscious and alive, like plasm. She could not know what it was. She could not remember what it had been. . . . And afterwards she was utterly still, utterly unknowing. . . . And he was still with her, in an unfathomable silence along with her. And of this they would never speak. (230–1)

Yet earlier in her affair with Mellors Connie does not trust her instincts in this 'utterly unknowing' manner. For instance, the day after 'she willed herself' into the separateness that prevents her orgasm; still harbouring her blend of desire and antagonism for

Mellors, she goes with Clifford to visit an elderly and aristocratic bachelor. This older man has an awareness of Connie's sexual charm, and he expresses it much in the manner of a connoisseur's evaluation of fine wine; his glib, class-conscious 'kindness' to a titled Lady temporarily confounds Connie's sense of what she slowly learns from Mellors about real and unpretentious erotic appreciation. Connie forgets that Mellors's homage to the womb *must* come first, as she now momentarily regresses to the fashionable platitudes of her Fabian womanhood and to the uncaring evasions of androgynous personhood:

> Winter called her 'dear child' and gave her a rather lovely miniature of an eighteenth-century lady, rather against her will.
> But Connie was preoccupied with her affair with the keeper. After all Mr. Winter, who was really a gentleman and a man of the world, treated her as a person and a discriminating individual; he did not lump her together with all the rest of his female womanhood in his 'thee' and 'tha'. (178)

Fortunately the logic of Connie's soul cannot sustain these trite and demeaning rationalizations about her passion for Mellors. As part of that characteristic 'ebb and flow' pattern that Lawrence in Chapter Nine relates both to the form of the novel and to its erotic preoccupations, Lady Chatterley's appreciation of the loving she gets from Mellors is revived when she sees Mrs Flint and her baby. Later she thinks fondly of her visit to Mrs Flint, and her illuminating self-realization occurs just before a fateful visit to Mellors: 'Yes, Mrs. Flint had flaunted her motherhood. And Connie had been just a bit, just a little bit jealous. She couldn't help it' (181).

Her sex with Mellors in the woods that follows the acknowledgement of a healthy and primitive envy of motherhood provides the first experience for Connie of vaginal orgasm; the metaphoric overlapping circles that Lawrence employs to chart this passion are meant to circumscribe the limited arcs of clitorally induced sensation that have characterized her mode of loving with Michaelis and with her former lovers on the continent. Connie's womb finally becomes open to response ('Whilst all her womb was open and soft, and softly clamoring . . . in her womb and bowels she was flowing and alive now' 183, 185) because the circumstances of the visit with Mrs Flint – an encounter that func-

guilt" 3

tions not unlike the second hunt for Macomber – has enabled her
to respond to Mellors from her instinctual centre and to suspend
the engrained patterns of her will and fear during intercourse. To
employ Mailer's terminology here, the orgasm is hers because the
jealousy over the baby was her residue of 'guilt', as she thus
appropriates the biles of her envy into the Lawrencian magic with
Mellors of sexual transcendence and developing self-definition.
Connie does not go to Wragby and talk out her jealousy with the
anti-life babblers who await her anecdotes; nor does she dismiss
the passion of her feeling for Mellors with the apologetics of her
political indoctrination as a liberated female. All she does is what
she senses she must do: she takes the burden of the Flint tension
to bed with Mellors, where she uses such guilt as the 'existential
edge' of sex. It is an edge sharp enough this one time to give her
the sexual gratification that opens up the potential of her emotional
life. Later in the novel, Connie's conversion to the visionary splen-
dours and silent passion of sex-with-guilt is evident when she
contemptuously ponders her sister Hilda's use of the term
'complete intimacy'. Connie thinks with an unequivocal value
judgement that would warm the hearts of Hemingway and Mailer
and irritate the advocates of Marie Stopes's campaigns in the 1920s:

> Complete intimacy. She supposed that meant revealing every-
> thing concerning yourself to the other person, and his revealing
> everything concerning himself. But that was a bore. All that
> weary self-consciousness between a man and woman! a disease!
>   'I think you're too conscious of yourself all the time, with
> everybody,' she said to her sister. (318)

Mellors is primarily responsible for Connie's gradual embrace
of instinctual knowledge over the security of wilful, mentalized
conditioning. Lawrence also cautions us against the facile belief
that, if it were not Oliver Mellors loving Lady Chatterley so wisely
and so well, it would have been any mature and sexually energetic
man available at the time. For Connie herself shows evidence of
the discriminating education she receives about men from her
embracings by Mellors. Here she makes a perfectly balanced judgement of the men in the pits, as she shows an awareness of their
primitive strength and – more importantly – an unsentimental
recognition of their inert sensual condition:

The common people were so many, and really, so terrible. So
she thought as she was going home, and saw the colliers trailing
from the pits, grey-black, distorted, one shoulder higher than
the other, slurring their heavy, iron-shod boots. Underground
grey faces, whites of eyes rolling, necks emerging from the pit
roof, shoulders out of shape. Men! Men! alas, in some ways
patient and good men. In other ways non-existent. Something
that men *should* have was bred and killed out of them. Yet they
were men. They begot children. One might bear a child to them.
Terrible, terrible thought! (212–13)

Connie easily puts to rest the romantic stereotype of the begrimed
and sexy man in the pits. What sounds like class snobbery in Lady
Chatterley is really a blunt and accurate appraisal by a woman
who has begun to understand the full measure of male sexual
responsibility, and modern man's increasing inability to meet it in
this age of machines and androgyny. What is killed off in these
men, as she captures so well, is any sense of phallic *imagination*,
any sense that they can, like Mellors, find the source of their
fundamental strength and enter the life and body of a Ladyship.
But unlike Mellors they are described as passive creatures of a
contemporary underworld, as robots who can only ride down
poisonous, mechanical shafts to violate mother earth. They are
dying under the ground and forsaking the blood knowledge that
knows better. They are without the ambitious fires of Mellors's
loins.

VIII

Connie's explicit awareness of the interrelation between the
colliers' degradation by industry and the poverty of their sensual
energy bespeaks a seminal concern by Lawrence that he exhibits
throughout *Lady Chatterley's Lover*: it is his prescient understanding
in post-war England of the developing threat to the instinctual life
of man, a threat Lawrence sees embodied in the snowballing
alliance among powerful corporations, inventive technologists,
and the various purveyors of utilitarian ethics who influence public
opinion. His fear is other than the old nineteenth-century warnings about the dire implications of an industrial revolution; Lawrence more subtly suggests how the increasing mechanization and

standardization of society has spill-over effects for intimate areas of private life previously felt to be relatively insulated from the influence of cultural and economic pressure. In several episodes of the novel, furthermore, Lawrence's illustration of this eminently modern threat *both* precisely echoes the fears of a celebrated, visionary British novelist, Charles Dickens, whose many works Lawrence read intensely, *and* exactly anticipates the sound of Norman Mailer's apocalyptic fears about contemporary America. The similarity among these novelists on this crucial theme, its adorning metaphors, and its urgent rhetorical expression deserves some illustration and comment. Perhaps the compelling resemblance may further suggest – in the boldness, accuracy, and integrity of the three novelists' concerns – the parochial quality of those feminist obsessions with *Lady Chatterley's Lover* I have sketched in this chapter.

Mailer's *The Armies of the Night* does considerably more than outline his theory of sex-with-guilt. It is a meta-fictional dramatization of his gradual willingness to involve himself fully in an open-ended protest against the Vietnam War; it is also a lyrical documentation and explanation – largely through Mailer's ruminations on his past and the varied aspects of the covered 'event' – of the cancerous assault on American life that finally prompts his participation in the protest. He locates his country's disease in its persistent willingness not to see beyond the demands of military paranoia, corporate technology, and economic self-interest; he sees the result as an increasing adulteration of the texture of current life and the nobility of our ambitions. Here is Mailer's description of the Pentagon, a Manichean passage that manages to be both prophetic and topical in its synthesis of the metaphors of hell, fairy-tale horror, and macho feature films:

> In some part of himself at least, he had grown; if less innocent, less timid – the cold flame of a perfectly contained exaltation warmed old asthmas of gravel in the heart, and the sense that they were going to face the symbol, the embodiment, no, call it the true and high church of the military-industrial complex, the Pentagon, blind five-sided eye of a subtle oppression which had come to America out of the very air of the century (this evil twentieth century with its curse on the species, its oppressive Faustian lusts, its technological excrement all over the conduits of nature, its entrapment of the innocence of the best – for which

young American soldiers hot out of high school and in love with
a hot rod and his Marine buddies in his platoon in Vietnam
could begin to know the devil of the oppression which would
steal his soul before he knew he had one).[73]

His phrase 'military-industrial complex' implies that it is not just
the Pentagon that is at the centre of Mailer's wrath. Here and
throughout *The Armies of the Night* he argues that the ravaging of
our potential greatness is abetted by a ravenous corporate
mentality in America, and by that he means more than any standard Marxist critique. We are 'corporate' to Mailer in the dictionary
sense that we are now 'combined as a whole', and thus we lack
a keen sense of differentiation and individual identity; that is, we
willingly accept deadening sameness if it is cost effective, or
tolerate the demise of art and style if we can have more leisure,
or sacrifice our sexual force if we can sublimate it in overseas
adventurism. Mailer sees the superstructures of our culture as
lacking in achieved grace, necessary risk, or any defining edge –
indeed, shall we coin the happy phrase for a future Aquarius,
'architecture-without-guilt', and use it to help him indict the landscape of America:

> He had written for years about American architecture and its
> functional disease – that *one could not tell the new colleges from the*
> *new prisons from the new hospitals* from the new factories from the
> new airports. Separate institutions were being replaced by one
> institution. . . . Floods of totalitarian architecture, totalitarian
> superhighways, totalitarian smog, totalitarian food (yes, frozen),
> totalitarian communications. . . . The machine would work,
> grinding out mass man.[74] (my emphasis)

Thus the cyclopean devil that Mailer associates with the Pentagon
stares intently from its 'five-sided eye' to set up curses that bewitch
America in the most fundamental way: we no longer care,
according to Mailer, that it is difficult to know from the outside
whether a 'place' is educating our children or punishing our crimi-
nals. We are numb to the touchstone, instinctual discriminations
of existence.

Forty years before *The Armies of the Night*, Lawrence reveals in
Lady Chatterley's Lover an emphasis on comparable symptoms of
industrial blight, money madness, and anesthetizing conformity.

In the midst of Connie's education about the value of sex-with-guilt, and on top of her developing realization of the full extent of what industry extracts from its men, she contemplates the awful sameness of the company's buildings; it is a perspective that reveals an infernal landscape that surrounds lost souls, and it highlights the metastasizing architecture of many areas in the mining belt of England:

> The Congregational chapel, which thought itself superior, was built of rusticated sandstone and had a steeple, but not a very high one. Just beyond were the new school buildings, expensive pink brick, and gravelled playgrounds inside iron railings, all very imposing, *and mixing the suggestion of a chapel and a prison.* . . . Tevershall! . . . It was producing a new race of mankind, over-conscious in the money and social and political side, on the spontaneous, intuitive side dead, but dead! Half-corpses all of them: but with a terrible insistent consciousness on the other half. There was something uncanny and underground about it all. It was an underworld . . . But if you looked, you saw on the left rows of handsome 'modern' dwellings, set down like a game of dominoes. (204, 205, 206, my emphasis)

Again the lingering malaise that the church and jail seem to share the same existential space in this real but futuristic society; it is a land evoked as an underworld of devilish indistinctness, as a miasma of the soul that keeps its prisoners in the morbid fog of their daily labour. Earlier Connie's lover prepares a similar insidious portrait of his environment, as his ruminations about mining soon encompass a metaphor that moves directly to thoughts about machines. The images are so close to Mailer's evocation of the 'Faustian lusts' emanating from that 'high church' of the defence establishment, that we must think, perhaps, of karmic power and the possibility of Mellors-Mailer marching to the Pentagon in 1967:

> The fault lay there, out there, in those evil electric lights and the diabolical rattling of engines. There, in the world of the mechanical greedy, greedy mechanism and mechanized greed, sparkling with lights and gushing hot metal and roaring with traffic, there lay the vast evil thing, ready to destroy whatever did not conform. (167)

These intense patterns of fear by Lawrence and Mailer were expressed by Charles Dickens, and with comparable details, in *Hard Times* (1854). That novel is Dickens's poignant, comic, and angry depiction of the dangers in the utilitarian consensus of his society; he recreates a world of conditioned behaviour and routinized learning in the thinly disguised Coketown of his novel. That town is a 'triumph of fact' in its painful resemblance to various nineteenth-century settings in the industrial north of England. This sharply evoked mining community is also not unlike the Tevershall of *Lady Chatterley's Lover*: the workers are similarly exploited by pit managers, and their love-life is often 'undermined' by a lack of spirit and ambition intrinsically related to the deadening sameness of their daily life. In passages on the shape of buildings and the detritus of industry, Dickens uses a series of Dantean metaphors and a tone of urgency that apparently influence at least two novelists in the next century. But the precision of his influence is something to behold. The same sense of presiding Devils as if near a Stygian river, the same revulsion at architectural deadness, the same horror at a mechanized infinity, and – of course – the same telling confusion about the jail:

It was a town of machinery and tall chimneys, out of which interminable serpents of smoke trailed themselves for ever and ever, and never go uncoiled. It has a black canal in it, and a river that ran purple with ill-smelling dye, and vast piles of buildings full of windows where there was a rattling and a trembling all day long, and where the piston of the steam-engine worked monotonously up and down. . . . It contained several large streets all very like one another, and many small streets, still more like one another, inhabited by people equally like one another. . . . All the public inscriptions in the town were painted alike, in severe characters of black and white. *The jail might have been the infirmary, the infirmary might have been the jail*, the town-hall might have been either.[75] (my emphasis)

In the midst of an era's notorious reticence, Dickens still manages a forceful indictment of society's mammonism and its deadly treatment of human passion. If in 1854 he cannot employ the dialectical insight of Mailer's sex-with-guilt, or the explicit power of Lawrence's sexual scenes, the tell-tale confutation of the distinction between the jail and the infirmary is a sign that he knows his country's malaise: he describes a venomous land in *Hard Times* where industrial pollution, cacophonous metallic sounds, and insidiously designed streets are all rationalized by the society's bromides on national progress and the public good.

F. R. Leavis's excellent discussion of *Hard Times* describes the novel's dramatized faith in the claims of instinct and love as Dickens's major answer to the encroachment of machines; Leavis isolates the central importance of the circus performers, and he concludes that they 'represent human spontaneity', and that their skill may 'have no value for the utilitarian calculus, but they express vital human impulse and they minister to vital human needs'.[76] Leavis's explanation of Bitzer's unfeeling, factual definition of a horse in the opening scene of the novel is pertinent but insufficiently examined, for the critic does not also consider the fascinating words of Sissy Jupe. Her honest answer is the naive and unadorned celebration of an existential imperative in *Hard Times*, for it announces her right to declare (in anticipation of Mellors and Lt. Henry) the absolute primacy of feelings. 'If it feels good it is good' is Mailer's reading of the Hemingway dictum, and Lawrence's review of Hemingway stressed the young writer's resolute ability to portray characters who build themselves on 'exactly and sincerely what they feel'.[77] When asked by an angry Gradgrind to elaborate on her expressed desire to use flowers on a carpet, she can only reply, 'if you please, sir, I am very fond of flowers'.[78] Gradgrind's ensuing perplexity is reflected in the black and white 'public inscriptions' of Coketown, for Sissy's words are not amenable to any standard of preference but her own. Just a few pages later, when Louisa is caught peeking by her father at the circus people, she is asked to explain her motive: 'Wanted to see what it was like'[79] is all she offers, and thus she refuses to offer more waste material for those ominously 'tall chimneys' and their 'serpents of smoke'.

It is not far from the locale that produces the naked, rebellious answers of Sissy and Louisa in *Hard Times* to the couplings of Mellors and Connie near the mine pits of Tevershall. But the issue that is joined is more compelling, of course, than that of mere geographical proximity. Lawrence and Dickens try to subvert the dominant notions of their country's 'progress', and in each novel they suggest not a political agenda but a return to fundamental expressions of love, desire, and unhampered imagination. Louisa's desire 'to see what it was like' is a rare articulation in Coketown of a young woman's right to explore and celebrate without the compulsion to memorize, pragmatize, or even build for the future. Mellors's notion, 'if people could fuck with warm hearts', is similar to that affirmation of honest sentiment contained in Sissy's radical assertion of instinctual primacy evident in her answer about the flowers. In a sense, Connie and Mellors seventy-five years later take that same fondness for flowers and baptize their passion through the zaniness of genital decoration. Such an unorthodox gesture of communion appropriately joins the natural world outside with the adamant prerogatives of their own sexual definition. There is a machine-world not far from the doors of the gamekeeper's hut, and its 'up and down' sounds of 'rattling and trembling' (as Dickens describes them a century earlier) may some day overwhelm the rhythms of passion that the lovers enjoy inside. Here Mellors 'properly handles' Connie in the 'passional secret places' mentioned in Chapter Nine of the novel. While feminists may express displeasure at his gestures and language, Lawrence knows better, as the moment declares the large stakes incumbent on the phallic imagination:

'Tha's got a proper, woman's arse, proud of itself. It's none ashamed of itself, this isna.'

He laid his hand close and firm over her secret places, in a kind of close greeting.

'I like it,' he said. 'I like it! An' if I only lived ten minutes, an' stroked thy arse and' got to know it, I should reckon I'd lived *one* life, sees ter! Industrial system or not!' (285)

Notes

1. Lawrence, 'A Propos of *Lady Chatterley's Lover*', in Harry T. Moore (ed.), *Sex, Literature, and Censorship* (New York: Viking, 1959), 87.
2. Carolyn Heilbrun, *Towards a Recognition of Androgyny* (New York: Harper & Row, 1974), 101.
3. 'A New Adam and a New Eve – Lawrence and Women: A Biographical Overview', in Anne Smith (ed.), *Lawrence and Women* (New York: Barnes & Noble; London: Vision, 1978), 45.
4. Near the end of his life, in a discussion with his friend, Earl Brewster – reported by Harry T. Moore, in his biography of Lawrence – Lawrence explained the significance of the symbolism in his 'pictures', and implicitly commented on his intentions in *Lady Chatterley's Lover*:

'I try,' Lawrence told his Buddhistic friend, 'to keep the *Middle* of me harmonious to the *Middle* of the universe. Outwardly I know I'm in a bad temper, and let it go at that.' But he stuck to his beliefs 'and put a phallus, a lingam you call it, in each one of my pictures somewhere. And I paint no picture that won't shock people's castrated social spirituality.' But this man's motive was never obscenity: 'I do this out of positive belief that the phallus is a great sacred image: it represents a deep, deep life which has been denied in us, and still is denied. Women deny it horribly, with a grinning travesty of sex. But pazienza! pazienza! One can still believe. And with the lingam, and the mystery behind it, goes beauty.' *The Priest of Love: A Life of D. H. Lawrence*, rev. edn (New York: Farrar, Straus & Giroux, 1974; Harmondsworth: Penguin, 1980), 328.

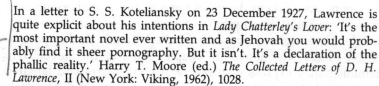

In a letter to S. S. Koteliansky on 23 December 1927, Lawrence is quite explicit about his intentions in *Lady Chatterley's Lover*: 'It's the most important novel ever written and as Jehovah you would probably find it sheer pornography. But it isn't. It's a declaration of the phallic reality.' Harry T. Moore (ed.) *The Collected Letters of D. H. Lawrence*, II (New York: Viking, 1962), 1028.

5. Lawrence, 'Why the Novel Matters', in Edward D. McDonald (ed.), *Phoenix: The Posthumous Papers of D. H. Lawrence* (New York: Viking, 1972), 535.
6. Lawrence, *Lady Chatterley's Lover* (New York: Grove, 1959; London: Heinemann, 1963), 146. Page numbers in my text refer to the Grove edition.
7. Kate Millett, *Sexual Politics* (Garden City: Doubleday, 1970; London: Virago, 1977), 240.
8. Ibid., 239, 240.
9. Juliet Mitchell, *Psychoanalysis and Feminism* (New York: Random House, 1975), 351–5.
10. Millett, *Sexual Politics*, 238.
11. Simone de Beauvoir, *The Second Sex* (New York: Random House, 1974; Harmondsworth: Penguin, 1972), 246.
12. Ibid., 242.
13. Robert Scholes, *Semiotics and Interpretation* (New Haven: Yale University Press, 1982), 140.
14. Ibid., 141.
15. Hilary Simpson, *D. H. Lawrence and Feminism* (Dekalb: Northern Illinois University Press; London: Croom Helm, 1982), 17.
16. Ibid., 131.
17. Ibid., 137.
18. Ernest Hemingway, *A Farewell to Arms* (New York: Scribners, 1957), 243.
19. Lawrence, '*In Our Time*: A Review', in *Phoenix*, 366.
20. Lawrence, 'A Propos of *Lady Chatterley's Lover*', 89.
21. Norman Mailer, *Advertisements for Myself* (New York: Putnam, 1959; London: Panther, 1980), 23.

22. Ernest Hemingway, *The Sun Also Rises* (New York: Scribners, 1954), 15.
23. Ibid., 26.
24. Norman Mailer, *The Prisoner of Sex* (New York: New American Library, 1971), 118.
25. Hemingway, *A Farewell to Arms*, 16.
26. Ibid., 31.
27. I shall deal with Millett's indictment of Lawrence in the body of this essay, but I must note here that the recent response to Hemingway is comparably instructive. Much recent criticism often ignores any sustained analysis of Hemingway's fictional heroines, and is content to make *ad hominem* attacks on what it regards as the inappropriateness of his preoccupations with war, courage, and sexual achievement. For instance, in a frenetic and politicized essay, that dismisses Saul Bellow and Norman Mailer from a list of acceptable writers, Vivian Gornick, the co-editor of the widely used college anthology, *Woman in Sexist Society*, reflects an approach similar to Florence Howe's confident dismissal, in the 1980s American Association of Colleges report, of Lawrence's purported message. She describes the 'emotional adolescence' of Hemingway, and then berates what she calls a 'misogynistic culture' that 'subscribed to the same adolescent truths about men and women as Hemingway did, and experienced these truths as a metaphor for life'. Gornick uses the past tense, of course, in her proud recognition that she writes in the 1970s, and that 'the culture no longer' subscribes to these adolescent truths. In 'Why Do These Men Hate Women?: American Novelists and Misogyny', *The Village Voice*, 6 December 1976, 12–15.

Even widely anthologized and more academic attempts to debunk Hemingway's work evade an understanding of characters like Catherine Barkley. Wendy Martin, for instance, sees *A Farewell to Arms* as a 'contemporary re-enactment of Eden', a metaphor that she uses to pursue her view of Catherine as tainted with original sin, a mere 'compliant companion', whose death 'expiates' her sin of sleeping with Henry. Martin shows little concern for the strength that Catherine manifests throughout her ordeal, nor does Martin explain how the novel's depiction of modern warfare functions in her strained allegorical reading. In 'Seduced and Abandoned in the New World: The Image of Woman in American Fiction', from Vivian Gornick and Barbara Moran (eds), *Woman in Sexist Society* (New York: Basic Books, 1971), 226–39. More recently Joyce Wexler, in 'E.R.A. for Hemingway: A Feminist Defense of *A Farewell to Arms*', in *The Georgia Review*, 35 (Spring 1981), 111–23, does understand what she properly regards as the 'development' of Catherine's character, and she demonstrates the inadequacy of angry feminist attacks on Hemingway, typified by their inability 'to regard Catherine as a distinct character' (112). But as the politicized title of Wexler's essay suggests, she is more interested in calming her feminist colleagues by indicating ways in which Catherine's character can be accommodated to contemporary notions of the liberated woman. Her argument ultimately ignores the essence of

Catherine's poetic acceptance of the archetypal feminine, as Wexler implicitly pursues the totalitarian notion that only *some form* of variant feminism, operating in *A Farewell to Arms*, could make this work palatable. Such a response resembles the feminist analysis of Connie Chatterley that prefers her single sex life on the continent to her monogamous affair with Mellors.

28. Mailer, *The Prisoner of Sex*, 121.
29. Ibid., 35.
30. Millett, *Sexual Politics*, 243.
31. Mailer, *Advertisements for Myself*, 340.
32. Hemingway, *A Farewell to Arms*, 31.
33. Mailer, 'The White Negro', in *Advertisements for Myself*, 342.
34. Hemingway, *A Farewell to Arms*, 185.
35. Mailer, *The Prisoner of Sex*, 36.
36. Lawrence, 'Nathaniel Hawthorne and *The Scarlet Letter*', in *Studies in Classic American Literature* (New York: Viking, 1964), 83–99.
37. Hemingway, 'The Short Happy Life of Francis Macomber', in *The Short Stories of Ernest Hemingway* (New York: Scribner's 1966), 21.
38. Ibid., 33.
39. Ibid.
40. Ibid.
41. Mailer, *The Armies of the Night* (New York: New American Library, 1968), 36.
42. Mailer, *Marilyn* (New York: Warner Books, 1975), 102.
43. Mailer, *The Prisoner of Sex*, 107.
44. Mailer, *The Deer Park* (New York: Putnam, 1955; London: Deutsch, 1959), 294.
45. Lawrence, 'A Propos of *Lady Chatterley's Lover*', 89.
46. Mailer, *Marilyn*, 77.
47. For an interesting study of Stopes's life and work, see Ruth Hall, *Passionate Crusader: The Life of Marie Stopes* (New York: Harcourt Brace Jovanovich, 1977).
48. Lawrence, 'Pornography and Obscenity', in *Sex, Literature, and Censorship*, 76.
49. Simpson, *D. H. Lawrence and Feminism*, 162.
50. Lawrence, 'Pornography and Obscenity', 76.
51. Mailer, *The Armies of the Night*, 36.
52. Ibid.
53. Mailer, *The Prisoner of Sex*, 25.
54. Ibid., 52.
55. Ti-Grace Atkinson, 'The Institution of Sexual Intercourse', in *Women's Liberation: Notes from the Second Year* (1970), 12. Quoted by Mailer in *The Prisoner of Sex*, 50.
56. Lawrence, *The Collected Letters*, I, 251.
57. W. D. Snodgrass, 'A Rocking-Horse: The Symbol, the Pattern, the Way to Live', in *The Hudson Review* 11 (1958), 191–200, and reprinted in Mark Spilka (ed.), *D. H. Lawrence: A Collection of Critical Essays* (Englewood Cliffs: Prentice Hall, 1963), 117–26.
58. Lawrence, 'Pornography and Obscenity', 73.

59. Mailer, *The Prisoner of Sex*, 135–6.
60. Mark Spilka, *The Love Ethic of D. H. Lawrence* (Bloomington: Indiana University Press, 1955), 177–204.
61. Mailer, *The Prisoner of Sex*, 36.
62. Millett, *Sexual Politics*, 239–40.
63. Mailer, *The Prisoner of Sex*, 92.
64. Lawrence, 'Making Love to Music', in *Sex, Literature, and Censorship*, 44.
65. Mailer, *The Prisoner of Sex*, 66.
66. Both Lawrence's anger at society and his related prophetic impulse for the creation of *Lady Chatterley's Lover* are reflected in a letter about the novel sent to G. R. G. Conway on 15 March 1928:

> It is – in the latter half at least – a phallic novel, but tender and delicate. You know I believe in the phallic reality, and the phallic consciousness: as distinct from our irritable cerebral consciousness of today. That's why I do the book – and it's not just *sex*. Sex alas is one of the worst phenomena of today: all cerebral reaction, the whole thing worked from mental processes and itch, and not a bit of the real phallic insouciance and spontaneity. But in my novel there is. (Moore, *The Priest of Love*, 424.)

67. Simpson, *D. H. Lawrence and Feminism*, 128.
68. Ibid., 131.
69. Millett, *Sexual Politics*, 62.
70. Mailer, *The Prisoner of Sex*, 122.
71. Millett, *Sexual Politics*, 243.
72. See Mailer, *The Prisoner of Sex*, 93–115, and Patricia Meyer Spacks, *The Female Imagination* (New York: Avon, 1976), 34–41.
73. Mailer, *The Armies of the Night*, 132.
74. Ibid., 198–9.
75. Charles Dickens, *Hard Times*, edited by George Ford and Sylvere Monod (New York: Norton, 1966), 17.
76. F. R. Leavis, *The Great Tradition* (London: Chatto & Windus, 1948), 227–48, and reprinted in part in *Hard Times*, 339–59. In this essay and in his first study of Lawrence, *D. H. Lawrence: Novelist* (New York: Knopf, 1955; Harmondsworth: Penguin, 1970), Leavis does establish several provocative insights into Lawrence's work by noting the apparent influence of Dickens on the later novelist. The essay in *The Great Tradition* on *Hard Times* makes note of the similar environments of Coketown and Tevershall, although Leavis does not pursue my notions about the relation between the 'machine' and sexual passivity.
77. Lawrence, 'In Our Time: A Review', 366.
78. Dickens, *Hard Times*, 5.
79. Ibid., 10.

Index